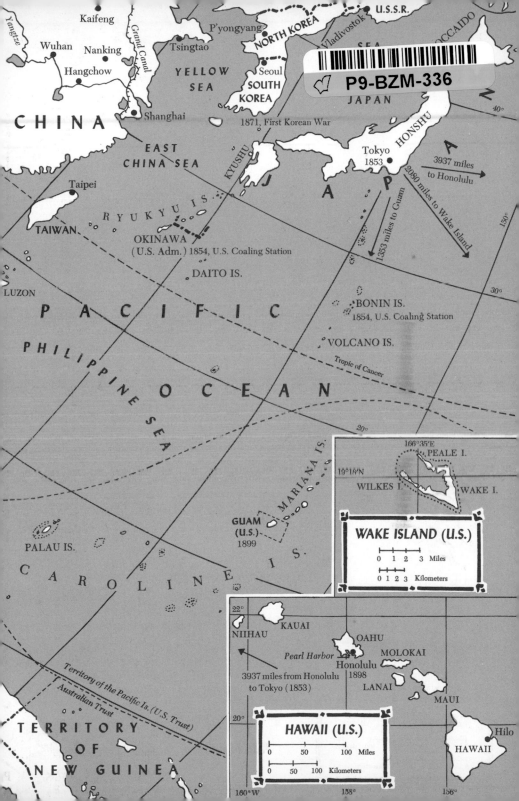

ROOTS OF INVOLVEMENT

The U.S. in Asia
1784-1971

By Marvin Kalb

EASTERN EXPOSURE
DRAGON IN THE KREMLIN
THE VOLGA, A POLITICAL JOURNEY THROUGH RUSSIA

Introduction to

ONE DAY IN THE LIFE OF IVAN DENISOVICH
by Alexander Solzhenitsyn

By Elie Abel

THE MISSILE CRISIS

ROOTS OF INVOLVEMENT

The U.S. in Asia
1784-1971

MARVIN KALB / ELIE ABEL

W · W · NORTON & COMPANY · INC ·
NEW YORK

Library of Congress Catalog Card No. 73-139381
SBN 393 05440 3
2 3 4 5 6 7 8 9 0

To those young Americans
who have fallen in Asia

Contents

Introduction

THE ROOTS of American involvement in the Far East go deep, far deeper than most citizens imagine. In our time it has become fashionable to blame President Lyndon Johnson primarily for committing more than a half million American troops to the endless war in Vietnam. Johnson defenders, on the other hand, have contended that President John Kennedy ought to bear the main responsibility. There is—as Robert Kennedy once observed —more than enough blame to go around. But any conscientious effort to apportion it fairly must reach back to the Truman and Eisenhower Administrations and even farther back in American history.

It seems curious that certain left-of-center critics (who showed little admiration for Dwight Eisenhower during his two-term Presidency) should now, in retrospect, credit him with a stubborn, enlightened refusal to take up the French colonial burden in Indochina. In fact, the United States started to pick up that burden more or less piecemeal during the predecessor administration of Harry Truman—a process that Eisenhower greatly expanded. The figures are instructive. As far back as 1951, when Truman sat in the White House and Dean Acheson presided over the Department of State, American aid to the French forces fighting in Indochina already exceeded a half-billion dollars a year. By the spring of 1954, with Eisenhower in office and John Foster Dulles in charge of the State Department, American aid for Indochina was running at $1,133,000,000, almost exactly one-third of the total foreign-aid budget.

At that early stage there was no talk in Washington of a

national commitment to Vietnam. The commitment was to
France. Its prime justification was the belief that France could
not be expected to pull her weight in the Marshall Plan program
for European reconstruction and—at the same time—pay the
full cost of her own doomed war. In short, it was to protect a
European investment amounting to many billions of dollars that
the United States took its first steps toward military involvement
in Southeast Asia. The link was ideological: should the Marshall
Plan fail, or the French lose Indochina, then Russia would surely
expand her power and influence, in the Far East as well as Europe. The conventional wisdom of the time did not allow for
differences between a Communist-ruled China (or an Indochina
ruled by Ho Chi Minh) and the Soviet Union.

It was General Eisenhower, the peace President, who five
years after the French defeat at Dienbienphu declared that the
survival of an anti-Communist regime in Saigon had become a
matter affecting "our own national interests." His speech at
Gettysburg College on April 4, 1959, was widely ignored at the
time. More than anything said by his successors in later years,
the Gettysburg speech fits the description of a national commitment, openly declared.

In our search for understanding of the American role in
the Far East, we have gone back to the early days of the Republic, the Yankee Clipper trade and America's 19th-century
commercial rivalry with Britain and Germany, through the era
of Manifest Destiny and the Open Door in China—all the way
to the Nixon Doctrine of today. We were struck by several remarkable parallels between the annexation of the Philippines at
the turn of the century and the Vietnam War of the Sixties.
Unlike Professor Samuel Flagg Bemis, who considered the
acquisition of the Philippines a "great aberration," we believe
that the Vietnam War was no aberration but a logical consequence—however regrettable—of certain long-held American
attitudes and assumptions, some of them plainly mistaken.

The Vietnam involvement was undertaken in massive
American ignorance of Southeast Asia, compounded by failures
of military and political judgment, questionable intelligence,
dubious and frequently overblown Presidential rhetoric, together with a steadfast refusal to recognize that the national

interest of the United States cannot be stretched to encompass the whole of the great blue globe without risking disaster at home.

We have traced the rising curve of American involvement from the beginning and, in the last two chapters, have attempted to recapture the frustrations, approaching despair, of two Presidents—Johnson and Nixon—each determined late in the day upon the far more difficult task of winding down the war while refusing to acknowledge defeat or failure. Under close scrutiny, the process of Presidential decision-making often appeared to be out of touch with the real world: President Johnson, for example, fearful that he would be accused of playing politics if he stopped bombing North Vietnam; or the Joint Chiefs of Staff enlisting General Westmoreland in a clumsy maneuver to wring from the reluctant President massive troop reinforcements, a call-up of reserves, and a win-the-war-now strategy at the very moment when the Tet offensive had all but totally undermined public support for the war.

We are grateful to a succession of former and present Washington officials (see Acknowledgments) who consented to share with us their recollections and, in so doing, helped to chronicle the dismaying story, including the disaffection of Robert McNamara; the surprising transformation of Clark Clifford from a complacent hawk to an embattled dove; Lyndon Johnson's astonishing statement to a White House aide that any new President—Richard Nixon, Robert Kennedy, or Eugene McCarthy—would have more clout than he with the Congress; and a great many more intimate glimpses behind the official curtain.

We found no substantial evidence that the United States was driven by imperialist motives—as the neo-Marxists would have us believe—to search for markets and raw materials—*i.e.,* profits—in Vietnam. Instead, we found a rich, generous, and powerful nation stumbling, step by downward step, into the longest, most costly, and most disruptive war Americans have ever fought, in the misguided belief that when things go wrong anywhere in the world the commitment of sufficient American dollars and—if need be—of American soldiers, must surely put them right.

M. K. / E. A.

Acknowledgments

WE ARE INDEBTED to a great number of present and former officials for generously sharing with us their recollections. Among these are: Dean Rusk; Clark Clifford; Henry Fowler; Paul Nitze; Averell Harriman; Cyrus Vance; Paul Warnke; George W. Ball; McGeorge Bundy; Nicholas deB. Katzenbach; William P. Bundy; Senator Mike Mansfield; General William Westmoreland; General Maxwell D. Taylor; Brigadier General Winant Sidle; Harry C. McPherson, Jr.; Joseph A. Califano, Jr.; Daniel Z. Henkin; and Robert J. McCloskey.

In addition, we have drawn upon notes of lengthy conversations with Dr. Henry Kissinger, Nguyen Cao Ky, Marshall Green, William Sullivan, Ambassador Bui Diem, and many other officials who are still engaged in policy-making and prefer the back rooms of anonymity.

Henry Raymont made a significant contribution by turning over to us tapes of an interview with Walt W. Rostow, part of which was published earlier in *The New York Times*.

We have read and profited from the published recollections of Charles de Gaulle; Arthur Schlesinger, Jr.; Theodore C. Sorensen; George Christian; Mrs. Lyndon B. Johnson; Kenneth P. O'Donnell; Townsend Hoopes; and Chester Cooper; and the biography of Richard Nixon by Earl Mazo and Stephen Hess. We have also profited from Walter Cronkite's television interviews with former President Lyndon B. Johnson as broadcast by CBS.

William Small, Washington bureau manager of CBS News, earned our gratitude for the understanding and forbearance he showed while this book was being researched and written. Sara Evans of the British Broadcasting Corporation and Marina Di Filippo of Columbia University helped mightily in the tedious business of transcribing taped interviews and typing the manuscript.

We acknowledge a debt to Richard O'Connor, whose *Pacific Destiny* inspired us to try to go further.

Finally, our eternal gratitude to Corinne Prevost Abel and Madeleine Green Kalb, who—not for the first time—have suffered the turmoils and dislocations that a book in progress necessarily imposes within the family circle. Without their unfailing encouragement and support, this book could not have been written.

M. K. / E. A.

ROOTS OF INVOLVEMENT

The U.S. in Asia

1784-1971

ONE

The Reluctant Imperialists

IN THE BEGINNING, America's romance with Asia combined a lust for wealth with a yearning for God. The American Republic was still a toddler among sovereign nations when the sea captains of Salem and Boston began to fire businessmen and bankers, politicians, poets, and preachers with visions of a grander national destiny to be fulfilled far from New England and Virginia, across the wide Pacific. The promise of earthly wealth was so compelling, the hope of heavenly reward so powerful, that ordinary men put to sea from the harbors of the northeastern United States in little sailing ships for the unknown Orient—all the way around Cape Horn or eastward across the Atlantic, then round the Cape of Good Hope and through the Indian Ocean—forgetting the hazards. They carried furs and hardware from the New World to be exchanged for silks and spices. It was a time for visionaries.

One such dreamer, young John Ledyard of Connecticut, haunted lower Manhattan in the 1780s, exhorting bankers and businessmen to get rich quick in the China trade. There were skeptics among the bankers particularly—until they saw the hard evidence of rich profits carried home from voyages to China or Java. Elias Hasket Derby, an early convert, sent whole fleets of sailing ships to China. Derby built a fortune and a great reputation in the land, to the point where they called him King Derby of Salem. The poets and politicians were not far behind.

There was John L. O'Sullivan, an Irish immigrant, who sang of America's "Manifest Destiny." All but overwhelmed by the sweep of his new homeland, the open space as far as human eye could see, O'Sullivan wrote in November, 1839:

The far-reaching, the boundless future will be the era of American greatness. In its magnificent domain of space and time, the nation of many nations is destined to manifest to mankind the excellence of divine principles; to establish on Earth the noblest temple ever dedicated to the worship of the Most High—the Sacred and the True. Its floor shall be a hemisphere—its roof the firmament of the star-studded heavens, and its congregation a Union of many Republics, comprising hundreds of happy millions, calling no man master but governed by God's natural and moral law of equality, the law of brotherhood—of "peace and good will amongst men."

The Almighty had blessed America. And He seemed to move with the Americans as they moved into the Pacific. President William McKinley, for example, had no reason to doubt that the annexation of the Philippines in 1898 was God's own will. Before God made his will known, McKinley had opposed "forcible annexation." That would be nothing more nor less, he said, than "criminal aggression." He later explained his change of heart to a White House meeting of Methodist and Episcopal missionaries.

"I didn't want the Philippines and, when they came to us as a gift from the gods, I did not know what to do with them," he said. Night after night, McKinley recalled, he paced the floors of the White House, puzzling over his problem and sometimes dropping to his knees in prayer. One night, he said:

It came to me . . . that (1) We could not give them back to Spain. That would be cowardly and dishonorable; (2) that we could not turn them over to France or Germany—our commercial rivals in the Orient. That would be bad business and discreditable; (3) that we could not leave them to themselves. They were unfit for self-government—and they would soon have anarchy and misrule over there worse than Spain's was; and (4) that there was nothing left for us to do but to take them all, and to educate the Filipinos, and uplift and civilize and Christianize them, and by God's grace do the very best we could by them, as our fellow men for whom Christ also died. And then I went to sleep and slept soundly.

Spain, in fact, had Christianized the Philippines some 300 years before the Americans landed. But McKinley was not troubled by awkward facts. The wicked European powers had moved into Asia long before the United States, acquiring colonies and assured markets and national glory. Americans, from childhood, had been taught that the Europeans had no right, moral or legal, to be there. If America, too, had now become a power in Asia, ruling over millions of Filipinos, her reasons were bound to be more elevated: nothing less than the will of God.

The United States can be said to have slipped into its involvement with Asia in recoil from the embroilments of Europe. George Washington had warned his countrymen, in his Farewell Address on September 17, 1796, against taking sides in European quarrels. He said nothing about the dangers of getting involved in Asia. Washington had led the colonies to nationhood, after a successful revolutionary war against Britain. The central idea of the American Revolution, a truly revolutionary idea for the time, was that those Englishmen and Europeans who had settled in the New World possessed the right, by their own declaration, to dissolve their bonds with the Old World and proclaim their independence. So they founded a new nation where, in contrast to the stratified societies of Europe, "all men are created equal." Washington admonished his fellow Americans to make the most of their "detached and distant situation"—detached and distant from Europe, that is—to enjoy with him "the benign influence of good laws under a free government." To Washington and his contemporaries freedom in the national sense meant freedom from Europe. The context is vital.

"Europe has a set of primary interests," Washington wrote, "which to us have none or a very remote relation. Hence she must be engaged in frequent controversies, the causes of which are essentially foreign to our concerns."

He put a rhetorical question: "Why, by interweaving our destiny with that of any part of Europe, entangle our peace and prosperity in the toils of European ambition, rivalship, interest, humor or caprice?" America's answer was "why indeed?"

The Americans promptly turned their backs on Europe, facing westward to that vast continent their destiny commanded them to explore and settle, and to the great ocean beyond. Thomas Jefferson, the third President, fully shared Washington's conviction. Upon assuming the Presidency, at the turn of the

19th century, he set about the giant task of exploring, possessing, and taming the continent. He concluded the Louisiana Purchase, which added one million square miles of territory to America's domain. He dispatched the Lewis and Clark Expedition beyond the Mississippi to the West. He also encouraged the German-born fur trader, John Jacob Astor, to establish trading posts in the Northwest.

America was on the march to Manifest Destiny. Exploration and conquest of the western reaches became part of the heady politics of the age. Clearly, the political party that could identify itself with the westward thrust and bring new wealth and glory to the United States would win the nation's confidence and its votes. Thus the poets and sloganeers of the fledgling Democratic Party in the 1840s became intoxicated with visions of grandeur. Whether the battle cry was "Fifty-four forty or fight" or "On to Mexico City" or "Manifest Destiny," the people responded. *The Democratic Review* pressed the Polk Administration to seize California and Texas from Mexico and to oust the hated British from Oregon.

This pursuit of national grandeur did not go unopposed in Congress. In the feisty 1840s, as at the time of the Philippine adventure in the 1890s and of Indochina in the time of Lyndon Johnson, Congress hotly debated the issue of intervention. Then, as now, there were Senators and Representatives who questioned whether the plunge was worth the cost, whether it would not lead to wider wars and degrade America's moral standing. Then, as now, the argument for intervention was that American honor or the validity of America's word was somehow at stake. While John O'Sullivan was preaching expansion, with the as-sured blessing of the Almighty, Congressman Robert C. Winthrop of Massachusetts pleaded for prudence and patience. Winthrop, like Senator Fulbright more than a century later, believed that the outward thrust of American policy would inevitably lead to conflict with other nations. Like Fulbright, denouncing America's "arrogance of power," Winthrop warned that other nations could never accept the notion that America possessed a divine license to put together, in the words of one Democratic spokesman, a "universal Yankee nation." Winthrop argued persuasively but he lost.

Thus the United States, in the 19th century, became a continental nation, washed by two oceans. Avarice and politics may have provided part of the push. But once America's writ extended westward as far as California, geography exposed her to Pacific responsibilities and commitments. Dean Rusk used to argue, in defense of America's involvement in Indochina, that the United States (unlike France, for example) had a right to be there: it was a two-ocean country with two-ocean commitments. The contention that a Pacific coastline entitles the United States to intervene in Southeast Asia falls of its own weight, however. Applying the same logic, Japan could have argued that as an acknowledged Pacific power she had every right to land troops in Hawaii. It has never been easy for Americans to see themselves as others see them, or to concede to foreign nations the particular rights they claim for themselves. Their view of Asia, as we shall see, has often been self-righteous.

It was in 1784 that the first Yankee Clipper sailed from New York to China. She was somewhat brashly named *The Empress of China*. The 360-ton privateer moved in on Britain's lucrative trade in Canton, delighting in the rancor she caused among the British and playing on the sensibilities of the Chinese merchants by extending full courtesies to them. In the *Journals of Major Samuel Shaw*, the first U.S. consul in China, Shaw tells of a conversation with one of the Chinese.

"You are not an Englishman?" the Chinese asked.

"No," Shaw replied.

"But you speak English word," the Chinese continued, "and when you first come, I no can tell difference, but now I understand very well. When I speak Englishman his price, he say, 'So much—take it—let me alone.' I tell him, 'No, my friend, I give you so much.' He look at me. 'Go to hell, you damned rascal. What! You come here and set a price on *my* goods!' Truly, Massa Taipan, I see very well you no hap Englishman. All Chinamen very much love your country."

Pleased by the merchant's ability to distinguish superior

qualities in Americans, Shaw established an amicable relationship with him, even though a lingering Chinese skepticism remained. "All men come first time China very good gentlemen,
all same you. I think two, three more time you come Canton, you
make all same Englishmen too."

The Americans came "two, three more time," and over the
years and decades they kept coming. Starting with the success
of King Derby of Salem and other venturesome businessmen
from New England and New York, the China trade slowly became big business and the stuff of legend. Even when the trade
dipped, or war intervened, it still acted as a magnet for the new
moneymen from lower Manhattan.

There was a kind of China craze in those years. Wealthy
matrons bought Chinese porcelain from returning skippers and
showed it at fancy dinners to impress their guests. To shift
from pewter to china became a status symbol. The Chinese
exploited the trend. They produced special dishes and tureens
for export, which gradually made their way into the cupboards
of American society. Today, in the elegant eighth-floor reception
rooms of the Department of State, there are proud displays of
Chinese export porcelain. These are regarded as pieces of Americana, no less than the portraits of Washington, Adams, and
Jefferson that hang on the walls.

Alarmed by America's early success in the Pacific trade,
London instructed the British East India Company "to prevent
the subjects of Great Britain from assisting or encouraging in
any shape the American commerce." The Americans saw this as
a challenge, worthy of defiance. The clipper ships plunged into
the pepper and spice trade of the Indies, plowed the waters off
the Malayan peninsula, visited ports in Cochin China, and eyed
new markets farther east and north—in the Philippines and the
island chain of Japan.

Those were exciting years. As the continent was being explored, the ocean beyond it was being exploited. The Yankee
Clipper ship became a symbol of American superiority. It quickened the pulse of the poet. "Under full sail, with a favoring
wind," Richard O'Connor writes, "the American clipper seemed

to skim just over the waves, half-bird, half-fish, traveling on canvas wings." Or, as Samuel Eliot Morison has written:

The long-suppressed artistic impulse of a practical, hard-worked race burst into flower. . . . Never, in these United States, has the brain of man conceived, or the hand of man fashioned, so perfect a thing as the clipper ship. . . . The *Flying Cloud* was our Rheims, the *Sovereign of the Seas* our Parthenon, the *Lightning* our Amiens.

The Yankee Clipper became the very expression of this new nation—thrusting outward, ever expanding, full of promise. Senator William Henry Seward, evoking the spirit of the time in Old Testament rhetoric, said: "Multiply your ships and send them forth to the East!"

America lost no time multiplying her ships and sending them forth. Soon they were calling in the central Pacific, at the Samoan Islands. To the northeast lay the Sandwich Islands, better known as the Hawaiian Islands. Much farther north lay Alaska and the Aleutians, a natural northern approach to the islands and peninsulas off the Asian mainland: Japan, Korea, Taiwan, the Philippines, Cochin China, the East Indies. A pattern developed. First the clippers came—with their crews and cargoes. Then the consuls came—to look after the commercial interests of the clippers and the national interests of the United States. With the consuls, of course, came the flag; and if that flag was dishonored, then there could be little question that warships would follow the Yankee Clippers to restore the nation's honor. Finally, if the blood of American sons was spilled on foreign shores, then Congress would demand just retribution, and more ships and sons would be sent to right the wrong.

It was seldom hard to frame a policy, or a rationalization, for one Asian action or another. In the early 19th century the age of ideology had not yet dawned. In the mid-19th century there was "Manifest Destiny," which could mean anything. By the latter part of the 19th century there was the "Open Door"— designed to protect traders and missionaries and all of those American interests that had accumulated over the preceding decades. Whatever the ideological rationalization, the United

States managed to establish a far-flung trading empire from one end of the Pacific to the other.

SAMOA. The Samoan Islands were the key to the South Seas. In 1839, Commodore Charles Wilkes visited the serene harbor of Pago Pago. He befriended an American trader, one of many who used the Samoan Islands for commerce and pleasure, and designated him "agent" of the U.S. Government. Over the next three decades the United States vied with Britain and Germany for control of the islands. In 1871 some American shipping companies explored the possibility of setting up a naval and coaling base at Pago Pago, "the most perfectly land-locked harbor that exists in the Pacific Ocean." Britain did not have the power to object; and Germany was too absorbed in fighting the French at Metz to raise any meaningful objections. So, by a treaty signed in February, 1872, the United States acquired Pago Pago. Actually, the Senate never ratified that treaty. But no matter. American ships continued to use Pago Pago. Finally, on April 12, 1890, J. C. Williams, the U.S. consul in Samoa, signed a new treaty in Apia with Malietoa, Tamalangi, Matetau, Reea, Tooa, Moli, and Saga, the ruling chiefs of Samoa. Malietoa signed for all the chiefs with a single "X." And, after much hesitation, the United States took final and formal control of the "American Samoas" in 1899.

THE SANDWICH ISLANDS. Of them, Mark Twain once wrote:

No alien land in all the world has any deep, strong charm for me but that one; no other land could so longingly and beseechingly haunt me sleeping and waking, through half a lifetime, as that one has. Other things leave me, but it abides; other things change, but it remains the same. For me its balmy airs are always blowing, its summer seas flashing in the sun; the pulsing of its surfbeat is in my ear; I can see its garlanded crags, its leaping cascades, its plumy palms drowsing by the shore; its remote summits floating like islands above the cloudrack; I can feel the spirit of its woodland solitudes; in my nostrils still lives the breath of flowers that perished twenty years ago.

These were the magnificent islands introduced to the world early in the 19th century by sailors from many lands. By the 1840s whalers, missionaries, and merchants filled Honolulu. The native rulers were so baffled by the commercial and religious onslaught that they almost accepted a British protectorate in

1843; but the British were too preoccupied in India and China to impose their political will on the Hawaiian Islands. Besides, with each passing year, more and more Americans reached the islands, gradually introducing their customs and setting up their businesses. By the 1860s the Hawaiian Islands were thoroughly Americanized. In September, 1867, after the United States took possession of Midway Island, farther west across the Pacific, Secretary of State Seward wrote: "A lawful and peaceful annexation of the islands to the United States with the consent of the people of the Sandwich Islands is deemed desirable by this government."

But it did not happen, not then. It happened in stages. In 1875 the United States extended a kind of protectorate over Hawaii, obtained extensive trading privileges, and acquired Pearl Harbor as a naval base. American capital flowed to the islands. Huge sugar and pineapple industries flourished, even if the people did not. In 1800 the native population was estimated at 400,000; by 1880 it was down to 55,000.

In 1891, when Queen Liliuokalani, a poetess and songwriter, came to the throne, she tried to stop the spread of Westernization. She failed dismally. American business now controlled the islanders' livelihood. Moreover, President Benjamin Harrison and Secretary of State James G. Blaine favored American expansionism. When it became clear to them that Queen Liliuokalani was determined to expel American power from the Hawaiian Islands, they encouraged a powerful coalition of American businessmen and native dissidents to depose her and to set up a provisional government. In mid-January, 1893, Harrison dispatched the Marines to Honolulu and a treaty of annexation to the Senate. The Senate did not act quickly, chiefly because Harrison was by then a lame duck. He had been defeated by Grover Cleveland, returning to the White House for a second term. Five days after taking office, on March 9, Cleveland tried to defy public opinion by recalling the annexation treaty from the Senate. He succeeded only in touching off a slashing congressional debate "over the merits of imperialism," to quote Allan Nevins.

This time Cleveland sought to "vindicate national honor,

conscience, and love of justice." Carl Schurz and Charles Francis
Adams, Jr. praised Cleveland's "defiance of jingoism." "It is not
easy to see," Adams wrote, "how the United States can protest
against the policy of force pursued by England and France in
their dealings with semi-civilized natives if we ourselves are
quite unable to resist the temptation to have a hack at them on
our own account." But, in the 1890s, while Japan revealed her
far-reaching imperial designs, the European powers hacked at
China, and a war with Spain was just over the horizon, Adams's
voice was drowned in the clamor for still wider expansion of
American influence and power. The Republicans enlisted a Navy
captain, Alfred T. Mahan, to launch a patriotic and successful
counterattack. His article, "Hawaii and Our Future Sea-Power,"
made the point that the United States simply could not do
without Hawaii. One expansionist journal exploded: "President
Cleveland turned back the hands on the dial of civilization.
Native rule, ignorant, naked, heathen, is re-established; and the
dream of an American republic at the crossroads of the Pacific
. . . has been shattered by Grover Cleveland, a Buffalo Lilli-
putian."

The argument between Adams and Mahan, between the
doves and the hawks, was to be repeated in less than a decade,
when the United States suppressed a nationalist uprising in the
Philippines. Again the doves lost. On July 7, 1898, despite lingering misgivings among many Congressmen and writers, the
Hawaiian Islands were formally annexed by the United States.

ALASKA. Secretary of State William Seward had big dreams
for America. One of those dreams was to possess Alaska, or
Russian America. The story may be apocryphal but, according
to his son, Frederick Seward, the Secretary was playing whist
one March night in 1867, when the Czar's minister in Washington was announced. "I have a dispatch, Mr. Seward, from my
government by cable. The Emperor gives his consent to the
cession. Tomorrow, if you like, I will come to the Department,
and we can enter upon the Treaty." Seward smiled, pushed away
the whist table, and said: "Why wait until tomorrow, Mr.
Stoeckl? Let us make the treaty tonight."

The two went to the State Department. Seward invited

Senator Charles Sumner, chairman of the Foreign Relations Committee, to join the discussions. By the time dawn rose over Washington, Seward and Stoeckl had signed an agreement under which the United States was to purchase Alaska for $7,200,000. The Democratic press denounced the deal as "Seward's Folly," disparaging Alaska as "Seward's Polar-Bear Garden." Seward ignored the criticism and shrewdly steered the deal through a skeptical Congress, helped by clever propaganda and Stoeckl's bribing of several influential Senators. Sumner compared the deal to the Louisiana Purchase, called the Aleutian Islands "a friendly hand to Asia," and applauded Republican vision. On July 14, 1868, more than one year after Seward struck his late-night bargain with Stoeckl, Congress appropriated the money, and the United States acquired control over Alaska and the Aleutians. It was, in retrospect, a brilliant deal for the United States, a colossal loss to Russia.

JAPAN AND KOREA. Japan had been closed to outsiders for more than 200 years by a xenophobic shogunate, which deeply distrusted the West. Every now and then a shipwrecked American sailor, cast up on Japanese shores, would be maltreated. This provided the pretext for American intervention. Commodore Matthew Calbraith Perry was entrusted with the mission of "opening the door to Japan." His instructions from the State Department became a significant expression of American policy in the Pacific:

Recent events—the navigation of the ocean by steam, the acquisition and rapid settlement by this country of a vast territory on the Pacific, the discovery of gold in that region, the rapid communication established across the Isthmus which separates the two oceans—have practically brought the countries of the East in closer proximity to our own; although the consequences of these events have scarcely begun to be felt, the intercourse between them has already greatly increased and no limits can be assigned to its future extension.

Commodore Perry steamed into Tokyo on July 8, 1853 in the lead ship of a squadron of four black warships. His orders were to get an agreement with the Japanese that would protect American seamen, open several ports, and establish a coaling depot for American ships on their way to China. The fact that

Britain had managed to wrest control of Hong Kong and to open several ports in China, a result of the Treaty of Nanking in 1842, goaded the United States to seek similar concessions in Japan. As Commodore Perry wrote en route to Japan: "When we look at the possessions in the East of our great maritime rival, England, and of the rapid and constant increase of their fortified ports, we should be admonished of the necessity of prompt measures on our part."

On his way to Japan, Perry stopped off at Okinawa and the Bonin Islands in order to set up a coaling station for American ships. He returned to Okinawa after his historic entry into Tokyo harbor, then set course for Macao and Hong Kong. A few months later, in February, Perry returned to Tokyo and, within a month, signed a treaty with the confused Japanese, who still regarded him as a barbarian—but a strong one, from whom Japan must learn. The Japanese opened the port of Nagasaki and promised humane treatment for shipwrecked American sailors.

THE FIRST KOREAN WAR. No sooner had the United States established coaling stations on Okinawa and opened ports in Japan than American ships began to move toward Korea, the Hermit Kingdom. It proved to be a more difficult operation. The Koreans, like the Japanese, had been cut off from the West. But, unlike the Japanese, they insisted upon remaining cut off. When a foreign ship sailed into a Korean port, its cargo was generally confiscated and its crew murdered. In August, 1866, an American trading schooner, *General Sherman,* sailed into a Korean port with a cargo of cotton goods, tinplate, and glass. The crew was slaughtered. At roughly the same time, a small group of French missionaries was massacred by the Koreans. In the spring of 1867 Secretary Seward proposed a joint American-French attack on Korea. The French refused. Four years later Seward's successor, Hamilton Fish, ordered a small American naval force to attack Korea. In May, 1871, this squadron sailed from Nagasaki, where America's Asiatic Fleet was based, to the mouth of the Han River, where it anchored. Upstream were several forts. One was called The Citadel. On June 10, two American gunboats, carrying 546 sailors and 105 Marines, sailed upstream to attack The Citadel. By midday the American flag was raised over

The Citadel. Three hundred and fifty Koreans had been killed. American losses were put at three dead and ten wounded. Thus, after eleven long years of on-again, off-again negotiations, in 1882, the United States signed a treaty with Korea opening the Hermit Kingdom to Yankee traders.

THE PHILIPPINES. By 1898 the United States was a major Pacific power—with island holdings or ports from the Aleutians in the north to American Samoa in the south, from Honolulu in the central Pacific to Midway and Okinawa closer to the Asian mainland. The major European powers were carving up China. With the extraordinary exception of Japan, which learned from the West in order to teach "the barbarians" a lesson much later on, all of the smaller countries on the periphery of China, including Cochin China, or Indochina, were fair game. (Thailand was fair game, too, but by some accident of geography and diplomacy escaped colonial subjugation.) Among these was the Philippines, a possession of Spain since the middle of the 16th century. Toward the end of the 19th century, as a Filipino middle class developed and as more and more Spaniards intermarried with the natives, a spirit of revolt swept the islands. In 1896 the Spanish rulers killed Dr. José Rizal, a nationalist leader, and and many of his supporters in the Young Filipino Party. Open rebellion followed. Some nationalists proclaimed a "declaration of independence," after the example of the American Revolution.

Spain refused to recognize the declaration. She was thoroughly absorbed in a threatening conflict with the United States over Cuba. In both Madrid and Washington the Philippines seemed far away. War could perhaps have been avoided, despite powerful jingoist pressures for American intervention to save Cuban patriots from Spanish persecution, and that pervasive American sympathy for colonial peoples struggling for independence from the domination of other powers. But in December, 1897, major rioting erupted in Havana, producing widespread demonstrations of concern in Congress. In February, 1898, the *New York Journal*, a sensation-seeking newspaper recently founded by William Randolph Hearst, published a private letter from the Spanish minister to Washington, Depuy De Lome, describing McKinley as "weak and a popularity-hunter."

De Lome instantly resigned. But publication of the letter enraged McKinley. Finally, on February 15, 1898, an unexplained explosion sank the powerful American battleship *Maine* near Havana. More than 260 U.S. seamen died. "Remember the Maine, to hell with Spain" became the popular battle cry.

Intervention was inevitable, given the temper of the times. On April 11, McKinley sent a message to Congress demanding that "the war in Cuba must be stopped." He asked authority to use the armed forces of the United States "to secure a full and final termination of hostilities between the Government of Spain and the people of Cuba." On April 20, Congress passed several resolutions, declaring that "the people of Cuba are, and of right ought to be, free and independent." On April 24, Spain broke relations with the United States and declared war. On April 25, Congress declared war against Spain but made the declaration retroactive to April 21, to make it seem as though Spain had been reacting to an American initiative.

The Spanish forces in Cuba were defeated in short order. The American people thrilled to the exploits of the Rough Riders and their charismatic leader, Theodore Roosevelt. When they stormed San Juan Hill and there planted the American flag, it was a moment to savor. America had come of age. By August, Spain was decisively beaten. She asked France to arrange peace terms. Spain surrendered Cuba, ceded both Puerto Rico and Guam and, by an armistice protocol, accepted American occupation of the city and harbor of Manila, pending a final peace treaty.

Plans for occupying the 7,000-island Philippine archipelago had been hatched by Teddy Roosevelt himself months before war was declared against Spain. Roosevelt was an activist Assistant Secretary of War. He dreamed of empire. "All of the great masterful races," he told a graduating class in June, 1897, "have been fighting races." In the fall, as war clouds were gathering over Cuba, he secretly summoned Admiral George Dewey to his office and offered him the job of Commander of the Asiatic Fleet. Dewey was sixty-one years old, tough and determined. He agreed with Roosevelt that war with Spain was inevitable and that the conquest of the Philippines was necessary for American interests in the Pacific.

Dewey proceeded to Nagasaki. There he refitted his squadron for battle. On February 25, 1898, he received instructions to set sail for Hong Kong and to be ready for action at a moment's notice. On April 27, two days after Congress had declared war against Spain, Dewey received orders to "proceed at once to Philippine Islands" and to "commence operations at once against the Spanish fleet." His Asiatic Squadron left immediately. On May 1, as dawn rose over the magnificent harbor of Manila, Dewey came within easy range of the Spanish fleet and opened fire. When a morning breeze cleared the smoke of battle, the Spanish fleet lay in ruins.

Filipino nationalists cheered the American victory. Their fiery leader, Emilio Aguinaldo, issued a proclamation to his people. "The Americans, not from mercenary motives, but for the sake of humanity and the lamentations of so many persecuted people, have considered it opportune," Aguinaldo naïvely stated, "to extend their protecting mantle to our beloved country. . . . There where you see the American flag flying, assemble in numbers; they are our redeemers!" Aguinaldo headed for Manila, where he conferred "almost daily" with Dewey. Assured of American blessings and arms, Aguinaldo rallied his forces and fought the Spaniards.

On June 12 the Filipinos proclaimed a provisional republic with Aguinaldo as president. On September 29 a revolutionary assembly ratified the independence of the island republic. Part of the reason for this legislative haste lay in Aguinaldo's growing suspicion that the United States, despite its fine rhetoric and material support, had no serious intention of recognizing the independence of the Philippines. He had heard reports from Washington that Roosevelt and his influential friend, Senator Henry Cabot Lodge of Massachusetts, both devotees of Captain Mahan's sea-power doctrines, wanted to convert Manila into the largest American naval base in the Pacific. Dewey's easy victory gave substance to this strategic vision. American businessmen feared that European aggression against China would rob them of their investments there; they looked upon the Philippines as a fine fallback position. In addition, Protestant missionaries saw the Manila victory as a divine summons for God's work in the Philippines, where the Catholic Church had been predominant for 300 years. The British and Japanese governments, fearful of growing German and Russian power in the Pacific, promptly let it be known that they would have no objections to American control over the Philippines.

On December 10, 1898, the United States and Spain signed a peace treaty. By its terms Washington got the Philippines, and Madrid got $20,000,000 as a kind of reward for defeat. McKinley signaled his defiance of Aguinaldo's proclamation of Philippine independence. The usually weak President, who once had so little heart for "forcible annexation," had sniffed the political winds and decided that "there was nothing left for us to do but to take them all, and to educate the Filipinos, and uplift and civilize and Christianize them."

Neither he nor Roosevelt—nor any of the other supporters of empire—had any idea of the political, psychological, and physical anguish that lay just ahead. McKinley was an honorable, upright man; so was Roosevelt, soon to be his vice-presidential running mate. So also Lodge and Mahan and Beveridge, the young Senator from Indiana, who told a Boston club, "We are a conquering race." All wanted what was best for America, and all combined, perhaps unwittingly, to create a climate in which annexation of the Philippines was somehow made to appear acceptable, sensible, truly American; more acceptable than the much older belief, dating back to the Revolution itself, that a colonial people had the right to rebel against a foreign oppressor, to be encouraged in the process, and to be recognized in the result by the United States.

Before the Spanish Treaty was approved by Congress on February 6, 1899—by one vote—a stormy and momentous debate raged in the U.S. Senate. It resembled the debate over the Hawaiian annexation earlier in the decade, but was sharper in tone and much more significant. The hard-liners dazzled the Senate with visions of wealth, power, and glory. The flag, once raised, must never be hauled down, they said; the battle, once joined, must be won. The doves, led by an elderly Senator, Hoar of Massachusetts, questioned the wisdom of the entire venture: the presumed need to squander human lives and material treasure in seemingly never-ending contributions to a dubious and somewhat shabby cause. "You make the American flag, in the eyes of numerous people," Hoar thundered, "the emblem of sacrilege in Christian churches, and of the burning of human dwellings, and of the horror of the water torture."

The doves had the eloquence, but the hawks had the votes, enough to carry the day. McKinley and Roosevelt had no master plan for running the Philippines. If they had known in 1898 what they learned by 1902, many arguments and many lives later, they might have taken different decisions.

Aguinaldo's disappointment was understandable. His redeemer, Dewey, had become, in his mind, the aggressor. The Filipino nationalist ordered his troops, who by that time had won the allegiance of most of the people, to turn on the Americans. On February 4, 1899, two days before Congress approved the Spanish Treaty, Aguinaldo declared war on the United States. His soldiers outnumbered the Americans, but they were outgunned and outfought. They retreated from Manila and fled northward—into the jungles. By November they resorted to guerrilla warfare, which challenged the American troops to the utmost. Those with combat experience against the Mexican insurgents or in the Indian wars did better than the greenhorn recruits from the eastern cities. But it was a trying, exhausting, and bitter struggle in a hot, sticky climate against a stubborn enemy. In March, 1901, Aguinaldo was captured. This broke the back of the insurrection in Luzon, although fighting continued for another year and a half on that island and for a decade and more on the southern, Moslem islands of the archipelago.

It was called an insurrection, but it was a major war. For the first time a large-scale expeditionary force left the American hemisphere to fight in a distant land; not all at one time but slowly, in small increments, over a substantial period. It was not that officials in those days were trying to delude the American people; they were themselves deluded. They had no idea from one decision to the next how many men would be needed to complete the job. By May, 1898, General Nelson A. Miles, Army Chief of Staff, had sent three infantry regiments and three artillery battalions, about 5,000 men, to Manila. By June the number had increased to 8,500 men. By December there were 25,000

men. By the following December there were 64,000 men; and
over the next several years the head count climbed to more
than 100,000.

It was a bloody victory. The Filipinos resisted bitterly once
they had retreated into the jungles. They ambushed American
troops; they burned village headquarters; and for a time they
fought the Americans to a standstill. U.S. military commanders
claimed they were killing the enemy at a ratio of 20 to 1. A reporter for the *New York Evening Post* wrote: "The twenty is
guesswork." Another reporter avoided censorship by filing from
Hong Kong a dispatch in which he countered official claims of
military success: "We have been floundering about in the wil-
derness for months without accomplishing anything." Worse, the
reporter told how American troops often became so frustrated
and embittered that they burned entire villages. He described
how "one or two of our scouts made a practice of cutting off
the ears of the insurgents they killed, and preserving them as
trophies." (Had television existed at the time, to bring these
events home to the American people every evening in their turn-
of-the-century parlors, there might well have been an outcry anticipating the popular turn against the Vietnam war in 1968.)

In 1901, after Aguinaldo's capture, an American Congressman traveled through Luzon to check on official reports that it
had been thoroughly pacified. He found the reports to be accurate. "They never rebel in northern Luzon," he said, "because
there isn't anybody there to rebel. The country was marched
over and cleaned in a most resolute manner. The good Lord in
heaven only knows the number of Filipinos that were put under
the ground. Our soldiers took no prisoners, they kept no records;
they simply swept the country, and wherever or whenever they
could get hold of a Filipino they killed him. The women and
children were spared."

Generals made names for themselves. One of them, General
Jacob Smith, made headlines as "hell-roaring Jake." He ordered
all Filipinos into camps soon after his arrival on the island of
Samar, with its population of 250,000 people. One day, a U.S.
infantry company was surprised and killed by a band of rebel
Filipinos. General Smith demanded retaliation. "I want no pris-

oners," he said. "I wish you to kill and burn; the more you kill and burn the better you will please me." All males on the island over the age of ten he ordered killed. There is no reliable estimate of the number of Filipinos slaughtered. But, because Smith made the mistake of putting his order in writing, a touring correspondent discovered the massacre and reported it; the Army court-martialed "hell-roaring Jake."

As the war continued, domestic anguish deepened. Senator Hoar intensified his attack on the administration. "You have wasted nearly six hundred millions of treasure," Hoar thundered. "You have sacrificed nearly ten thousand American lives, the flower of our youth. You have devastated provinces. You have slain uncounted thousands of people you desire to benefit. You have established reconcentration camps. Your generals are coming home from their harvest, bringing their sheaves with them, in the shape of other thousands of sick and wounded and insane, to drag out miserable lives, wrecked in body and mind." The hawks counterattacked. Senator Albert Beveridge, who was clearly running for the Presidency, noted: "Just beyond the Philippines are China's illimitable markets. We will not retreat from either. The Pacific is the ocean of commerce of the future, and most future wars will be conflicts of commerce."

As casualties mounted with no end to the bloodletting in sight, the debate moved into the streets. A half-million Americans joined the Anti-Imperialist League. They staged demonstrations in Washington, New York, Baltimore, San Francisco, and other major cities. Mark Twain suggested the American flag be redesigned with "the white stripes painted black, and the stars replaced by a skull and crossbones." Editorial writers attacked the administration's policy in the Philippines and wondered aloud what had happened to the American conscience.

When, in 1902, the war began to "fade away," Elihu Root, the Secretary of War, journeyed to the Philippines. His mission was not to grant the islands their independence (even in victory this was out of the question) but to survey the war's devastation and to propose a costly program of reconstruction. Over the next ten years, as many as 10,000 Americans went out to the Philippines to help in this effort of restitution.

They comprised, in effect, the first Peace Corps: not tourists come to visit a now-notorious place but dedicated workers who came to help the Filipinos recover from a miserable war. There were doctors who battled the plague; teachers who started schools in small villages, deep in the interior; nutrition experts who fought beriberi. These Americans have never been celebrated—perhaps because their countrymen preferred to forget the Philippine experience, the good as well as the bad; perhaps because they could not balance the help that was being extended against the harm that had been inflicted.

It has always been a strong and, to some, a possibly strange feature of American policy that the effort to right a particular wrong must be made; sometimes even as the wrong was being inflicted. For example, at the very height of the Philippine fighting, when native insurgents were being slaughtered, President McKinley was instructing his generals and diplomats to make sure they understood that "the mission of the United States is one of 'benevolent assimilation.'" American troops offhandedly referred to the Filipinos as "niggers" and "googoos." "Gooks" had not yet come into use. Yet there were numerous examples of the same troops giving food and shelter to Filipinos, because, as one soldier is quoted as having said, "we are all Christians." Even as General Pershing brutalized the Moros on the southern islands, killing hundreds and thousands of them for not accepting Americanization, his colleagues were contributing personal funds to start schools and hospitals in Luzon. The good and the bad have always mixed curiously in American policy and action—then as now, as though the pull of conscience were never far behind the presumed necessities of policy.

By the turn of the 20th century America had fought her first guerrilla war; dispatched her first large-scale expeditionary force to a foreign country, to be followed years later by her first Peace Corps; listened wearily to a prolonged Senate debate on the wisdom of intervention; and, in her way, gloried in the global visions of her first modern President. America had acquired an empire and lost her innocence.

TWO

The Rise to World Power

FROM THE ACQUISITION of the Philippines in 1898 until the close
of World War II in 1945, the United States advanced steadily
into the ranks of the Great Powers. London, Paris, Berlin, and
Moscow could no longer ignore the American presence in Asia.
A few years after the outbreak of the Great War, America sent
her first expeditionary force to Europe, just as twenty years
earlier she had sent an expeditionary force to the Philippines.
Now the European powers had to reckon with American power
as a new fact of 20th century life. The Great Power club swung
open its heavy doors to a new member.

Foreign diplomats were quicker to perceive the new, global
role of the United States, however, than the American people.
They were totally unprepared for world leadership and responsibility. The American dream, as the people understood it, had
never involved becoming a power like other powers; that much
of Washington's early teaching still lodged in the American soul.
If America were to be great in wealth and military power, she
had equally to stand for higher values than other nations, never
stooping to those cynical manipulations that Americans associated with the worldly, corrupt older nations of Europe.

Professor Samuel Flagg Bemis, troubled by the widening
gap between American belief and American action, concluded
that the Philippines acquisition must have been a "great aberration." He ignored America's earlier forays in Asia. Believing that
America's national interest lay in what later came to be called
the Atlantic community, Bemis dismissed Senator Beveridge's

ranting about "China's illimitable markets" as "dangerous." He
wrote:

If the expansionists of 1898 could have read the future as we
read the past, or if they had even taken the pains to study a few
statistics of trade and investment demonstrative of the small stake
which the United States had in the Far East compared with other
parts of the world, or the problems of strategy involved, we are constrained to believe that they would not have embarked so precipi-
tately upon the conspicuous but unprofitable and foolhardy venture
into the world politics of Asia, so alien to American traditions and
interests, so dangerous to the welfare of the United States.

Yet successive Presidents did little or nothing to correct the
"aberration" that so deeply troubled Professor Bemis. The U.S.
held its far-flung Asian position. The Philippines remained to
all intents a colony. And, in China, as Professor J. K. Fairbank
has pointed out in his classic study, *The United States and
China,* America established a new territorial frontier after the
last frontier at home had been conquered. Secretary of State
John Hay—a "fine figurehead," according to his boss, President
Roosevelt—called it the "Open Door." Playing on both strings of
America's newly-enunciated China policy, Hay first criticized the
Europeans for carving up China, then demanded "equality of
trading opportunity." Clearly he and Roosevelt felt that the
United States, fresh from its conquest of the Philippines, was
now entitled to at least an equal share of the China market.

Americans had long been drawn to China. They saw in the
men who wore gowns and the women who wore trousers an intriguing differentness that aroused their curiosity and sympathy
as much as their greed.

This "disconcerting split," in Professor Fairbank's words,
"between humanitarian ideals and strategic realism" was just as
evident in the Philippines as later also in Vietnam. It has remained a hallmark of the American approach to Asia.

Consider, for example, the extraordinary American response
to the Russo-Japanese war of 1905. For the first time in history
an Asian country had soundly defeated a great European power.
Here was a backward, island kingdom, so recently bullied and
bamboozled by the West, which had learned enough about how
Europeans fought to overcome the armies and navies of Imperial

Russia. The victory was a staggering setback for Czarism, which succumbed to Bolshevism within twelve years. It also set an electrifying example for other Asian nations. All yearned for the kind of respect Japan had so abruptly exacted from the West. Washington began to worry over the rise of a strong and potentially belligerent Japan. Teddy Roosevelt, the most imperial-minded of American Presidents, offered his mediation. Representatives of the two powers—Russia and Japan—met at Portsmouth, New Hampshire, to agree upon the terms of a peace treaty. Japan acquired Port Arthur and the Liaotung Peninsula (both won and lost in the 1895 war against China), a preferred position in Manchuria, a protectorate over Korea, and the southern half of Sakhalin Island. The victory over Russia was so complete that, had the Japanese pressed their advantage, they might have got even more. But Roosevelt, the mediator, was not eager to oblige them further. He shrewdly struck a balance between the minimum that Japan could accept and the maximum that Russia could tolerate, hailing the compromise as the "work of statesmanship." For these efforts—and his advocacy of the Hague Tribunal—T.R. in 1906 was awarded the Nobel Peace Prize.

As T.R. looked at Asia, American interest required that neither Japan nor Russia should acquire too much influence in North China. From that time on, Washington held fast to John Hay's contention that the "integrity" of China must not be compromised. It was, of course, compromised constantly. But the idea of Chinese integrity remained an increasingly compelling factor in American policy toward Asia.

From 1905 until 1914 the colonial powers devoted less attention to their Asian possessions—or to China—than to the gathering threat of war in Europe. Japan moved slowly at first, taking advantage of Europe's preoccupation with the Kaiser. If China's integrity was to be compromised still further, it was clear that Japan would do the compromising. She played that role until her shattering defeat in 1945.

Aiming to challenge Japan's rising stature in Asia, Roosevelt decided in 1908 to send a mammoth naval fleet into the Pacific. It paid a conspicuous visit to Japan, hoping to induce a submissive reaction from the emperor. If Roosevelt's design was to reenact the triumph of Commodore Perry, the tactic failed. In Tokyo's spacious harbor the American fleet was met with elaborate courtesy by a Japanese fleet of identical size. This bow-to-bow standoff demonstrated the rising power of both nations and the unwillingness of either to be intimidated by the other.

Within a few months, in the Root-Takahira note, the United States recognized Japan's "special interest" in Asian affairs. This was Washington's condescending way of admitting Japan to the Pacific club; in 1917, in the follow-up Lansing-Ishii note, the United States went one step further by acknowledging Japan's "special interests in China." The two nations were then allied against Germany. While the United States fought the common enemy in Europe, distracted for the time being from such historic developments as Dr. Sun Yat-sen's proclamation of a republic and his distressing inability to control China's competing warlords, Japan moved swiftly. She occupied all the German possessions in the Shantung Peninsula, turned Manchuria and most of northern China into a kind of Japanese protectorate, overran German-controlled islands in the Marshall and Caroline chains, and sent troops into Siberia as a hedge against a resurgent Russia.

Washington fretted but did nothing: a conference here, a conference there, but essentially nothing. There were efforts through the 1920s to limit Japan's growing military strength, especially her navy, but the efforts proved fruitless. Japan expanded her industrial base, captured many of the Asian markets formerly controlled by the Europeans, and developed a dynamic, driving, and ultimately desperate society. By the late 1920s Japan's high-powered modernization had wakened the appetites and ambitions that ultimately changed the character of the government—from a civilian, liberal, Western-oriented regime into an increasingly aggressive and militaristic clique. By 1931 the Japanese claimed that one of their officers had been killed in Mukden; and, accepting no satisfaction other than conquest, their army units based in southern Manchuria seized Chinese arsenals and spread northward over all of Manchuria. In 1932 the Japanese landed 70,000 troops in Shanghai and declared Manchuria to be an independent state under a ruler selected by them. The Chinese government of Generalissimo Chiang Kai-shek complained to the League of Nations. An investigating commission was quickly dispatched to China. It established the obvious—that Japan was guilty of "disturbing the peace." This report encouraged certain smaller powers to call for military sanctions. But the larger powers, paralyzed by an economic depression and frightened by the sudden rise of Hitler, had little stomach for a showdown with the aggressive Japanese. There was, as always, a certain sympathy for China. But she got no help, none at all. For China, World War II began in 1931.

Washington upheld its honor by refusing to recognize the new Japanese-puppet state of Manchukuo, consistent with its long-standing policy of supporting the "integrity" of China. Throughout the 1930s it joined collective diplomatic efforts to discourage Japan from further aggression. Americans grieved when they learned of Japanese atrocities against the people of China. The grief was sincere enough. It suited a national mood of despair, symbolized on the economic side by mass unemployment and on the psychological side by a feeling of helplessness and frustration unknown in the nation's history. These were not the times to mobilize America's resources in China's behalf. Had an order of national priorities been drawn up in the mid-1930s, China would have been near the bottom—after the Great Depression, Hitler's rise in Europe, Mussolini's attack on Ethiopia, and the bloody civil war in Spain.

There was, overall, so little appetite for any kind of foreign entanglement that Congress passed the Neutrality Act of 1935, specifically depriving the President of the right to discriminate between "aggressor" and "nonaggressor" in international conflicts. Even as Washington bemoaned Japan's aggression against China, it allowed the sale of scrap metal to the aggressor. In a most peculiar way, neutrality reigned supreme. What made it most peculiar was that mixed with the policy of neutrality was an attitude of self-righteous morality. Neutrality and morality coexisted through the 1930s, producing a policy of strong words and weak action. After Japan, in the summer of 1937, had conquered Peking and bombed Shanghai, President Franklin D.

Roosevelt delivered his famous quarantine-the-aggressor speech
in Chicago: "War is a contagion, whether it be declared or undeclared," he said. "It can engulf states and people remote from
the original scene of the hostilities." FDR seemed to be testing
public opinion to determine whether the nation would tolerate
the quarantining of Japan in order to save China. The answer
was no. Even Henry L. Stimson, Secretary of State in the Hoover
Administration and the primary advocate of strong collective action to check Japanese aggression, declared: "Let me make it
perfectly clear that in my opinion this is not a case where there
should be any thought of America sending arms to participate
in the strife going on in Asia."

Some American businessmen admired Japan—they had,
after all, invested about $250,000,000 there. But many other
Americans, perhaps most of them, were deeply suspicious of
Japan. They distrusted her reckless expansionism.

Sumner Welles, who was Roosevelt's Under Secretary of
State during World War II, recalled the President's strong anti-
Japanese feelings, even back in the Twenties, when he was Assistant Secretary of the Navy. "He had become imbued with the
Navy's conviction," Welles wrote, "that Japan was America's
Number 1 antagonist. And no one close to the President could
have failed to recognize the deep feeling of friendship for China
he had inherited from his mother's side of the family. His mother,
in fact, had lived in China as a small girl, and he himself loved
to tell over and over again stories of the dealings members of his
family had had with various Chinese dignitaries and merchants
in the earlier decades of the nineteenth century."

"A personal equation of this kind," Welles said, "undeni-
ably influences the thinking of a man even in high office. . . .
He became ever more incensed by Japan's conduct as the years
passed."

If there was suspicion of Japan, there was the deepest res-
ervoir of sympathy for China. Here Americans had made their
heaviest emotional investments. Sun Yat-sen had been schooled
by Americans in the Hawaiian Islands. He believed, as he wrote
in *The Three People's Principles,* in democracy, nationalism, and
social well-being. Like many of his American friends, Sun Yat-sen

never accepted the Treaty of Versailles at the end of World War I, because none of the major signatories would agree to abandon the "treaty system" which had been imposed upon China in 1842. He linked European capitalism inescapably with colonialist exploitation and, moved by the Russian revolution, turned to Moscow for help in restoring the dignity of China. In historical terms, he saw the Chinese and Russian revolutions as part of the same mass movement of oppressed peoples. Soon he allowed members of the Chinese Communist Party, formed in 1921, to join the Kuomintang, his nationalist party. He also accepted Soviet military and political advisers, most notably the professional revolutionary Borodin.

Sun Yat-sen died in 1925, a bitterly disappointed man. He had hoped for American help in modernizing China, but he was forced to settle for Soviet help. "America was the inspiration and example," he wrote, "when we started the revolution to abolish autocracy and corruption in high places. We might well have expected that an American Lafayette would fight on our side in this good cause. In the 12th year of our struggle towards liberty, there comes not a Lafayette but an American admiral with more ships of war than any other nation in our waters."

The more Sun Yat-sen's disappointment deepened, the more he leaned on the Russians; and the more he leaned on the Russians, the more the Americans distrusted him. This cycle gained strength from America's fear of Bolshevism—Washington had refused to recognize the Soviet Union until 1933—and from a missionary-inspired belief that the future of China lay with those leaders, as one missionary put it, who "have been touched by Christ."

Such a leader was Chiang Kai-shek, who had the good sense to marry a sister-in-law of Sun Yat-sen. Madame Chiang was a graduate of Wellesley College and a Christian. In 1927— just as Stalin swung Soviet policy away from Trotsky's notions of world revolution toward his own doctrine of "socialism in one country"—the Kuomintang split in two. The anti-Communists, captained by Chiang, turned abruptly on the Communists and drove them from the seat of power into the villages of north and central China, where they slowly acquired a "good reputation" by giving land to the peasants and fighting not only the tax-hungry warlords but later the invading Japanese. Thus did the Chinese civil war begin. It was to last until 1949, when the Communists triumphed.

It would be hard to overstate the influence of the American missionaries in China: not so much in terms of their success in bringing God's word to the "heathen masses," but rather in terms of their impact upon American thinking about China. These missionaries began arriving in China in 1829. One hundred years later, there were twenty-seven missionary colleges and universities in China. There were 300,000 Chinese students in Protestant high schools and 260,000 in Catholic schools. In all of China there were an estimated 750,000 Protestants, and a million and a half Catholics.

Statistics tell only a fraction of the story. The missionaries brought a message of God and freedom to the Chinese people. They became, as Earl Cressy once wrote, "an intermediary between two great civilizations" and "an embodiment of the strivings of the West to attain its ideals of social justice and world brotherhood." Pearl Buck, a daughter of missionary parents in China, put the same thought in more personal terms: "I can only believe that my parents reflected the spirit of their generation, which was of an America bright with the glory of a new nation, rising united from the ashes of [civil] war, and confident of the power to 'save' the world. Meantime they had no conception of the fact that they were in reality helping to light a revolutionary fire, the height of which we still have not seen, nor can foresee." When she wrote, the Communists had not yet taken power.

Gradually, as the Christian gospel reached a limited number of Chinese, a more sophisticated awareness of Chinese civilization reached the American people through the missionaries. Americans became more inquiring, more respectful of Chinese civilization. Tens of thousands of them traveled to China and lived there. They went as teachers, journalists, businessmen, and soldiers. Entire Army and Marine Corps units were based in China, protecting American commercial interests, for the first four decades of this century. The 15th "Can-Do" Regiment was stationed at Tientsin for twenty-eight years, graduating an impressive corps of American officers, including George C. Marshall, Joseph W. Stilwell, and Matthew B. Ridgway.

American influence and interest in China peaked in the early Thirties. Alice Tisdale Hobart's *Oil for the Lamps of China* was a best-seller; so were the early works of Lin Yutang, among them, *My Country and My People*. Charlie Chan, a Chinese detective, became an American folk hero. The family-oriented *Saturday Evening Post* featured his exploits, and Sidney Toler immortalized him for the Saturday-afternoon movie crowd. In *The Good Earth,* first the book and later the movie, Pearl Buck created a powerfully sympathetic account of the Chinese people. "It can almost be said," Harold Isaacs, the journalist turned historian, has written, "that for a whole generation of Americans she 'created' the Chinese, in the same sense that Dickens 'created' for so many of us the people who lived in the slums of Victorian England." The book sold more than 2,000,000 copies. The movie was seen by an estimated 23,000,000 Americans and 20,000,000 foreigners.

Other children of missionary parents brought their vision of China to the American people. Henry R. Luce, a giant of journalism, who started *Time, Life,* and *Fortune* magazines, constantly propagated his dream of a Christian and democratic China. Generalissimo and Madame Chiang Kai-shek were his heroes; their enemies became his enemies. In 1938 *Time* selected them as Man and Woman of the Year.

China was "in." No longer a nation of illiterate and unsympathetic heathens, China had become, at least in American eyes, a country well on its way to Christianity and democracy; no longer just a marketplace.

It was in this emotional context that Japan, "America's Number 1 antagonist," went to war against China. Roosevelt was furious. He watched with dismay the outbreak of conflict in Europe on September 1, 1939, when Germany marched into Poland. He had tried to maintain a posture of neutrality, consistent with the will of Congress and the mood of the American people. But it became increasingly difficult—in Europe as in Asia. On October 27, 1939, he persuaded Congress to lift the embargo on the shipment of arms to friendly nonaggressors. Within a year Britain had received fifty destroyers and when, in September, 1940, Japan invaded French Indochina, Roosevelt quickly imposed an embargo on the sale of scrap iron and steel to Japan. His suspicions of the 1920s looked sounder every day as Japanese armies stretched their attack against Indochina to a more general assault on Southeast Asia. Somewhere in the far Pacific, American officers expected a Japanese attack. But they were shocked and surprised when the Japanese targeted Pearl Harbor. In a daring air attack, Japanese planes flew out of the early morning sky on December 7, 1941. They destroyed three battleships, sixteen cruisers and destroyers, shot up dozens of warplanes lined up like sitting ducks at an air base, and inflicted about 3,000 casualties.

At approximately the same time, the Japanese struck at the Philippines, the Malayan peninsula, the East Indies, Wake, Guam, and Midway—a stunning series of well-executed campaigns. On December 8, President Roosevelt asked for a declaration of war against Japan—and got it instantly. Similar declarations against Germany and Italy soon followed. America went on a wartime footing. Around the clock her mighty industrial machine produced the weapons of war for Britain and Russia and China as well.

By early 1943 the tide had turned—against the Italians and the Germans in Europe, against the Japanese in Asia. From his headquarters in Australia, General MacArthur directed the American counterattack. One after another the island fortresses of Japan fell to the Allies. General Eisenhower directed the allied counterattack against Nazi Germany. First North Africa was secured; then Italy; and finally France. Relentlessly, from the East, came the Russians—determined, in this grandest of all Slav-Teuton confrontations, to destroy forever Germany's capacity to make war. In both theaters of conflict—Asia and Europe—the Allied demand was "unconditional surrender." Roosevelt, the chief architect of this policy, died on April 12, 1945, as the Axis powers were on the verge of defeat. Harry Truman, once a Missouri haberdasher, succeeded to the Presidency and the problems of a postwar world. On April 25 the

United Nations was born in San Francisco. On May 7 Germany surrendered. On July 16, at 5:30 A.M., the first atomic blast was detonated on top of a steel tower on the Alamogordo air base 120 miles south of Albuquerque, New Mexico. On July 26, in Potsdam, the three Allied leaders—Truman, Attlee (who had just replaced Churchill), and Stalin—issued an ultimatum to Japan: accept "unconditional surrender" or risk "utter destruction." Truman was prepared to use the bomb. In fact, preparations for its use were underway. Although some Japanese leaders made an unconvincing peace gesture in those hectic final weeks of the war, it came to nothing. Japan's fanatical military leadership pressed the course of war, sending kamikaze (suicide) planes against American targets and battling American troops until death.

On August 6 the United States Army Air Force dropped the first atomic bomb on the Japanese city of Hiroshima. It had the power of 20,000 tons of TNT. The bomb totally devastated four square miles of the city and killed 66,000 people, injuring 69,000 more. Truman barely gave the Japanese time to digest the significance of the explosion. On August 9 he ordered a second atomic bomb dropped on Nagasaki. Half the city was destroyed, and 39,000 Japanese were killed, 25,000 more injured. Later that day, by prearrangement with Roosevelt and Churchill at Yalta, Stalin ordered the Red Army to attack Japanese forces in Manchuria and, at that late hour, formally declared war against Japan. On August 10 the Japanese emperor himself broadcast an appeal for peace. On August 15 the war ended.

Japan was stripped of Formosa, Korea, Manchuria, vast stretches of China, Southeast Asia, and all her island conquests in the central and south Pacific and forced to retreat to her home islands. Forty years before, she had inflicted a humiliating defeat on a white, European nation, and to a degree changed the course of world history. Now she lay in dreadful purgatory, under clouds of atomic dust, her home islands occupied by a western nation that had returned to take a terrible revenge.

President Truman felt that he had given Japan fair warning. As Commander-in-Chief, he wanted to save the tens of thousands of American lives that—so his generals told him—

would have been lost in the scheduled invasion of the Japanese home islands. Still, questions arise. Could he not have given Japan a little more time after the first atomic attack? Or issued another warning? If Japan had capitulated before Germany, would Truman have ordered atomic-bomb attacks on Germany? We cannot *know* the answers to these hypothetical questions. We know that many Asian intellectuals over the years have persuaded themselves that the United States had fewer qualms about dropping atomic bombs on Asians than on Europeans. There is some evidence that in 1945 the men who governed the United States had more regard for Germany, even in defeat, than for Japan. Like Roosevelt himself, they shared an anti-Japanese bias that had a strong, perhaps suppressed, racial coloration. During the war, the American people had no difficulty accepting the Hollywood image of a bucktoothed, fiendish, unbridled Japan; largely because her military actions were so brutally effective; partly because her chopping-up of China during the 1930s had conditioned Americans to think the worst of Japan. When finally the atomic bombs were dropped on Japan, there was little public anguish and much joy. Everyone had known that one day those "little yellow bastards" would have to be taught a lesson!

Had Americans truly been the "conquering race" that Teddy Roosevelt implored them to be, then 1945 was the time, it seemed, to impose a Pax Americana upon the world. No other nation possessed the atomic bomb. (Russia was still four years away.) No other nation had so phenomenal an industrial base and one that was intact. No other nation had its forces so widely deployed around the world. No nation could have stopped the United States, not even Russia. But America lacked the desire to impose a "universal Yankee nation" upon the world. Some Americans, admittedly, were ready then to take on the Russians in hopes of restoring a comfortable, pre-Communist order to the world. But they were a tiny minority. Most Americans wanted nothing more than to "bring the boys home," to put their muscle to peacetime work. There were homes to be built, and jobs to be got, skills to be mastered, families to be raised. By 1945, this deep-seated yearning for a return to "normalcy" was, however, doomed to frustration. The experience of World War II had been too wrenching; the world looked too dangerous. Americans remembered that "neutrality" had afforded no safeguard against Germany and Japan. The United States had become a world leader. The change was startling and it was ineradicable. It produced a sudden sense of global responsibility and a generation of new leaders who realized, perhaps for the first time, that history had laid a heavy, special burden on the American people— a burden they could not put down for decades to come.

THREE

The Burdens of the Mighty

ROOSEVELT had less than ten weeks to live when he arrived at Yalta. Churchill thought he looked "frail and old." Together they talked with Stalin about the many problems of making peace; the shape of the new United Nations organization; whether Germany ought to be dismembered in defeat; when and under what conditions Russia should join the war against Japan; free elections in Poland. Through these long, difficult, and detailed discussions, Roosevelt's interest appeared to flag at times. But the old fires within him flared when he argued that colonialism had no place in the brave new postwar world. It was a point on which he had bullyragged Churchill in past encounters. The British, he insisted, ought to grasp the movement of history and free their colonies now.

On February 8, 1945, Roosevelt and Stalin met without Churchill at the Livadia Palace. Roosevelt told Stalin that he would like to see United Nations trusteeships established for Korea and Indochina. Such a decision would have prevented a return to French colonial rule in Indochina after the defeat of Japan. The British, Roosevelt said, did not approve of his trusteeship idea because they were afraid of its implications for Burma.

Charles E. Bohlen, Roosevelt's interpreter, has recorded the gist of the conversation that followed:

Marshal Stalin remarked that the British had lost Burma once through reliance on Indo-China, and it was not his opinion that Britain was a sure country to protect this area. He added that he thought Indo-China was a very important area.

The President said the Indochinese were people of small stature, like the Javanese and Burmese, and were not warlike. He added that France had done nothing to improve the natives since she had the colony. He said that General de Gaulle has asked for ships to transport French forces to Indo-China.

Marshal Stalin inquired where de Gaulle was going to get the troops.

The President replied that de Gaulle said he was going to find the troops when the President could find the ships, but the President added that up to the present he had been unable to find the ships.*

Churchill was not there to defend himself, or the French. That summer, moreover, he was swept out of office in favor of Clement Attlee's Labor Government. Attlee promptly embarked upon that "liquidation of the British Empire" which Churchill, in 1942, had vowed to prevent. As for de Gaulle, who was not invited to Yalta, he had long since determined that France would rush troops back into Indochina as soon as that became possible. In the summer of 1945, when such Gaullist stalwarts as Jacques Soustelle, Georges Pompidou, and Michel Debré urged him to consider freeing Indochina, de Gaulle refused. He argued forcefully that France needed Indochina to help restore her former position of power and influence in the world.

Indochina had been a French colony from the expansionist 1880s until the Japanese conquest in World War II. With the French gone, the flag of resistance to Japanese rule was raised by a group of Vietnamese Communists and nationalists. In May, 1941, they had met on Chinese territory, in the little town of Chingsi, Kwangsi Province, under the chairmanship of a Communist refugee leader named Nguyen Ai Quoc, who later changed his name to Ho Chi Minh (He Who Enlightens).

Together they established a League for the Independence of Vietnam, which became known as the Viet Minh. Its political platform subordinated the class struggle to the goal of national independence, looking to Nationalist China and the United States for support. In 1944, Ho boldly moved his headquarters from South China into Tonkin "to intensify the struggle" against the Japanese. In the final weeks of the war against

* "The Conferences at Malta and Yalta, 1945," *Foreign Relations of the United States* (Washington: Department of State), page 770.

Japan, his underground forces had the admiring support of the American Office of Strategic Services.

But the death of Roosevelt on April 12 doomed any possible design to dissuade the French from returning to Indochina in force. On May 28, 1945, Ambassador Patrick J. Hurley wrote President Truman:

In my last conference with President Roosevelt . . . I told him that the French, British, and Dutch were cooperating to prevent the establishment of a United Nations trusteeship for Indochina. . . . The President said that in the coming San Francisco Conference, there would be set up a United Nations trusteeship that would make effective the right of colonial people to choose the form of government under which they will live as soon as in the opinion of the United Nations they are qualified for independence.

With Roosevelt dead and Truman beset by massive, new responsibilities, the notion of a trusteeship for Indochina was soon forgotten.

At Potsdam, in July and August, Truman had little time to think about Indochina. A man who could order his priorities easily, and stick to them, he was plotting Japan's defeat. Indochina could wait. A secret interim arrangement was formalized at Potsdam. After Japan's defeat, Chinese nationalist forces were to occupy Indochina north of the 16th parallel and the British were to take over the territory south of the parallel. Presumably, the French in time would reestablish their control over Indochina.

Ho Chi Minh had other ideas. The moment Japan surrendered, he ordered his fighters into Hanoi. Like de Gaulle himself in liberated Paris, Ho received the acclaim due a wartime hero. Some Americans were with him; among them, General Gallagher and Major Patti of the OSS, who were so moved by the spirit of the occasion that they raised the Stars and Stripes near the Communists' revolutionary banner. Like Sun Yat-sen years before, Ho had looked to the United States for help. On September 2, anticipating allied support, ignorant of the Potsdam decision and encouraged by the OSS, Ho issued his own Declaration of Independence. It read in part: "All men are created equal. They are endowed by their creator with certain inalienable rights, among these are Life, Liberty and the pursuit of Happiness."

On September 12 the British arrived in Saigon. Soon afterward the Chinese reached Hanoi. The French came in strength in early 1946 and promptly took command. The British were pleased to get rid of their Vietnam obligation, as were the Chinese Nationalists, already so deeply involved in their own losing struggle with Mao Tse-tung's Communists. By March, 1946, the French, under General Leclerc, had reluctantly concluded that Ho's strength throughout Vietnam was considerable and his popularity enormous. General Leclerc then proposed, and Paris agreed, that Annam and Tonkin should be incorporated into a single territory (present-day North Vietnam); that it be recognized as a "free state" within the French Union, having its own parliament, army, and finances. But the future of Cochin China (now South Vietnam) was to be decided by a popular plebiscite at a later, unspecified date. This distressed the Communists, who disapproved of any administrative change that would have the effect of dividing the country. Ho, nevertheless, swallowed his objections. He was still hoping that France ultimately would transfer sovereignty to his provisional government. There is reason to think that Ho, in addition, believed his forces were still too weak to fight the French. As a result, he agreed not to oppose the return of French forces for a period of no more than five years.

Later in the year Ho went to Paris. It was a gesture of conciliation toward the French that displeased certain of his Communist colleagues. At Fontainebleau, in September, he signed a set of accords the chief aim of which was to avoid fighting between his revolutionary forces and the returning French troops. But the reconciliation was doomed from the start. The French were intent on reasserting their colonial rule, and the Viet Minh was intent on independence. The new high commissioner, Admiral d'Argenlieu, was an old-style French colonialist. In October the newly proclaimed French Constitution specifically named Vietnam, Laos, and Cambodia as "associated states" of the far-flung French Union. Ho and his friends felt betrayed. Fighting between the French and the Viet Minh increased. According to

official British records, "on the night of 19 December, the Viet
Minh launched a general attack on French posts and French-
occupied houses in Hanoi, the capital of northern Vietnam, and
from that moment a state of general civil war prevailed."

In Washington, all this made little impression. Churchill had
already spoken at Fulton, Missouri, about an "iron curtain" de-
scending in Eastern Europe. The Communist parties of France
and Italy were quickly gaining influence. The Red Army stood
fast throughout Eastern Europe. Greece was racked by civil war.
Stalin made alarming speeches. As perceived in Washington, the
major threat came from Eastern Europe. Washington focused on
ways of strengthening Western Europe to contain and defeat the
Communist challenge. "As we saw our role in Southeast Asia,"
Dean Acheson recalls, "it was to help toward solving the colo-
nial-nationalist conflict in a way that would satisfy nationalist
aims and minimize the strain on our West European allies. This
meant supporting the French presence in the area [Indochina]
as a guide and help to the three states in moving towards genuine independence within (for the present, at least) the French
Union. It was not an easy or a popular role."

Nor was it an inescapable role. Bernard Fall, the French-
born chronicler of the Vietnam tragedy who was killed in 1967
when he tripped over a Vietcong mine, strongly disagreed with
this line of Achesonian reasoning. In the Introduction to his
Viet Nam Witness, Fall wrote:

Back in 1946, a moderate amount of American pressure on the
French to rein in their "hawks" in Saigon, and an equal amount of
pressure on Ho and his Chinese Nationalist backers . . . by the
American mission in Hanoi, guided by a firm hand in Washington,
might have brought about an entirely different situation. Ho might
have become a Tito even before Communist China reached the Vietnamese border in December, 1949, or shortly afterward. Or, on the
other hand, he would have revealed his aggressive tendencies far earlier, and to an American-French combination backing a non-Communist
regime, just as an American-British combination backed such a regime in Greece at precisely that time. In either case, a French-fought
colonial war could have been avoided.

But there was no American pressure on the French. Europe,
not Indochina, was the main arena. The Acheson policy pre-

vailed. Washington had taken the first in a number of crucial steps—none taken with enthusiasm—which, over the years, drew the United States into the long, wasting struggle for control of Indochina.

The original mistake, according to William H. Sullivan, a career foreign service officer who helped to negotiate the Laos accords of 1962 and later served as ambassador to Laos, dates all the way back to the immediate postwar period. Before a Senate subcommittee in 1969, Sullivan testified: "By having, as a result of that [mistake] polarized the political situation in that region to the point where the United States assumed responsibilities for the region that went beyond what we had previously had, we have set ourselves on a track which has been a very expensive one. . . . The original promise that we made in World War II, and that we left with most people in the region, was that, as a result of our military action, these people would achieve independence." The problems in Indochina, a quarter century later, according to Sullivan, "stem very largely from the fact that this independence was frustrated." Ironically, the Europe-first strategy, so galling to General MacArthur throughout World War II, can be held to a degree responsible for America's eventual involvement in the Vietnam War.

President Truman's decision to support the French in Indochina doubtless seemed natural, not to say inevitable, in the Washington climate of 1946. Here was a new, untested President, inheriting burdens he was scarcely prepared to carry. Stalin appeared to threaten all of Western Europe, including France, America's oldest ally. Moreover, the leader of the movement for independence in Indochina was, like Stalin himself, a Communist. It was easy—for some policy-makers perhaps automatic—to look upon the French campaign against Ho Chi Minh as another front in the world-wide struggle to block the expansion of Russian power and Russian doctrine.

All these calculations, regrettably, had little to do with the facts of life in Hanoi. When Ho Chi Minh entered the city in August, 1945, the Emperor of Annam, Bao Dai, abdicated. He shuttled after that between France and Hong Kong, nominally a member of Ho's broadly based, anticolonial coalition, called the Viet Minh.

In 1947 the French sent tens of thousands more troops to Indo-china. Many of them were to die fighting the Viet Minh. The French were strong in the big cities. The Viet Minh controlled almost all of the northern provinces and much of the countryside. There was no end in sight. French liberals were disheartened and embarrassed by their new colonial war—particularly as Britain was yielding independence to Gandhi in India and the Dutch were giving up the East Indies. They brought pressure on the government to grant Ho his independence, but they failed. The more hawkish French politicians and generals hated Ho, distrusted communism, and persuaded themselves (quite accurately, as it turned out), that if Vietnam were to be given her independence, then Laos, Cambodia, Morocco, Algeria, Tunisia, Madagascar, and other French colonies would quickly demand theirs. Doves and hawks did strike a compromise, however. They proposed that Annam, Tonkin, and Cochin China could, if they wished, form a single state of Vietnam (the French considered this proposal a major concession to Ho), which would enjoy complete local autonomy within the French Union. Although the Communists denounced this proposal, Bao Dai accepted it. He led a band of Vietnamese nationalists into negotiations with the French High Commissioner, Emile Bollaert. On June 5, 1948, Bao Dai was appointed Chief of State of Vietnam. Theoretically his jurisdiction was to run from the Chinese border in the north to the rich Delta in the south. It was, as Jean Lacouture says, a "phantom state." But in time thirty pro-Western nations "recognized" its anomalous position as a "free state" within the French Union moving towards "independence." This "solution" satisfied the Truman Administration.

The Vietnamese Communists reacted in predictable fashion. They ridiculed Bao Dai's provisional government, directing their fire with equal ferocity at the French and their "puppet." The civil war intensified throughout this period of diplomatic finagling.

Washington officials, slowly adjusting to the strategic needs of the cold war, were becoming more and more sympathetic to those Frenchmen who saw dangers of communism spreading throughout the world. There was, after all, ample evidence. In

China, Mao Tse-tung's forces were winning one major battle after another. In French Indochina, Ho Chi Minh's troops were proving remarkably resistant to French pressure. In Europe, east of Churchill's Iron Curtain, Stalin was solidifying his socialist empire. It started on December 12, 1943, with a Treaty of Alliance with Czechoslovakia; then, in quick succession, similar treaties were signed with Yugoslavia on April 11, 1945; with Poland, April 21, 1945; with Rumania, February 4, 1948; with Hungary, February 18, 1948; with Bulgaria, March 18, 1948. The Communist Information Bureau, or Cominform, was established in September, 1947, to coordinate Communist propaganda. Stalin's agents had Jan Masaryk murdered in Prague. Russia blockaded all land traffic between West Berlin and West Germany. The United States met this frontal challenge to its war-won rights in the divided city in an imaginative way. It avoided unnecessary military provocation but secured its rights by instituting a massive airlift of food and supplies into West Berlin, finally breaking the back of the blockade in May, 1949.

This was consistent with the evolving policy of "containment," recently drafted by George Kennan, a controversial American expert on Russia who was then a high official at the State Department. In rough terms, the policy meant that the West should strengthen its "sphere of influence" by building up its economy and its defenses, and not allow the Soviet Union to expand westward. This was the point of the Truman Doctrine, under which in 1947 Congress appropriated $400,000,000 for economic and military aid to Greece and Turkey, both countries threatened by Communist domination. It also became the spirit of the Marshall Plan. In April, 1948, Congress began to appropriate literally billions of dollars for economic aid to war-devastated Western Europe. George C. Marshall, then Secretary of State, had invited the countries of Eastern Europe to share in this largesse. Poland and Czechoslovakia showed interest, but Stalin forbade them to take part. As much as anything else Stalin did in the postwar years, this flat denial of the proposition that East and West could cooperate even in the limited sphere of economic reconstruction killed Wendell Willkie's endearing notion of "one world" and confirmed the reality of "two worlds" locked in a struggle for survival. The cold war had become a fact of life.

Kennan had discerned and diagnosed the East-West confrontation—first from his diplomatic vantage point in Moscow
and, later, from his policy-making position in Washington. He
believed, in effect, that the West should not concede any additional territory to the Soviet Union, then presumed to be the
leader of a monolithic international Communist movement. At
the same time, Kennan had no thought of rolling back the Iron
Curtain. "Spheres of interest" would naturally evolve, according
to Kennan, and in time the leadership of each sphere would develop a strong vested interest in the maintenance of its own
political preserve. "Should the democracies prove able to take
in their stride the worst efforts of the disciplined and unscrupulous minorities pledged to the service of the political interests of
the Soviet Union," he observed, "Moscow would have played its
last real card." Kennan looked back into Russian history, into the
Russian soul as he understood it, and concluded that the iron
discipline associated with Stalinist rule in Eastern Europe would
gradually give way to a more moderate form of government, not
only in the Soviet Union but also throughout Eastern Europe,
thus, little by little, dissolving the Stalinist bloc. "If our policies
are wise and nonprovocative," Kennan wrote, the West should
be able "to contain" the outward thrust of Soviet power "both
militarily and politically for a long time to come."

Kennan has contended, more recently, that he never had
military power in mind when he advocated this "policy of
containment." He never, for example, favored the stationing of
hundreds of thousands of troops along the frontiers of the new
Communist empire in one vast encircling movement. Kennan
argued that economic and spiritual supremacy in the West would
suffice to produce healthy social and political changes in the
East. Seldom has any articulate man been so widely misunderstood and his teaching so thoroughly misapplied. For by containment, Kennan says he meant a peaceful mobilization against
communism. Instead he saw his policy ideas used to rationalize
a great military confrontation with the Russians. Moreover,
containment (without Kennan's consent) came to stand for a
policy of armed western reaction to every Communist threat,

real or imaginary. Mutual trust had been in short supply even when the United States and Russia were comrades in arms. In the new postwar climate the last trace of it vanished. American policy-makers and politicians made the simple assumption that in any dealings with Communists the West had to be assured of military supremacy.

It did not help matters that in this bleak, sword's-point situation of 1949, the Soviet Union should have tested its first nuclear bomb, breaking the United States monopoly. At the same time Mao's Communist armies finally thrashed the demoralized remnants of Chiang Kai-shek's forces, which promptly took refuge on the island of Formosa. Both events produced shudders in Washington. Communism appeared to loom over the Eurasian continent with one foot in the Baltic and the other in the South China Sea: one billion people, governed by Marxists, who in turn appeared to be governed by an insatiable appetite for further conquest. In India and Indonesia the Communists made their bids for power—but failed. In Malaya the Communists opened a guerrilla war against the British, matching for a time Ho's efforts against the French and later the Americans. In France and Italy the Communist parties attracted one out of every three or four voters. The entire Western World seemed threatened. As for Ho Chi Minh, in January, 1950, Acheson declared that Ho, by accepting Chinese military aid, had shown his "true colors" and was to be regarded as the "mortal enemy of native independence in Indochina."

Stalin's decision to build the bomb was not seen in Washington as a defensive measure—which, in part, it was—but rather as additional evidence of his "disciplined and unscrupulous" quest for more and more power. Mao's conquest of the mainland was seen as nothing less than a catastrophe. It instantly produced a national trauma, the dimensions of which are difficult to grasp or appreciate at this time. The "loss of China" became a powerful political issue. Accusing fingers were pointed, and the question posed: "Who lost China?" A Senator from Wisconsin named McCarthy charged there were Communists hidden in the government bureaucracy, especially in the State Department. He had a list of names to "prove" it, he warned.

As McCarthy mounted his attack against "Communists in government," even some conservative American officials with recent experience in China found themselves under suspicion, their careers in jeopardy over the "loss of China." Anyone who had uttered a kind word about Mao or an unkind word about Chiang Kai-shek was pronounced unreliable. In bureaucratic terms, the upshot of this witchhunt was that the nation's leading China specialists were hounded out of the government. Once out, they were generally silenced. Their knowledge of Asia, so desperately needed in the 1960s during the plunge into Vietnam, was absent from government decision-making. In the intervening years a new generation of China specialists was developing; but these were younger men, lacking direct experience of China. The big decisions were left to politicians or to Soviet specialists, such as Ambassador Llewellyn E. Thompson, Jr., who would be the first to admit his lack of experience in Asia. John Paton Davies, among others, had the experience, but he was kicked out of the State Department during the McCarthy purge. Thompson knew the Russians, especially Nikita Khrushchev, intimately; his insights into Khrushchev's behavior during the Cuban missile crisis proved to be invaluable guides to action and policy for President Kennedy. But "Tommy" Thompson was incapable of providing President Johnson with similar insights into Mao's judgments and Ho's policies. For a time Johnson had no single China expert sitting at his side to help him reach the big war-and-peace decisions on Vietnam.

In policy terms, the unfortunate conjunction of such major events as the "loss of China" trauma and the rise of McCarthyism meant that the United States through almost two tragic decades would grope and fumble for a policy that might make possible a *modus vivendi* with China. Such a policy is still proving to be elusive; at least McCarthyism is dead, and the "who lost China?" disorder—symbolized until recent years by a rigid, unrealistic, and paralyzing attachment to Chiang Kai-shek on Formosa— is fading. A nation that had invested so much love, treasure, and missionary zeal in another could not easily accept rejection. When Mao raised his red banner over the Square of Heavenly Peace, it was a moment of sheer panic for all American romantics about China—and they were many. It was, in a way, a love spurned.

Some wanted to punish China, as an adult would punish a child who had done a foolish thing. Others, including Henry Luce, came to favor a deal with the "new" China, perhaps because they could not accept a world in which contact with China would be cut. On February 14, 1950, after ten weeks of tough bargaining, Mao Tse-tung and Joseph Stalin signed a thirty-year pact, which seemed to commit China to support of Russia's hardening policy against the West. Emboldened, China then launched a strong propaganda attack against the American occupation of Japan, its support of Chiang Kai-shek and of France in "stifling the national liberation movement" in Indochina. The increasingly anti-American tone of Peking's propaganda coincided with a strident reaffirmation of China's faith in the strategy of "local wars" and "armed insurrections" then articulated by such party leaders as Liu Shao-chi and Li Li-san. In the spring of 1950, the Chinese massed hundreds of thousands of troops in the Chekiang-Fukien coastal provinces opposite Chiang's base on Formosa. Washington gloomily estimated that Chiang's days were numbered. O. Edmund Clubb, the last United States consul general in Peking, felt that the Communist regime would "coordinate any move in the Formosa Strait with Communist actions planned for other sectors." No one could say where.

Washington's worry deepened as reports circulated that the few remaining American consuls in China were being harassed and in some cases beaten. The rising tension snapped on June 25, 1950. On that day the lingering debate over China policy was choked off—prematurely, it now appears—by the start of an Asian war involving the use of American ground combat troops. Again unwittingly, the United States took another step —in fact, a series of steps—which led to direct American engagement in Vietnam.

The Communists struck in Korea. On June 25, North Korean troops, supported by Moscow and encouraged by Peking, crashed across the 38th parallel, dividing the peninsula that American gunboats had helped to open seventy-odd years before. The Communist advance was swift and startling. Within several weeks it had crushed the South Korean defenses. Anti-Communist troops retreated to the southern part of the peninsula. President Truman wasted little time. He went to the United Nations, where he took advantage of the deliberate absence of the Soviet delegate to push through a Security Council resolution authorizing immediate intervention by a UN force and condemning North Korea's "aggression." At roughly the same time he ordered General Douglas MacArthur, Supreme Allied Commander in Japan, to move American troops into Korea to repel the Communist attack. After several initial setbacks, MacArthur's forces drove the North Koreans back across the 38th parallel. Truman, fearing the Communist attack in Korea was only the opening shot of an Asia-wide campaign, moved the United States Seventh Fleet into the Formosa Strait. This was a unilateral action; it had no UN backing. On June 27 he also beefed up U.S. defenses in the Philippines and for the first time, in a presidential statement, addressed himself to Indochina. "The attack upon Korea," the President stated, "makes it plain beyond all doubt that Communism has passed beyond the use of subversion to conquer independent nations and will now use armed invasion and war." Truman then acted. "Accordingly," he said, with characteristic firmness, "I have directed acceleration in the furnishing of military assistance to the forces of France and the Associated States in Indochina and the dispatch of a military mission to provide close working relations with those forces."

This was a fateful decision; no one yet realized how fateful. Nor did anyone raise the implied question: if Truman was now *accelerating* the "furnishing of military assistance" to Indochina, when had this program begun?

Everyone's attention was riveted on Korea, not Indochina. By midsummer General MacArthur held the clear edge. Peking was obviously worried that he might decide to carry the fight into China. It was, in *his* mind, a definite possibility. Here was a possible opportunity to defeat the Communists and reinstate Generalissimo Chiang Kai-shek. On August 1, General Chu Teh, head of the People's Liberation Army, stated: "We Chinese people recognize that the Korean people's struggle is entirely just. We definitely come to the relief of the Korean people, and definitely oppose the American government's aggression against Korea!" MacArthur pressed the UN attack. On September 15 he ordered a brilliant landing at Inchon, behind enemy lines.

General James Gavin, the paratrooper who later became a Vietnam dove, led an assault battalion, which quickly seized Kimpo airfield on the outskirts of Inchon. As he later recalled, "I was surprised to find that it had recently been thoroughly prepared for the introduction of modern air power. Huge U-shaped freshly constructed revetments to house fighter-bombers were newly built and scattered around the periphery of the field." Gavin assumed the North Koreans were expecting "the intervention of a modern air force, and it most likely would be Chinese." He returned to Tokyo within several days and reported to General Willoughby, MacArthur's intelligence chief, that the Chinese were "most likely" on the threshold of intervention. Willoughby dismissed Gavin's report.

But the Chinese were in fact on the threshold. A quick series of statements seemed to confirm the impression. On September 24, Kuo Mo-jo, chairman of the Chinese World Peace Salvation Society, warned: "We should, in the name of the progressive youth of the whole world, oppose American imperialism's aggression and use *practical actions* to come forward to support the Korean people's just struggle." On September 29 the Chinese Aliens Association of North Korea sent Chairman Mao Tse-tung a telegram, which said in part: "We desire, under the brave and enlightened leadership of yourself and the Central People's Government, to manifest a spirit of internationalism and patriotism and directly to support the Korean people's war to liberation, and to overwhelm the common public enemy of the two countries China and Korea—the American imperialists—in order to protect our Fatherland and to protect Korea, and to fight to protect world peace." Public organizations demanded that Peking "protect" China from "blatant violations of Chinese territory." On September 30 China capped this crescendo of warnings by formally publishing and ratifying the Treaty of Alliance with the Soviet Union.

Were the warnings bluff? In Washington, at the time, most

people thought they were. On October 1, MacArthur issued a
surrender order to North Korea. "Lay down your arms and cease
hostility," he said, "under such military supervisions as I may
direct." On the same day, Premier Chou En-lai issued what was
in effect an answer. "The Chinese people definitely cannot
tolerate foreign aggression," he asserted, and "cannot allow
imperialists recklessly to aggress against their own neighbor and
disregard it." On October 3 Chou told the Indian Ambassador,
K. M. Panikkar, that China would "definitely" intervene if UN
forces continued their drive toward the Manchurian frontier.
India relayed this final warning to Washington. It too was
ignored. On October 25 hundreds of thousands of Chinese troops,
many of them equipped with American weapons captured during the long civil war against the Nationalists, swarmed across
the Yalu River, separating China from North Korea, and met the
advancing United Nations, but mostly American, forces.

Congress quickly appropriated fresh funds for a gigantic,
crash program of national defense. On December 16 Truman
proclaimed a state of national emergency. Consistent with the
spirit of this proclamation, which envisaged an aggressive world-
wide Communist conspiracy and the desperate need to resist it,
Truman moved deeper into Vietnam. On December 23 he formalized his fledgling program of military aid to Indochina by
signing a Mutual Defense Assistance Agreement with France for
indirect U.S. military aid to Vietnam, Cambodia, and Laos.
He feared a similar Chinese move into Indochina.

After several months of bloody fighting in North Korea, the
Chinese successfully repelled the American threat to Manchuria
and restored the military situation in the Korean peninsula to
roughly what it had been before June 25. A long, frustrating
stalemate followed, which saw Truman fire MacArthur in a
sharp disagreement over military strategy and presidential pre-
rogatives. The armistice was finally signed in July, 1953.

The Korean War took a terrible toll. More than 1,000,000
people were killed; more than twice that number left homeless;
and more than one billion dollars' worth of property destroyed.
The war also had a profound effect upon Far Eastern diplomacy.
It froze Sino-American relations in a posture of rigid, mutual

hostility, inducing wild distortions of reality. Witness Dean Rusk's unfortunate description of China in 1951: "We do not recognize the authorities in Peiping for what they pretend to be. The Peiping regime may be a colonial Russian government—a slavonic Manchukuo on a larger scale. It is not the government of China. It does not pass the first test. It is not Chinese. It is not entitled to speak for China in the community of nations." The war also had the effect of pushing both countries into conflicting policies in Southeast Asia, where, as Clubb observed, "the United States supported the French in their colonial war in Indochina and the Chinese gave aid to the revolutionary Vietminh."

To the northeast and to the southeast of China there were now two small Asian nations, each divided along ideological lines, each bloodied by conflict. In Korea the conflict subsided, but in Vietnam it continued and grew.

The French still clung stubbornly to their Associated States in Indochina, yielding only limited sovereignty to Emperor Bao Dai. On March 8, 1949, after long and intricate negotiations, Bao Dai and President Vincent Auriol reached a series of general agreements on Vietnam. They extended a small role to Vietnam in foreign and domestic affairs, promised to help build an indigenous, anti-Communist army for internal security, and granted membership in the French Union. These agreements satisfied Washington, even though few knowledgeable officials at the State Department believed they would be implemented in time to meet the Communist challenge.

In June, Bao Dai became Chief of State (and later Head of Government). Washington sent him a "message of welcome," a first step toward *de jure* recognition. The Chinese conquest of the mainland accelerated this diplomatic process. On December 30 the French formally transferred internal authority over Vietnam to Emperor Bao Dai. In January, 1950, the French National Assembly voted to treat Vietnam, Laos, and Cambodia as "independent" states within the French Union. The Soviet Union and China then recognized North Vietnam; a month later, on February 7, Washington and London extended *de jure* recognition to the Bao Dai regime, encouraged other nations to

do the same, and underscored their "fundamental policy of giving
support to the peaceful and democratic evolution of dependent
peoples towards self-government and independence."

Thus, the Big Two of the East lined up solidly behind
Ho, and the Big Three of the West squarely behind Bao Dai.
There was little question that South Vietnam needed help. Soon
after the Communist conquest of China, General Chu Teh had
concentrated several of his best army units on the Chinese side
of the Vietnamese border and quickly began an extensive program of military assistance to North Vietnam. Under Ho's orders,
General Giap then opened a broad military offensive against
French outposts on the Vietnamese side of the border. One after
another, they fell to the Communists—until finally the entire
border was open to an unhindered flow of Chinese supplies.
This radically changed the nature of the war. North Vietnamese
troops soon became a match for the French and, as time passed,
more than a match.

By March, State and Defense Department officials worried
whether the French could hold out long enough for Bao Dai to
build and train an army—a process that had been indirectly
supported by the United States since 1946. American military
aid went to France, and from France to Vietnam. These U.S.
officials were also afraid that the Chinese Communists might
intervene in the Vietnam War. Late in April Truman opened
a program of direct American military aid for Vietnam, though
he yielded to French sensitivities by agreeing that it had to be
funneled through Paris. The French did not want to give the
Americans an opportunity to gain political influence over Bao
Dai. It was in June, after the outbreak of the Korean War, that
Truman accelerated American aid to Vietnam.

The aid had little immediate effect. French forces were
retreating   into   enclaves   as   the   Communists   intensified
their military pressure. In October the foreign ministers of the
newly created North Atlantic Treaty Organization came to
Washington, planning to enroll West Germany in the Atlantic
Alliance, but realizing they would also have to discuss Indochina. In a way the two problems were related. Washington
needed French cooperation in accepting the West Germans as

allies, and France desperately needed Washington's support in Indochina. This interdependence produced resentment, especially on Dean Acheson's part. The Secretary of State felt that France was dragging her feet on European security in order to pressure the United States into providing more military aid to Vietnam. For their part, the French resented American pressure to get out of Indochina. It was an unhappy situation all the way around. Many years later Acheson wrote:

Both during this period and after it our conduct was criticized as being a muddled hodgepodge. . . . The description is accurate enough. The criticism, however, fails to recognize the limits on the extent to which one may successfully coerce an ally. . . . So while we may have tried to muddle through and were certainly not successful, I could not think then or later of a better course. One can suggest, perhaps, doing nothing. That might have had merit, but as an attitude for the leader of a great alliance towards an important ally, indeed one essential to a critical endeavor [European unity], it had its demerits, too.

In October the French promised to add ten divisions to the French army in Europe and increase the number of Vietnamese battalions from twelve to thirty, but for this they needed more aid. In his memoir, *Present at the Creation,* Dean Acheson recalls:

Livingston Merchant, who had been working on French military problems, sent me through Dean Rusk an urgent memorandum stressing that the military situation in Vietnam was extremely serious; that military aid should receive the highest priority; that Prince Bao Dai should be pushed to assume maximum effective leadership; that although Indochina was an area of French responsibility, in view of French ineffectiveness it would be better for France to pull out if she could not provide sufficient force to hold; that we should strengthen a second line of defense in Thailand, Malaya, Laos, Cambodia, the Philippines, and Indonesia; that the military problem was essentially one of men and the sinews of war. We could supply the second; the first must come from national forces in Vietnam.

Acheson and Truman accepted Merchant's recommendation. Again U.S. aid to Vietnam was increased, this time significantly. In 1951 military aid alone amounted to more than $500,000,000. From Capitol Hill and from within the administration came warnings that the United States must not get more deeply involved in Vietnam. John F. Kennedy, a young Massachusetts Congressman, lamented the American attachment to French colonialism. "In Indochina we have allied ourselves to the desperate effort of the French regime to hang on to the remnants of Empire," he said. John Ohly, a career diplomat, warned Acheson that the United States ran a double risk in Vietnam: one, that the aid, no matter how substantial, might not achieve the stated goal of helping the French to defeat Ho Chi Minh; two, that as the volume of aid increased, American responsibilities would "tend to supplant rather than complement those of the French." Ohly's fear was that the United States could get sucked into direct intervention. "These situations have a way of snowballing," he warned.

No one except perhaps the French and Bao Dai wanted America's involvement in Vietnam to snowball. It simply did. On September 7 the United States signed an agreement with Saigon for *direct* economic aid to South Vietnam. The effect of this agreement was to increase the size of the American establishment in Saigon—to add civilian helpers to the military advisers already there. On September 8 the United States invited official representatives of Vietnam, Laos, and Cambodia to attend the formal signing of the Japanese Peace Treaty in San Francisco, thus elevating the diplomatic stature of the Associated States. At the same time General de Lattre de Tassigny, the new French High Commissioner and Commander-in-Chief in Indochina, visited Washington. His was supposed to be a courtesy call; it ended up a strategy session. The general argued that France was preventing a "red tide" from engulfing South Vietnam, the "barrier in Southeast Asia" against communism. He found many in Washington who agreed wholeheartedly with him.

American experts in guerrilla warfare, trained in the Philippines, ferried back and forth between Manila and Saigon, trying to persuade the French that the war in Vietnam was a "new kind of war" and they had better adjust to the tactics of a modern guerrilla movement, as the Americans had been forced to adjust to the tactics of an earlier struggle against Aguinaldo's guerrillas back in 1898. The French said they needed no American advice, thank you; just American aid. When the United States offered to send experienced instructors from Korea to Vietnam to train Vietnamese officers, the offer was gruffly declined as an "insult" to France.

It was a trying relationship. But for the fact that Washington was so committed to the defense of Western Europe and so obsessed by the possibility of Chinese intervention in Vietnam, many American officials would have been delighted to abandon the French. But exasperating though the French could be, this was a luxury of temperament that Washington felt it could not afford. The stakes seemed to be getting higher.

The military power of Mao's China had been effectively demonstrated in Korea. When Chinese units began to maneuver in the southern provinces, early in 1952, western military leaders checked their resources and despaired. At a Washington meeting in January the Joint Chiefs of Staff flatly declared that the United States, already committed to Korea and Western Europe, could not be counted on to provide ground troops to help the French in Vietnam. The JCS promised only air and naval support. The British, bled white during World War II, promised even less. The French began to feel more and more alone. At home, domestic pressures for disengagement increased. In Vietnam there was frustration: too many casualties for so little glory.

In May, before Acheson flew to Bonn to help launch the European Defense Community project, he was summoned to the White House to discuss the deteriorating situation in Vietnam with the President, Secretary of Defense Robert Lovett, and General Omar Bradley. Their particular concern was the continuing possibility of Chinese intervention. Acheson received instructions to raise the idea of a tripartite (American, British, and French) warning to Peking against committing "aggression" in Vietnam. If Peking ignored or rejected the warning, then the Big Three were to open urgent discussions on joint military action. The United States alone, however, was prepared for such discussions. So the idea of a Western warning to China was dropped.

Instead, on June 30 the Big Three issued a communiqué, categorizing the allied effort in Indochina as part of a world-wide

resistance to "Communist attempts at conquest and subversion."
It recognized that France had the "primary role in Indo-China,"
just as the United States had the primary role in Korea, and it
pledged more American aid to the French–Bao Dai cause in
Vietnam. By 1952 it had become the established western policy
line to link the actual struggle in Vietnam with a broader,
somewhat hypothetical defense against Chinese or Russian "aggression" and to keep pledging more United States aid each time.
A commitment, born of rhetorical repetition, was in the early
stages of development.

The commitment was to South Vietnam. In July the State
Department announced, in a matter-of-fact manner, that the
President had decided to raise the level of the American
legation in Saigon to an embassy. The South Vietnamese opened
an embassy in Washington. The diplomatic message was clear:
one sovereign country was dealing with another. In Paris the
message was read with irritation as another case of American interference in French affairs; in Hanoi it was read with disenchantment as another sign of American duplicity. Despite the
irritation and the disenchantment, American aid to South Vietnam continued. By October 12 the 200th American ship carrying military hardware for the French and Bao Dai arrived in
Saigon. The Americans, their sights fixed on China, could not
master their fear that one day the Chinese would storm across
the Vietnamese border, as they had crossed the Yalu, and inflict a crushing blow on the French. Few American officials
questioned the established dogma that a world-wide Communist
conspiracy, directed from Moscow and loyally supported by
Peking, was out to do the "free world" in.

In November, 1952, after Dwight Eisenhower's crushing
election victory over Adlai Stevenson, the Democratic governor
of Illinois, Acheson passed on this somber judgment of the
Indochina problem to the new administration:

There had been a noticeable lack of French aggressive attitude, from
a military point of view in Indochina. The central problem in Indochina was the fence-sitting of the population. They would never come
down on one side or another until they had a reasonable assurance of

who would be the victor and that their interests would be served by the victor.

We are helping France to the extent of carrying between one-third and one-half of the financial burden of the Indochinese war. We have had military discussions between the five powers—the United States, the United Kingdom, France, Australia, and New Zealand— which had not been effective in devising agreed military solutions against the contingency of *overt Chinese intervention in Indochina*. The French now sought political discussions to carry the matter forward.

This is an *urgent matter* upon which the new administration *must be prepared to act.*

This Achesonian advice, which Truman imparted to Eisenhower, proved remarkably similar to the advice and warnings on Indochina that Eisenhower imparted to President-elect Kennedy in January, 1961. The language was virtually interchangeable. In 1953 Eisenhower faced the unhappy possibility that he might have to commit American ground forces to Indochina, just as Truman had committed them to Korea. Eight years later Kennedy, having narrowly defeated Vice-President Nixon, faced the equally unhappy possibility that he might have to send troops to neighboring Laos. Like Truman before them, both new Presidents quickly found themselves pressed to make distasteful and difficult policy decisions concerning Indochina.

Eisenhower had promised the voters that he would go to Korea and end the war. Soon after his election he went to Korea. Six months after his inauguration, the war ended. No one can prove a direct cause and effect; but, because no one could disprove it either, the Republican Party was able to drape itself in the peacemaker's mantle. That was good politics. The Democrats got the country into war, the victorious GOP proclaimed, and it took the Republicans to restore peace.

The President, a novice at politics but a professional about war, accepted the implied wisdom of this position. The country needed a break from the tumult of wars and the trauma of losing China. Eisenhower determined early in his administration that he would strive for peace and quiet. He was not always successful. But, on at least one occasion, in April, 1954,

when the admirals and generals came pounding at the White
House door for permission to attack Communist positions in
Indochina—all of them supported by Vice-President Nixon,
Secretary of State Dulles, and Senator William Knowland—
Eisenhower did not yield under pressure. He attached conditions to his consent, which, as it turned out, they could not
meet. Eisenhower, no less than his predecessors and no more
than his successors, hated to appear weak or indifferent in the
face of an obvious Communist challenge. That is why he allowed
himself to embrace and support the idea of an anti-Communist
South Vietnam. Over the years that support matured into a
commitment. It made the Kennedy decision to send more military
advisers to South Vietnam and the Johnson decision to send
combat troops and to bomb North Vietnam appear consistent,
logical, perhaps even inevitable. In the postwar spirit of bipartisan foreign policy, with a cold war raging in Europe and Asia,
no President dared to disown the major undertakings of his
predecessors, no matter how deep their political antagonisms.
No President questioned the proposition that order, no matter
how imperfect, was infinitely preferable to chaos. Nor that the
Communist leaders, constantly probing for signs of American
weakness, had to be shown how superior American force could
be.

Secretary Acheson had riveted his attention on the building
of a strong Atlantic Alliance, with few exceptions seeing the
problems of Asia through the prism of Paris or London. Eisenhower's Secretary of State, John Foster Dulles, believed that Asia
deserved comparable attention. "When I became Secretary of
State," Dulles once told Andrew Berding, "NATO had already
been developed and was proving a barrier to further Soviet expansion in Europe. But there had been no similar development
in the Far East. I recall that when I was in the Senate [Dulles
served briefly by appointment from July, 1949 to January, 1950]
. . . I testified then that unless something comparable to NATO
were formed in Asia and a line were drawn beyond which the international communists knew they could advance only at their own
peril, we would face a serious situation in that area." In his mind,
Europe was reasonably secure, especially after a rearmed West

Germany had become a member of NATO. But Asia was in the grip of war, social strife, and political upheaval.

Dulles's sense of urgency was heightened by his absolute abhorrence of Communist China. A man of strong convictions, who impressed various of his contemporaries as being "stubborn," "moralistic," and "inflexible," Dulles had once believed the Peking regime ought to be admitted to the United Nations. He changed his mind after China entered the Korean War. From that moment Dulles showed a consistent hatred and distrust of Red China. His rhetoric reflected this animosity. United States recognition of China must depend, he said, "on the way they conduct themselves." He warned that if "Peiping's tentacles" were allowed to "stretch" through Asia, "tyranny" and "oppression" would follow. As for the Chinese people's communes, Dulles called them "abhorrent to our ideal of the Christian family and the dignity of the individual."

Such rhetoric was typical of the Eisenhower entourage, though not of the President himself. Richard Nixon had sprung onto the national scene—first as a Congressman, then as a Senator, and finally as Vice-President—with the justified reputation of a hard-line Communist hunter. The Republican leader of the Senate, Knowland of California, believed that Generalissimo and Madame Chiang Kai-shek represented "our ideal of the Christian family." Knowland championed the pro-Chiang "China Lobby" (and its natural offspring, the pro-Diem "Vietnam Lobby") through the 1950s. Walter Robertson, an Assistant Secretary of State, fought Chiang's fight in the policy councils of the administration. Admiral Arthur W. Radford, Chairman of the Joint Chiefs of Staff, felt that there was only one way to stop the march of communism in Asia: use nuclear weapons against North Vietnam and, if China intervened, use them against her, too.

There were so many anti-Communist crusaders in the upper echelons of the administration that Eisenhower was hard pressed to assert his own conviction that the U.S. needed peace, not dubious new battlefields in Asia.

Acheson had warned the incoming administration about the possibility of "overt Chinese intervention in Indochina." Dulles,

Nixon, Knowland, Robertson, Radford—all shared Acheson's apprehension. "If you are scared to go to the brink," Dulles once said, "you are lost." Happily, Dulles was not President; though, in the area of foreign policy, he sounded like the supreme authority.

Eisenhower did not devote a great deal of attention to Indochina until he had wrapped up the Korean War. Then, in the summer of 1953, before he would commit himself to any course of action, he dispatched Lieutenant General J. W. O'Daniel to South Vietnam. O'Daniel's mission was to find out how American military aid was being used, whether any more was needed, and what could be done to check Chinese expansionism. The President, a convert to containment, was not about to forfeit Indochina to the Communists. But he was less than passionate on the subject. From personal experience in Europe as NATO's first supreme commander, he knew the French were stubbornly committed to defeating Ho. He wanted to help them in every way— short of a direct American military role on the mainland of Asia. After Korea, he wanted to station American troops on island strongholds around the rim of China, helping Asians to fight the Chinese but not fighting their battles (or France's) for them. It was a strategic concept that, in a different context, one Asian war later, was to recur in President Nixon's Guam Doctrine in 1969.

O'Daniel held extensive talks with General Henri-Eugène Navarre, the French commander in Indochina. Navarre had a plan. With sufficient American military aid, and with a stepped-up program of training the Vietnamese ("Vietnamization," he told a UPI reporter many years later, "is an old idea. It was the basis of my own plan when I was first sent to Indochina in 1952."), Navarre sincerely believed he could crush the Communists. O'Daniel could not think of one good reason why Navarre would fail. He returned to Washington with a recommendation that, in addition to the $400,000,000 in military aid already earmarked for Vietnam, the U.S. should provide an additional $385,000,000. On September 30 Eisenhower approved that recommendation. As he said many times, he wanted to help. (In fact, the aid total went much higher. On April 7, 1954,

Harold Stassen, coordinator of the foreign aid program, submitted a $3,497,000,000 program to Congress. He disclosed that the "biggest single item" was $1,133,000,000 for Indochina, of which $500,000,000 would go for direct support of the anti-Communist fighting forces, allocated through France: $300,000,000 for military equipment; $21,185,000 for economic aid; the rest went for technical assistance.)

The aid, the French assured O'Daniel, would not be wasted. In 1953 a Vietnamese Army was formed. Within one year it numbered about 300,000 men, all trained by the French with American assistance. Some American advisers were in South Vietnam even then. Two hundred Air Force mechanics were sent to Da Nang in early 1954, to service American combat planes, flown by French pilots. There were many others. To their superiors they grumbled privately about ARVN—the Army of Vietnam. When Emperor Bao Dai heard about these grumblings, he would complain that the French were not giving ARVN sufficiently modern weapons; that they kept the best equipment in France (which was true), and sent only the second-rate equipment to Vietnam (which was also true).

Secretary Dulles, an early victim of the official Washington euphoria about Vietnam, believed that the Navarre Plan could "break the organized body of Communist aggression by the end of the 1955 fighting season." But many other supporters of the French cause in Indochina—especially in France—began to lose heart. Ho's forces had opened a new offensive, moving to the north and destroying one French bastion after another until finally the entire Chinese border was open. Communist military supplies poured into North Vietnam, bolstering the morale of Ho's blooded veterans. French forces tried to lure the Viet Minh into fighting classic set-piece battles. But the Communists time and again avoided these armored traps and vanished into the jungle. Often they bided their time; then, at an opportune moment, they would ambush a French company, cut it to ribbons, and disappear.

The French people became increasingly exasperated with the war. Many wanted to disengage from Vietnam, even if that meant Ho would win. The generals and many politicians re-

sisted this deepening defeatism. They insisted that Vietnamization
was going ahead and they promised victory by the end of the
"1955 fighting season." Navarre devised a plan to speed the inevitable French victory. More than 200 miles behind enemy lines,
in a steep valley known as Dienbienphu, the French assembled
15,000 of their finest troops. With their armor and big guns, they
were certain they could engage the enemy and defeat him. The
French command envisaged a defeat so staggering that it would
symbolize for Ho and his followers the utter futility of continuing the war. On March 13, 1954, the French engaged the enemy
at Dienbienphu. The battle was to last 56 days.

After the first five days, however, General Navarre must
have realized that he had gravely miscalculated. He had not
baited a trap for the enemy; the enemy had baited one for him.
Dienbienphu was surrounded by hardened Viet Minh, who
caught the sweet smell of victory. Navarre cabled the bitter
news to General Paul Ely in Paris: Dienbienphu was doomed,
with it all of Indochina, unless the United States should intervene. On March 20 General Ely carried this sobering message to
Washington. Secretary Dulles was shocked. He had believed in
the Navarre Plan, and he had persuaded Radford, Nixon, and
Robertson to believe in it. The President had his doubts—both
about the Navarre Plan and the Ely request—but he was prepared to listen to a Radford scheme for immediate American
military intervention in Indochina to save Dienbienphu. Eisenhower attached two conditions: The European allies must join
the operation (he had Great Britain in mind) and the Congress
(he had the Senate minority leader, Lyndon B. Johnson, in
mind) must approve.

The Radford plan looked deceptively simple. The Chairman
of the Joint Chiefs had first recommended the use of tactical
nuclear weapons against the Viet Minh near Dienbienphu. But
when General Ridgway, then Army Chief of Staff, raised violent
objection, Radford lowered his sights. His alternative recommendation was that the Allies, meaning the United States, should
launch one massive air strike against enemy positions around
Dienbienphu. The U.S. Navy carriers *Essex* and *Boxer*, both in
the 31,000-ton class, were then on a "training mission" in the

South China Sea. From their decks, and from Clark Air Force Base, some 1000 miles to the southeast in the Philippines, more than 200 American warplanes could quickly be launched. Radford had several contingency plans. If this "one massive air strike" did not break the enemy's "will to resist," then other strikes should be ordered. Should air power alone not do the job, then American paratroopers would be dropped into Dienbienphu. And, if the French needed additional help, then Haiphong Harbor should be mined and closed. General Gavin, who had been transferred to the Pentagon, pointed out that no military operation against Haiphong could succeed unless Hainan Island was first "neutralized." Hainan belonged to Communist China, and Gavin wanted no part of another Sino-American confrontation. Radford withdrew his Haiphong plan, but he persistently urged his civilian allies to accept, as a minimum, one major air attack against Communist forces near Dienbienphu. Radford believed that the United States could not allow Indochina to fall to the Communists. It was 1954, an off-year election in prospect, and his supporters, including Vice-President Nixon, agreed that this was no time to concede additional real estate to the Communists.

On March 25 the National Security Council approved the Radford plan. So did President Eisenhower, with the proviso, of course, that the Allies and the Congress must go along. Ike had not retreated one inch from his fundamental judgment that the country wanted peace and that the G.O.P., having ended the Korean War less than a year before, would profit enormously from a period of tranquility. Yet many of his civilian and military advisers favored a limited American intervention in Indochina to help an ally and, more important, to keep another piece of Asia from falling into Communist hands. Some of his political confidants rationalized the Radford plan as sound and sensible, even in an election year. It could be sold to the country—so the argument ran—as an example of G.O.P. firmness against communism in Indochina, as contrasted with Democratic weakness against communism in China. Ike had his doubts. He listened carefully to his hawkish advisers but again insisted that Britain and LBJ must approve. The United States had, in effect, taken a provisional decision to fight in Indochina on March 25, 1954. Not that the area was regarded as "vital" to the security of the nation, but rather that its loss could not be justified in political terms, given the passions of the McCarthy period and the American purpose of containing Communism.

On March 29 Secretary Dulles began to prepare the American people for a new war. Speaking in New York, he urged "united action" against Hanoi's "aggression" in Indochina, even if this should involve "serious risks" of again committing American troops to the Asian mainland. Dulles warned: "That possibility should not be passively accepted but should be met by united action."

His speech stimulated journalistic speculation. Had a decision been reached to save the French? Was Dienbienphu falling? If the United States intervened in Indochina, would the Chinese move? And, if they did, would the United States consider using nuclear weapons against China? What would be the political effects of intervention on the upcoming off-year elections? The administration offered no immediate enlightenment, but continued its private preparations for war.

Chalmers Roberts, a respected Washington reporter, recalls in a splendid recapitulation of this period that April 3 was a raw, windy day in the nation's capital. Even so, 100,000 visitors had come to Washington to admire the cherry blossoms. President Eisenhower had gone to Camp David for the weekend. He was said to be preparing a speech to be delivered on Monday. Secretary Dulles, who seldom rested, summoned eight members of Congress to a secret briefing at the State Department. They were Senate Majority leader Knowland, Senator Eugene Millikin of Colorado, Minority leader Lyndon Johnson, and Democratic Senators Richard Russell and Earle Clements, in addition to House speaker Joe Martin and Democrats John McCormack and C. Percy Priest. When they entered the fifth-floor conference room, they noticed a large map hanging on the wall behind Dulles's seat. They also noticed that Dulles had company: Admiral Radford, Under Secretary of Defense Roger Kyes, Navy Secretary Robert Anderson, and Assistant Secretary of State for

Congressional Relations, Thruston Morton. This was to be no
ordinary briefing.

"The President has asked me to call this meeting," Dulles
began. The atmosphere turned serious almost immediately. The
President wanted a joint resolution allowing him to use American
air and naval power in Indochina. Radford used the map to show
how important Indochina was to the whole Pacific region. He
said the Communists had only recently taken China and they had
to be stopped in Indochina. He added that he was not sure
whether Dienbienphu was still in French hands. The military situation was deteriorating rapidly. Dulles said that if Indochina
fell, so would all of Southeast Asia; and if Southeast Asia fell,
then the American defense perimeter would be pushed back to
Hawaii. Radford then outlined his plan for a massive air strike
against enemy positions near Dienbienphu.

The legislators had questions.

Would such action mean war? Yes, Radford answered.

If one strike did not succeed, would there be two and more?
Yes, Radford answered.

Would land forces have to be used? Radford's answer was
vague.

Clements asked: "Does this plan have the approval of the
other members of the Joint Chiefs of Staff?"

"No," replied Radford.

"How many of them agree with you?"

"None."

"How do you account for that?"

"I have spent more time in the Far East than any of them
and I understand the situation better."

Lyndon Johnson asked whether Dulles had consulted any of
the nations that might be America's allies in such an intervention
and whether he had gone to the United Nations. After Korea,
Johnson said, the nation had been sold on the idea that unilateral
intervention was bad. He advised Dulles to go shopping for allies if he hoped to get a joint resolution.

The Secretary lost no time. In Washington, he conferred
with the diplomatic representatives of Britain, France, Australia,

New Zealand, the Philippines, Thailand, and the three Associated
States of Indochina—Vietnam, Laos, and Cambodia. Dulles
wanted an allied statement of support for American air and
naval action in Indochina. He knew such support did not have
to be unanimous, but it had to include Britain. That was essential to the President, who respected Prime Minister Churchill
and Foreign Secretary Anthony Eden, both old and dear friends.

The President reinforced Dulles's lobbying effort on April 7.
At a news conference he discussed the importance of defending
Dienbienphu. "You have a row of dominoes set up," he said
(little realizing that he was baptizing a new policy line), "and
you knock over the first one and what will happen to the last
one is the certainty that it will go over very quickly. So you have
the beginning of a disintegration that will have the most profound influences." Thus the "domino theory" was born—the underlying policy justification for America's step-by-step intervention in Indochina.

On April 10 Dulles flew to London. He hoped to persuade
Churchill and Eden that immediate intervention was necessary
to save Dienbienphu. All he needed was their support. But they
did not share Dulles's sense of urgency. Eden said that Britain
wanted to give diplomacy a chance to end the war. After ardu-
ous negotiations with the Russians and the Chinese, he had managed to get their agreement—and Hanoi's—to open a peace conference in Geneva in late April. Eden refused categorically to
support any military action that would jeopardize the conference.
Dulles realized that the Radford plan was dying. Ever resourceful, he then asked the British if they would agree to the creation
of a Southeast Asia Treaty Organization that could, in time,
lead to "united action." Dulles was obviously seeking a diplomatic formula for circumventing the Geneva Conference. He had
no confidence in any conference accepted by the Chinese Communists. Eden nodded ambiguously.

When Dulles returned to Washington, assuming British
approval of the SEATO idea, the atmosphere was rife with reports and rumors of imminent American action in Indochina. On
April 15 Radford said that the loss of Indochina would be the
prelude to the "loss of all Southeast Asia and a threat to a far

wider area." On April 16 Vice-President Nixon told a convention of newspaper editors (what better forum to insure that an off-the-record speech would get front-page headlines?) that the United States would have to send troops to Indochina if there were no other way to prevent its collapse. A few days later Dulles called a SEATO drafting meeting. But Eden, informed of the Radford-Nixon comments, instructed his ambassador not to attend. Dulles smelled betrayal.

On April 23 Dulles was back in Europe, conferring with the French foreign minister, Georges Bidault. There was another desperate cable from General Navarre. Dienbienphu would fall, the general warned, without immediate air support. Dulles advised Bidault that the United States wanted to help but, without Allied (*i.e.*, British) approval, such help would be impossible. On April 24 Radford joined Dulles in Paris. Together they saw Eden. They told him that the French needed help desperately, that more than 200 American warplanes were ready to strike at enemy positions near Dienbienphu, that the President was prepared to ask the Congress on April 26 (the day the Geneva Conference was set to open) for a joint resolution authorizing the strike, and that if the Congress acted quickly, which they expected, the strike would take place on April 28. All they asked was Eden's agreement.

The British foreign secretary said he personally opposed such action and could not in any case commit his government. Churchill called his Cabinet together and summed up the Dulles proposal, as he understood it:

What we are being asked to do is assist in misleading the Congress [of the United States] into approving a military operation which would be in itself ineffective, and might well bring the world to the verge of a major war.

The British Cabinet, in an extraordinary Sunday-morning session on April 25, firmly rejected any immediate military intervention; Eden so informed Dulles the same day. On April 26, as the Geneva Conference opened, Eisenhower formally buried the Radford plan by expressing his "personal" hope that the Communists would accept a *modus vivendi* with the anti-Communists in Indochina. At the same time, Dulles privately advised

Bidault that the United States "reluctantly" must reject the
French bid for military help.

It was a near miss. If the British had supported the President, Congress would almost certainly have gone along. So persuaded were Washington's leaders of the need to resist Communist expansionism—so politically rewarding and safe had this
position become in American politics—that they were ready to
commit American forces in order to salvage the crumbling
French colonial empire without first considering the costly implications of such a venture.

Only General Ridgway appeared to be fully aware of the
political implications. He argued that an American air strike
would not suffice, that troops would have to be sent; and that
the expedition would be doomed from the start because Asians
would see it as a desperate effort by the United States to save
white colonial rule. Most other officials preferred to think of the
proposed intervention as a laudable—perhaps essential—move
to build a dike against international communism.

That was the view of Dulles, Radford, and Nixon. Dulles
saw himself as a tough man who was not squeamish about "going to the brink." He distrusted the British; he did not think
they had the "stuff" to defeat communism. He had grave doubts
about the French and the Italians, who willingly coexisted with
Communist parties at home. Dulles believed the United States
could not depend upon any of them in the crunch. Nor could he
conceal his profound distaste for the "neutrals" of the developing world—Nehru, U Nu, and Sukarno—who seemed unable or
unwilling to choose between an Eisenhower and a Khrushchev.
It was a life-and-death struggle, as he saw it, against atheistic
communism. Neutrality in those circumstances was to him im-
moral. Dulles admitted to no doubts. "We would face a serious
situation" in Asia, he warned, unless "a line were drawn beyond
which the international Communists knew they could advance
only at their own peril."

Viewing his allies as unreliable and the neutrals as im-
moral, Dulles devised a purely American plan. He would do all
he could at Geneva to block total Communist control of Indochina; then he would set about building an anti-Communist al-

liance in Asia, similar to NATO, to checkmate Peking and Hanoi.

For General Vo Nguyen Giap, Ho Chi Minh's military commander, the Geneva conference meant an approaching deadline for decisive action. He needed just one sensational victory to persuade the French that their cause in Indochina was lost. General Navarre was reinforcing the French garrison at Dienbienphu. Giap allowed Navarre to build up his strength to 15,000 men. Then he started to tighten the noose.

FOUR

In for a Penny, In for a Pound

THE SIEGE OF DIENBIENPHU, so humiliating to France, left General Giap holding the trump card at Geneva. The conference opened on April 26. Dulles, for all his protestations, was there at the start; along with Anthony Eden for Britain; Georges Bidault for France; Chou En-lai, China; Vyacheslav Molotov, the Soviet Union; Brigadier Ta Quang Buu, an Oxford-trained scholar, for Ho Chi Minh's Democratic Republic of Vietnam; Dr. Tran Van Do for Bao Dai's regime in Saigon; and a scattering of delegates from Laos and Cambodia.

At the start, the discussion centered upon another divided Asian country, Korea. There was talk of armistice arrangements. In time, though, the delegates focused on what was happening at Dienbienphu and the inevitable impact of that climactic battle upon the Vietnam settlement they had assembled to negotiate.

Eight days after the start of the conference, on May 4, Dulles decided he had had enough. He flew home to Washington. Bidault and Eden were thunderstruck. They had counted on the presence of a powerful United States delegation to hold the line against the combined pressures of Russia, China, and the Vietnamese Communists. Eden promptly telephoned Churchill, and the Prime Minister, in turn, called President Eisenhower in Washington. Churchill pleaded with the President to send Dulles back. Eisenhower said Dulles was adamant. When Churchill protested that the absence of an American delegate would gravely weaken the Western position, the President asked whom he could send.

"Send Bedell," Churchill barked.

So General Walter Bedell Smith, Eisenhower's wartime Chief of Staff, former director of the Central Intelligence Agency, former ambassador to Moscow, now Under Secretary of State, flew to Geneva to sit in for Dulles. President Eisenhower explained that the United States mission was being downgraded to observer status. It was as if Dulles and Eisenhower, fully expecting a sellout to communism at Geneva, were disclaiming in advance any responsibility for what might happen there.

On May 8 General Navarre announced the fall of Dienbienphu to the Communists. It was a moment of supreme tragedy for the French, of supreme elation for the Communists. Foreign Minister Bidault, eyes red and voice choked, opened the day's session with a eulogy to the fallen soldiers of France. Then he moved to the depressing business of negotiating an end to the war. Partition seemed unavoidable, at least from the big-power point of view. Both Vietnamese delegations resisted this solution. Saigon insisted on territorial unity and national elections under UN inspection. Hanoi also insisted on territorial unity and accepted the idea of nationwide elections although it wanted no UN inspection. Big-power pressure for partition increased. For the West, partition had the merit of salvaging half of Vietnam; from the Communist point of view, it solidified Ho's control over at least half of the country and held out the prospect of eventual control over the other half.

In June, halfway through the conference, Eden had to fly to Washington for another meeting. The other foreign ministers took advantage of his departure to recess the deliberations. They returned to their respective capitals—Bidault to Paris, Molotov to Moscow, and Chou to Peking by way of New Delhi and Rangoon. The shape of a solution was apparent to everyone. It had to be partition, even though Dr. Do, a Vietnamese of towering integrity, argued in vain against the division of his homeland.

During the break, the battered French Republic went through still another change of government. Pierre Mendès-France became Prime Minister and, in addition to promoting milk over wine in the French diet, pledged his new regime to end the war within a month. If not, he would resign, raising the possibility of a military coup in Paris and a new regime pledged to continue the war. The Russians and the Chinese decided the time had come to pressure the Viet Minh into accepting the partition of Vietnam. Molotov and Chou evidently felt Ho's standing throughout the country was so great, and Saigon's so weak, that Hanoi was virtually assured of total political control within a brief period. They reasoned that such an interim solution would erase the lingering possibility of direct American intervention.

Arguments continued as to where the line should be drawn. Finally, on July 20, the Viet Minh accepted the 17th parallel with the understanding that national elections would be held within two years. Separate arrangements for Laos and Cambodia still had to be detailed, but the Vietnam package was completed before dawn on July 21. At 3:43 A.M. the first phase of the Indochina war ended.

Brigadier General Henri Delteil signed the military cease-fire agreements for France, and Brigadier General Ta Quang Buu signed for the Viet Minh. When the "victor" invited the "vanquished" to share a glass of champagne, Delteil quietly declined. "I am sure," he said, "that you understand that this is not possible."

The document signed by the two generals was called "Agreement on the Cessation of Hostilities in Viet Nam." It covered the setting up of a demarcation line and a demilitarized zone; the technicalities of moving troops and equipment through two "regrouping zones"; the banning of reinforcements, that is, "all types of . . . war material, such as combat aircraft, naval craft, jet engines and jet weapons, and armored vehicles," and the prohibition of "new military bases throughout Viet Nam"; finally it provided for the establishment of an "International Commission for Supervision and Control," later known as the ICC, consisting of India, Canada, and Poland.

Political arrangements remained unresolved, though not for long. That afternoon, at a meeting chaired by Eden, all of the implied understandings were formalized and incorporated into the "Final Declaration of the Geneva Conference." One after another the foreign ministers expressed their general support of the Declaration—Britain, France, Laos, China, the Soviet Union, Cambodia, the Democratic Republic of Vietnam.

Then Under Secretary of State Bedell Smith, the American "observer" in place of Dulles, rose to speak. "My Government is not prepared to join in a Declaration by the Conference such as is submitted," he said. Instead, Smith submitted a separate declaration in which the United States promised that it would "refrain from the threat or the use of force to disturb" the agreements, stipulating, however, that it would view "any renewal of the aggression in violation of the aforesaid agreements with grave concern and as seriously threatening international peace and security." Smith concluded by supporting the position of the Saigon regime on election procedures. "In the case of nations divided against their will," he said, the United States believed in "unity through free elections, supervised by the United Nations."

No one signed the declaration. Jean Lacouture and Philippe Devillers, two French writers who covered the conference, noted that the absence of signatures "would permit [the participants] to act as if the organization of elections in Vietnam within two years had been a simple project" rather than a binding commitment. They added: "The Geneva Conference will thus have invented a new form of peaceful coexistence—that which results from the tacit consent of the negotiators—as well as a new form of legal obligation between states: the unsigned treaty."

Clearly, an unsigned settlement was better than no settlement or continued haggling. In any case, it was known that the United States and the State of (South) Vietnam would not sign the Declaration, and the Viet Minh agreed to this loose arrangement.

Articles 6 and 7 were to have deep meaning for the future of Vietnam:

6. The Conference recognizes that the essential purpose of the agreement relating to Viet Nam is to settle military questions with a view to ending hostilities and that *the military demarcation line is provisional and should not in any way be interpreted as constituting a political or territorial boundary.* The Conference expresses its conviction that the execution of the provisions set out in the present declaration and in the agreement on the cessation of hostilities creates the necessary basis for the achievement in the near future of a political settlement in Viet Nam.

7. The Conference declares that, so far as Viet Nam is concerned, the settlement of political problems, affected on the basis of

respect for the principles of independence, unity and territorial integrity, shall permit the Vietnamese people to enjoy the fundamental freedoms, guaranteed by democratic institutions established as a result of free general elections by secret ballot. In order to insure that sufficient progress in the restoration of peace has been made, and that all the necessary conditions obtain for free expression of the national will, *general elections shall be held in July, 1956, under the supervision of an international commission composed of representatives of the Member States of the International Supervisory Commission,* referred to in the agreement on the cessation of hostilities. Consultations will be held on this subject between the competent representative authorities of the two zones from 20 July 1955 onwards.

The two articles meant that North and South were to open consultations in exactly one year with a view to holding "general elections" under ICC supervision in two years. There was no solid evidence at the time to indicate that Washington favored this arrangement, and there was much to suggest that it did not. Thus the United States refused, even orally, to support the Final Declaration and felt the need to issue a separate declaration warning against "any renewal" of "aggression." Everyone knew that "general elections" would result in a Communist Vietnam. President Eisenhower himself recognized Ho's broad popularity. In his memoirs he wrote: "I have never talked nor corresponded with a person knowledgeable in Indochinese affairs who did not agree that had elections been held as of the time of the fighting, possibly 80 percent of the population would have voted for the Communist Ho Chi Minh as their leader rather than Chief of State Bao Dai."

This promise of eventual victory at the polls explains why the Viet Minh agreed to the Final Declaration—but only in part. The Communists controlled about three quarters of Vietnam at the time of the battle of Dienbienphu. The French, even before their grand defeat, had started to evacuate their forces from the vital Red River Delta around Hanoi and Haiphong. Within a year, the Viet Minh had every prospect of controlling the entire country. Why, then, did they agree to accept half of it? There are several reasons beyond their confident expectation of winning the "general elections" set for July, 1956. They also believed that the defeated and demoralized French would be responsible "for the conduct of civil administration" in the southern half of Vietnam pending "general elections." (To them this meant that the fledgling regime of Ngo Dinh Diem, recently appointed premier of the Republic of Vietnam, would not be allowed to sabotage the Geneva agreements.) Finally, Russian and Chinese pressure for a quick solution during Mendès-France's tenure in office seems to have been critically important. Tillman Durdin, an experienced Far Eastern correspondent for *The New York Times,* cabled from Geneva on July 24: "Viet Minh leaders are not entirely happy about the peace settlement in Vietnam. A number of members of the Viet Minh delegation have declared openly that pressure from Chinese Communist Premier Chou En-lai and Soviet Foreign Minister Vyacheslav Molotov forced their regime to accept less than it rightly should have obtained here." Durdin's dispatch continued: "Their revolution has been slowed down, if not halted, right on the verge of complete success."

Nothing could have pleased Dulles more. By refusing to cooperate in what he regarded as a western sellout at Geneva, Dulles felt that he had stymied Hanoi's drive to control all of Indochina. He was not particularly disturbed by those provisions of the Geneva agreements concerning Cambodia and Laos. Cambodia had been declared free and independent by the French in late 1953. The agreements provided that elections would be held there in September, 1955. The popular Socialist and Community Party, formed and led by Prince Norodom Sihanouk, won all of the seats to the National Assembly. In Laos, the Communist-backed Pathet Lao refused to relinquish control over the two northernmost provinces, bordering on North Vietnam and China, so elections were barred in this region of the country. Elections were held in the southern part of Laos in December, 1955, which put power in the hands of anti-Communist generals and politicians.

Dulles consoled himself with the thought that Geneva could have turned out much worse. "The important thing from now on," he said shortly after the Conference broke up, "is not to mourn the past but to seize the future opportunity to prevent the loss in northern Vietnam from leading to the extension of communism through Southeast Asia and the Southwest Pacific."

He proposed to accomplish this goal through the building of a defensive bulwark against the "extension of communism" throughout Asia; and by supporting the Diem regime in southern Vietnam.

SEATO—the Southeast Asia Treaty Organization—was to be that bulwark. The ink was hardly dry on the "cessation of hostilities" agreement when Dulles took the diplomatic offensive. He asked Eden if Great Britain would now agree to take part in SEATO. Eden reluctantly agreed, pointing out first, however, that Britain would never accept in SEATO the kind of far-reaching commitments written into the NATO agreement—chiefly, that an attack on any of the signatories would be regarded as an attack on all. Dulles had no trouble with the French; not then. At the ANZUS (Australia, New Zealand, and the United States) meeting, the month before, Dulles had won the consent of Australia and New Zealand to his plan for a broader Asian system of collective security. Pakistan was heavily indebted to the United States for military equipment. Its emotional hostility to India ran hot and strong, a fact that did not displease Dulles; and when Dulles asked for its participation, Pakistan quickly jumped on the bandwagon. He had no difficulty with Thailand or the Philippines.

Within forty-nine days after the Geneva agreements were announced, Dulles was in a position to proclaim the creation of SEATO. At a Manila news conference he proudly announced that the United States, Great Britain, France, Australia, New Zealand, the Philippines, Pakistan, and Thailand had signed the new treaty. The SEATO language was less explicit than in the North Atlantic Treaty of 1949. It was obviously drafted to provide some legal justification for American support of anti-Communist regimes in Southeast Asia. Article IV, the operative section, stipulated in Section 1: "Each Party recognizes that aggression by means of armed attack in the Treaty area against any of the Parties or against any State or Territory which the Parties by unanimous agreement may hereafter designate, would endanger its own peace and safety, and agrees that it will in that event act to meet the common danger in accordance with its constitutional processes." The stress on *constitutional processes* was a deliberate braking device aimed at satisfying the British and a small group of skeptical Senators.

Section 2 of the same Article is also important to an understanding of American policy at that time. It read: "If, in the opinion of any of the Parties, the inviolability or the integrity of the territory or the sovereignty or political independence of any Party in the treaty area or of any other State or territory to which the provisions of paragraph 1 of this Article from time to time apply is threatened in any way other than armed attack or is affected or threatened by any fact or situation which might endanger the peace of the area, the Parties shall consult immediately in order to agree on the measures which should be taken for the common defense."

Other than armed attack later came to mean Communist subversion from the North; *the integrity of the territory* was a concept broad and vague enough to authorize full diplomatic relations with South Vietnam as a separate entity. The notion of a separate South Vietnam State or, for that matter, of a separate North Vietnam, was specifically ruled out in the Geneva agreements. The language of the SEATO treaty showed that the United States had little confidence in and even less use for those agreements.

A separate Protocol to SEATO, proclaimed on September 8, 1954, "unanimously" designated Laos, Cambodia, "and the free territory under the jurisdiction of the State of Vietnam" as being areas subject to the provisions of the treaty. Prince Sihanouk, anxious to improve his relations with North Vietnam and China, withdrew Cambodia from any association with SEATO within a year. And, Laos, in accordance with the Geneva agreements of July, 1962, had to reject the protection of "any alliance, or military coalition, including SEATO" as part of the price for her internationally sanctioned neutrality. But the "free territory under the jurisdiction of the State of Vietnam" clung to its association with SEATO for dear life. That link became one important way of tightening the ties between the United States and South Vietnam.

If SEATO was, in Dulles's mind anyway, one way of stopping the spread of communism in Asia, then the direct application of American military power was surely another. As the twenty-four man U.S. delegation was heading for Baguio, the pleasant summer capital of the Philippines, to help inaugurate the new treaty, a pocket war erupted between the two Chinas—the vast mainland on one side and the small island of Formosa on the other. At issue was control of the offshore islands of Quemoy and Matsu, and the Pescadores, which were in Nationalist hands.

After an exchange of blistering protests, the Communists bombarded Quemoy on September 3. During the attack, two Americans were killed. On September 4, one day before the Dulles-led U.S. delegation arrived in Baguio, the Seventh Fleet suddenly left Manila harbor for an "undisclosed destination." The fleet was supposed to be at Manila for the SEATO ceremony, but White House News Secretary James Hagerty explained the change in plans by saying there had been "no change in plans." There was quick speculation the fleet would enter the pocket war. Hagerty said that kind of speculation was "totally unfounded."

The U.S. delegation included two Senators—H. Alexander Smith, an elderly New Jersey Republican, and Mike Mansfield, a reflective Montana Democrat. They were tired from the long journey, but Dulles gave them no time to rest. There was an unexpected knock at the door. A messenger said the Secretary wanted to see the Senators immediately. Where? they asked. The messenger said he had orders to drive them to the residence of Ambassador Raymond A. Spruance. When they arrived, they were quickly escorted to the patio. Dulles was already there. He looked grim. He told them that he had information the Communists would soon assault Quemoy—obviously as a stepping-stone to Formosa. He said the time had come to teach Mao a "lesson." Mansfield asked Dulles what he meant. Dulles said that he had already decided to recommend an American air attack against Communist China; and he wanted the Senator's support. He added that Admiral Radford, Chairman of the JCS, and Vice-President Nixon agreed with him. Time was short. Communism had to be stopped. SEATO, he explained, could not act, because Formosa was "outside of its defense perimeter." The

United States had to act before the Communists again misread American determination.

Smith hesitated for just a minute. Like Dulles, he detested the Chinese Communists. If the Secretary felt that it was necessary to attack China, then he would go along. Mansfield did not hesitate. He told Dulles that he would not give his support, and he insisted that Dulles inform President Eisenhower of his strong belief that such an attack would be "madness," sure to invite a major war between China and the United States. Mansfield said that the defense of Matsu and Quemoy were not "vital" to the United States; for that matter, he did not think they were "vital" to Formosa. Moreover, Mansfield said that if the administration was bent on war with China, it had best go first to the Congress and test the will of the American people.

Mansfield did not know at the time that his argument had saved the day. Dulles had communicated the Senator's powerful arguments to the President, and Ike decided that he could not sanction an American attack against the Chinese mainland. But he told Dulles that he would encourage Chiang Kai-shek to launch a series of nuisance attacks and he would station the Seventh Fleet in the Taiwan Strait to prevent a Chinese attack on Formosa.

A few days later, on September 7 and again on September 8 and 9, as the Seventh Fleet steamed into the ninety-mile wide Strait, the Nationalists attacked the Communist harbor of Amoy and bombarded coastal fortifications in Fukien Province. Tension ran high for a time, but the distinct possibility of an American air attack against China, in support of the Nationalists, had mercifully died. Its death allowed Dulles, disappointed but never daunted, to redouble his efforts to link America's fortune to South Vietnam's. His vehicle, like Dean Rusk's a decade later, was the SEATO treaty.

The treaty was approved by the Senate and signed by President Eisenhower, in February, 1955. But, even before this formality was completed, the United States began an active program of direct economic and military support of the State of Vietnam. Very quickly, in official American pronouncements, the awkward treaty phraseology—the "free territory under the jurisdiction of the State of Vietnam"—was dropped. In its place the more direct term—South Vietnam—was used. In itself, this was not an important change but, like so many other seemingly unimportant changes in this period of growing American association with South Vietnam, it reflected a basic policy orientation. The United States began to think of South Vietnam as a separate entity, cut off from the northern part of the country by an international boundary. It began to treat South Vietnam as a separate country. In the back of its bureaucratic mind, Washington realized that one day South and North Vietnam might have to be merged into a single country; against that day South Vietnam had to be strengthened for the almost inevitable period of conflict that was to precede reunification. In any event, South Vietnam had been declared "free territory," which meant it was part of the "free world." It had to be helped, and it was.

On September 29, American and French officials meeting in Washington agreed that henceforth United States aid would be channeled directly to "free Vietnam." The French middleman was eliminated. Guy LaChambre, minister of state for relations with the Three Associated States, and Edgar Faure, minister of finance, spent hours with Bedell Smith discussing the best ways of "supporting the complete independence of Cambodia, Laos, and Vietnam." They decided to invite the "chiefs of diplomatic missions" of Cambodia, Laos, and Vietnam to join their deliberations. Smith and LaChambre wanted "to have an exchange of views and information." The final communiqué noted that the representatives of "all five countries" were "in complete agreement on the objectives of peace and freedom to be achieved in Indochina."

The agreements that diplomats write into communiqués are often painfully difficult to effect. Vietnam wanted massive economic aid. More than 860,000 refugees—almost 500,000 of them Catholics—began a mass exodus from the North into South Vietnam. They needed homes, food, and churches. Their accounts of horrors suffered under Communist rule infuriated Premier Diem, a devout Catholic himself, and hardened the conviction of his supporters that collaboration with the North was impossible. Diem took the position that the Geneva agreements, signed by a "foreign military command," namely, the French, "in contempt of Vietnamese national interests," could not bind him. When the North Vietnamese proposed repeatedly that the two "zones" normalize their economic and postal regulations, Diem coldly rejected them. "We cannot entertain any Communist proposal," he said, "as long as we do not have evidence that they place the interests of the Fatherland above those of communism."

Such tough talk pleased many Americans, liberal and conservative, who had met Diem during his long stay in the Maryknoll Seminary at Yonkers, New York, from 1950 until 1953. The late Francis Cardinal Spellman of New York had introduced Diem to Supreme Court Justice Douglas, Senators Mansfield, Kennedy, and Humphrey, and to State Department and White House officials. Spellman sponsored Diem as the "democratic alternative" to communism in Vietnam, organizing charities to help the Catholic refugees. When he had the opportunity, as, on August 31, 1954, before an American Legion convention, he denounced the Geneva agreements. "If Geneva and what was agreed upon there," he declared, "means anything at all, it means taps for the buried hopes of freedom in Southeast Asia! . . . Now the devilish techniques of brainwashing, forced confessions and rigged trials have a new locale for their exercise. . . . Communism has a world plan and it has been following a carefully set-up timetable for the achievement of that plan." Some of the Cardinal's Catholic charities encouraged the Air Force to drop propaganda leaflets over North Vietnam with such themes as "Christ has gone to the South" and "the Virgin Mary has departed from the North." Cardinal Spellman flew to Vietnam to deliver by hand the first check of Catholic charity.

The Cardinal was not alone among early visitors to Saigon. Wesley Fishel, a Michigan State University professor, moved into the Presidential Palace and became one of Diem's closest advisers. Wolf Ladejinsky, a New Dealer and an expert on land reform, became another adviser. Leo Cherne, President of the International Rescue Committee, visited Saigon and, after a long talk with Diem, returned to New York convinced that South Vietnam had found a new leader of great potential. There was Colonel Edward Lansdale, a former San Francisco advertising man who believed in "selling" the American way of life. Lans-

dale, later the hero of *The Ugly American* and the anti-hero
of Graham Greene's *The Quiet American,* met Diem and
agreed wholeheartedly with Cherne's estimate. Lansdale soon
persuaded his boss, CIA Director Allen Dulles, that Diem
was an excellent anchor for a large-scale American effort in
South Vietnam. Dulles then persuaded his brother, the Secretary
of State, though Foster Dulles needed little persuading. The
United States had found an Asian George Washington. True, he
was a difficult ally. There were problems of corruption, arbitrari-
ness, and a stubborn refusal to reform Saigon's way of doing
business. But these were generally overlooked or underestimated
in the American determination to make of South Vietnam an
anti-Communist redoubt.

President Eisenhower lost little time extending a personal
promise of support to Premier Diem. His now celebrated letter
of October 23, 1954, which President Johnson later solemnly
cited as the starting point of America's commitment to South
Vietnam, clearly never was intended to signal any kind of "commitment." Ike started by saying he was "glad" that the United
States had been able to help move and resettle "several hundred
thousand loyal Vietnamese citizens" who were fleeing from a
"political ideology which they abhor." He was instructing the
American ambassador, Eisenhower wrote to Diem, "to examine
with you, in your capacity as Chief of Government, how an intelligent program of American aid given directly to your government can serve to assist Viet Nam in its present hour of trial,
*provided that your government is prepared to give assurances as
to the standards of performance it would be able to maintain* in
the event such aid were supplied."

Thus as far back as 1954, with direct American aid to the
Government of South Vietnam just beginning, the United States
was conscious of Diem's shortcomings. But it was equally determined to build an anti-Communist regime around him. "The purpose of this offer is to assist the Government of Viet Nam in
developing and maintaining a strong, viable state, capable of
resisting attempted subversion or aggression through military
means," the Eisenhower letter continued. "The Government of
the United States expects that this aid will be met by perfor-

mance on the part of the Government of Viet Nam in undertaking needed reforms." In effect, Ike assured Diem that the United States would help his government and expected him to institute "needed reforms" so that South Vietnam could become a "strong, viable state, capable of resisting . . . subversion or aggression." Diem, of course, promised to reform South Vietnam. He pointed to Ladejinsky as proof that he meant to begin with land reform, always the most sensitive area when a Mandarin-like leader begins to tamper with a backward society.

That promise opened the gates to presidentially sanctioned American aid. On November 3 the White House announced that the President was sending General J. Lawton Collins, then U.S. representative on the military committee of NATO, to Indochina in order to "coordinate the operations of all U.S. agencies in that country." The White House stressed that it had been "particularly concerned over developments in Vietnam, a country ravaged by eight years of war, artificially divided into armistice zones, and confronted by dangerous forces threatening its independence and security." Little time was wasted. Collins dropped his NATO obligations and left for Saigon. Upon his arrival on November 17, he began a process of rhetorical escalation that was to plague succeeding administrations for years to come. "I have come to Vietnam," General Collins said, "to bring every possible aid to the Government of Diem and to his Government only." He added: "It is the legal government in Vietnam, and the aid which the United States will lend it ought to permit the Government to save the country." Collins thus became the first in a series of American generals who would arrive in Saigon, puffed with pride and confidence in the American military machine, only to fly home wondering what had gone wrong with its patent for success. "This American mission will soon take charge of instructing the Vietnam Army," he said, with barely concealed braggadocio, "in accordance with special American methods which have proved effective in Korea, Greece, and Turkey and other parts of the world."

Several questions come to mind in re-reading General Collins's exuberant prose after a lapse of many years. When, for example, and by whose decision did the Diem regime become

the "legal government" of Vietnam? When, and by whom, was
it decided that the United States would assist "his Government
only"? These are rhetorical questions, raised merely to alert the
reader to the ease with which a visiting general's loose language
can be made to appear, in retrospect, as the bedrock basis of a
solemn national commitment. Senator Mansfield, who is careful
about the meaning of words, said on December 1, 1954, that
Diem had "a theoretical mandate of full powers from the Chief
of State, Bao Dai, who in turn derives his authority from a combination of a French grant and the persistence of the symbolic
power of his former rule as Emperor." In short, there was nothing
"legal" about Diem's power; the people of South Vietnam had
never been consulted. Legality was assumed by those Washington officials already committed to the building of a bastion
against communism in South Vietnam. If not Diem, it might
have been Minh. If not Minh, then Khanh or Ky or Thieu would
do. (Not until 1967 did President Johnson insist that elections
be held in South Vietnam to give some semblance of legality to
the Thieu-Ky regime.)

Thus, barely five months after pledging itself not to "disturb"
the Geneva accords, the United States was beginning to act and
talk as though there were two Vietnam states, only one of which,
the Diem regime in Saigon, was legitimate.

Ironically, General Collins returned to Washington after his
brief Saigon mission, believing that the United States should not
link its fortunes in Southeast Asia to Ngo Dinh Diem. But the
Dulles brothers persuaded the President that Diem was the best
possible choice.

Small step by small step, starting in January 1, 1955, the
U.S. Military Aid and Advisory Group, known as MAAG, took
over the training and equipping of the South Vietnamese Army
from the French, who were delighted to abandon this responsibility. The French had developed problems with other nationalist movements in North Africa; having lost Indochina, they
were determined to hold Algeria. General Collins was pleased
with ARVN's progress, especially the dispatch and cold-blooded
efficiency with which Diem had liquidated the Binh-Xuyen po-

litical-military challenge and neutralized the political opposition
posed by the Cao Dai and Hoa Hao religious sects.

Diem, following his Mandarin instincts, surrounded himself
with relatives and friends. On May 10 he formed a new and congenial cabinet. On October 23 he deposed Bao Dai, then rigged
a national referendum in which 98 percent of the voters ostensibly pledged their loyalty to Ngo Dinh Diem. On October 26
Diem proclaimed the new Republic of Vietnam and appointed
himself its first president. Quickly he sent a note to the United
States Embassy in Saigon, expressing his "hope" that the "Government of the United States will continue as in the past to
entertain diplomatic relations with the new Government of the
State of Vietnam." Under instructions from Washington, Ambassador G. Frederick Reinhardt responded that the United States
"looks forward" to the "same cordial and friendly relations" with
the new Government as with the old. He added: "We are glad
to see the evolution of orderly and effective democratic processes
in an area of Southeast Asia which has been and continues to be
threatened by Communist efforts to impose totalitarian control."
Reinhardt, a sophisticated and experienced diplomat, may have
winced at the thought of equating the Diem referendum with
"orderly and effective democratic processes." But official Washington had made its choice and proposed to stick with Diem.
Not even the liberals on Capitol Hill were disposed to quibble.
Senator Hubert Humphrey said: "Diem is the best hope that we
have in South Vietnam. He is the leader of his people. He deserves and must have the wholehearted support of the American Government and our foreign policy." Diem was the hero of
the hour, even though he disdained free elections—a concept
dear to the hearts of Humphrey liberals. In their eyes, Diem was
satisfying a larger aim by frustrating a Communist takeover of
South Vietnam.

On July 20, 1955, as agreed at Geneva, "consultations" between the "competent representative authorities of the two
zones" were to have begun, leading to general elections the following year. Diem rejected the very notion of elections until
"conditions of freedom" should exist throughout Vietnam, mean-

ing North Vietnam. His somewhat brazen implication was that such conditions existed in the South. In taking this position, Diem had no problem with the United States, only with Hanoi. Ho Chi Minh, though bitterly disappointed, was not really surprised.

"All Vietnamese citizens, whether from the North or from the South," he told an Indian visitor, "have the right to canvass freely throughout the country through conference, leaflets, press, etc. The Government of the North and the authorities of the South should ensure the liberty and the security for all citizens during their activities for elections." In the North, of course, "all Vietnamese citizens" could have been expected to vote 100 percent for Ho. In the South, according to Eisenhower, 80 percent. Diem did not like the odds.

There was some gentle pressure from the British—if not for elections, then at least for negotiations that might lead to elections. "Her Majesty's Government has always regarded it as desirable that these elections should be held and has advised the Government of the Republic of Vietnam to enter into consultations with the Viet Minh authorities in order to ensure that all the necessary conditions obtained for a free expression of the national will as a preliminary to holding free general elections by secret ballot."

On September 21, 1955, Diem told a reporter for the *Times* of London: "There can be no question of a conference, even less of negotiations." There were to be no elections. The reason was clear. Elections, the State Department said a few years later, were a "trap," and the "authorities in South Vietnam refused to fall into this well-laid trap." The supposedly temporary demarcation line began to take on the look of a national boundary. In the South, Diem followed Ladejinsky's advice and launched a program of land reform. For a time it was the apple of his eye, earning praise from Washington and popularity from the peasantry. In the North, Ho started a program of collectivization that disrupted the countryside and led to swift and savage repression. Tens of thousands—perhaps hundreds of thousands—of "rich" peasants were slaughtered for resisting "the will of the people."

But Diem lost military strength as the French withdrew

much of their heavy equipment and most of their troops. His army was down to 150,000 men—no match for the armies of the North; even though his troops were beginning to receive American military aid and there was hope that in time they would improve. In the North, Ho concentrated on strengthening his army. It has been estimated that in July of 1954 he had only seven Viet Minh divisions. Two years later he had at least twenty. Arms from Russia and China continued to cross the Sino-Vietnamese border. Moral and ideological support followed. Both sides at the same time were strengthening their ties to their respective sponsors. While Chou En-lai visited Hanoi, John Foster Dulles visited Saigon. Each pledged support to his ally. In March, 1956, Assistant Secretary Walter Robertson accompanied Dulles to Saigon. He later told a Washington gathering of the American Friends of Vietnam that both of them had been struck by the "remarkable rise" of "Free Vietnam" and by the "dedication, courage, and resourcefulness of President Diem himself."

It was to become a rule of life in Washington that high officials would pay frequent visits to Saigon and, almost without exception, return "enormously impressed" by the progress that was being made in establishing "freedom, peace, and the good life" in South Vietnam. Robertson was doing what came naturally. ". . . Asia has given us in President Diem another great figure, and the entire free world has become the richer for his example of determination and moral fortitude, . . ." Robertson said. "In him, his country has found a truly worthy leader." The United States, Robertson went on, is proud to be "on the side of . . . the Vietnamese people under President Diem." He then blocked out the shape of United States policy:

"To support a friendly, non-Communist government in Vietnam and to help it diminish and eventually eradicate Communist subversion and influence.

"To help the Government of Vietnam establish the forces necessary for internal security.

"To encourage support for Free Vietnam by the non-Communist world."

At the time these were modest aims, even though Robertson's gushy rhetoric made them sound more far-reaching. He denounced Hanoi's "lies, propaganda, force, and deceit" and its "most blatant" violations of the Geneva accords; its "crimes against suffering humanity"; its adherence to "all the devious zigzags of the Communist-bloc line"; all this by way of stressing that it was "not possible" to hold "free elections." The United States, he seemed to be saying, must support "this staunch and valiant member of the free world fighting for its independence on the threshold of the Communist heartland of Asia." Out of sentiments such as these, commitments grow.

There was more of this rhetoric when, on July 6, Vice-President Nixon visited South Vietnam. He conferred at length with President Diem. Nixon handed Diem a letter from President Eisenhower, which said that the United States looked forward to many years of "partnership" between the two countries. Addressing the Constituent Assembly in Saigon, Nixon praised South Vietnam's efforts and announced, somewhat prematurely: "The militant march of communism has been halted."

Before Nixon left Saigon, he invited Diem to visit Washington. The state visit, designed to unveil Asia's "democratic alternative," was a block-busting success. Diem spent three days in Washington, from May 8 to May 11, 1957. He conferred at length with Eisenhower, Dulles, and other high officials. He addressed a joint session of the Congress, chatted with old friends, such as Cardinal Spellman, Mayor Robert Wagner of New York, Justice William O. Douglas, and Senator John Kennedy. At a New York luncheon, Wagner hailed Diem as a man "to whom freedom is the very breath of life itself." At a dinner that night, Angier Biddle Duke, representing Leo Cherne's International Rescue Committee and the American Friends of Vietnam, presented Diem with the Admiral Richard E. Byrd Award for "inspired leadership in the cause of the free world."

The White House communiqué said that the President had assured Diem of the "willingness of the United States to continue to offer effective assistance within the constitutional processes" in order to promote "political stability and economic welfare in the Republic of Viet Nam." The assurance approached a commitment. Its rationale was the "continued military buildup of the Chinese Communists, their refusal to renounce the use of force, and their unwillingness to subscribe to standards of conduct of civilized nations." The communiqué also pointed to "continuing Communist subversive capabilities." As a result, both Presidents referred to Article IV of the SEATO treaty, which they said covered the Republic of Vietnam (though the treaty text makes no specific mention of Vietnam) and they agreed that "aggression or subversion threatening the political independence of the Republic of Viet Nam would be considered as endangering peace and stability."

Eisenhower offered Diem his personal plane to fly to the West Coast—a sign of presidential favor and a symbol of the growing unity of purpose between Washington and Saigon. But, what pleased Eisenhower and delighted Diem was bound to worry Hanoi. The Viet Minh saw a powerful America replace a weak France as the major outside force in Indochina. This represented a major strategic change, requiring a shift in Communist tactics. From 1954 until 1957, the Viet Minh had been busy in the North, building up their armies, solidifying their political control, recouping some of the energy spent in eight years of warfare against the French. After the Diem visit to the United States, which capped three years of considerable social, economic, and political progress in South Vietnam, the shift became apparent. Hard-core guerrillas, some 6000 who had gone underground in 1954, began a program of systematic harassment, sabotage, and assassination, plainly designed to disrupt the progress that, they feared, would make reunification on their terms much more difficult.

There were few, if any, qualified American experts on Viet Minh affairs at the time. Experts or dilettantes, officials in Saigon and Washington took to arguing whether the recent upsurge in guerrilla activity was "a southern idea" or whether it had been ordered from North Vietnam. The argument continued for years, with no conclusion.

Diem decided to meet the Communist guerrilla challenge head on, by frontal attack. He increased the size of his army and the regional forces, sharply reducing at the same time his dedication to social reform. In fact, he grew suspicious of reformers. The Palace circle narrowed as the guerrilla challenge

in the countryside widened. Village chiefs were assassinated.
The Viet Minh became known as the Viet Cong, to distinguish
them from their counterparts in the North. They started to
collect taxes, cut roads, and blow bridges. Diem requested
more help from the United States and he got it. So many
millions had already been invested in South Vietnam that
Washington felt it had no choice but to increase the stake. "In
for a penny, in for a pound," was the official attitude. On April
4, 1959, when the Second Vietnam War had been raging for two
years, still undeclared and still widely ignored by the American
people, President Eisenhower spoke at Gettysburg College in
Gettysburg, Pennsylvania. Never before nor since had the President so clearly linked America's own "national interest" to the
survival of a non-Communist regime in South Vietnam. In the
long and tangled history of the American involvement, the Gettysburg speech stands out as a landmark.

(We italicize those phrases or passages of special relevance
in understanding United States policy during the transition
period between the Eisenhower and Kennedy administrations.)
Eisenhower began:

Vietnam is a country, divided into two parts like Korea and Germany. The southern half, with its twelve million people, is *free* but
poor. It is an underdeveloped country; its economy is weak, average
individual income being less than $200 a year. The northern half has
been turned over to communism. A line of demarcation running along
the 17th parallel separates the two. *To the north of this line stand
several Communist divisions.* These facts pose to South Vietnam two
great tasks: self-defense and economic growth.

Understandably the people of Vietnam want to make their country a thriving, self-sufficient member of the family of nations. This
means economic expansion.

For Vietnam's economic growth, the acquisition of capital is vi-
tally necessary. Now the nation could create the capital needed for
growth by stealing from the already meager rice bowls of its people
and regimenting them into work battalions. *This enslavement is the
commune system, adopted by the new overlords of Red China.* It
would mean of course the loss of freedom within the country without
any hostile outside action whatsoever.

Another way for Vietnam to get the necessary capital is through
private investments from the outside and through governmental loans

and, where necessary, grants from other and more fortunately situated nations.

In either of these ways the economic problem of Vietnam could be solved. But only the second way can preserve *freedom*.

And there is still the other of Vietnam's great problems—how to support the military forces it needs without crushing its economy.

Because of the *proximity of large Communist military formations in the North, Free Vietnam* must maintain substantial numbers of men under arms. Moreover, while the Government has shown real progress in cleaning out Communist guerrillas, those remaining continue to be a disruptive influence in the nation's life.

Unassisted, Vietnam cannot at this time produce and support the military formations essential to it, or, equally important, the morale, the hope, the confidence, the pride—necessary *to meet the dual threat of aggression from without and subversion within its borders.*

Still another fact! *Strategically South Vietnam's capture by the Communists would bring their power several hundred miles into a hitherto free region. The remaining countries in Southeast Asia would be menaced by a great flanking movement.* The freedom of 12 million people would be lost immediately and that of 150 million others in adjacent lands would be seriously endangered. *The loss of South Vietnam would set in motion a crumbling process that could, as it progressed, have grave consequences for us and for freedom.*

Vietnam must have a reasonable degree of safety now—both for her people and for her property. Because of these facts, military as well as economic help is currently needed in Vietnam.

We reach the *inescapable conclusion* that *our own national interests* demand some help from us in sustaining in Vietnam the morale, the economic progress, and *the military strength necessary to its continued existence in freedom.*

In short, by 1959 it was clear that the Eisenhower Administration would not—indeed felt that it could not—acquiesce in the loss of South Vietnam to communism. Ironically it was Eisenhower, the peace President, having once refused to intervene militarily at the time of Dienbienphu, who reached the conclusion five years later that the national interests of the United States were somehow at stake in South Vietnam. It remained for Presidents Kennedy, Johnson, and Nixon to expand and then contract the limits of America's involvement. But the basic commitment, in the name of national interest, had been made before Kennedy took office.

FIVE

There Is No Evil That Lasts
100 Years

An old Spanish proverb, a favorite of General Maxwell D. Taylor

ON JANUARY 19, 1961, the skies over Washington were charcoal gray. From the Oval Office of the White House, Dwight D. Eisenhower and John F. Kennedy could see the first flurries of an unwelcome snowstorm. For more than an hour the outgoing President shared with the incoming President some bipartisan secrets of the office. The session was both rewarding and sobering. Eisenhower, the last of the 19th-century Presidents, Texas-born, Kansas-reared, an admired soldier, a healing President, handing over the powers of his office to the first of the 20th-century Presidents: rich, Brookline-born, Harvard-trained, bursting with energy and promise, a Catholic who had overcome lingering prejudice to defeat Vice-President Nixon, at forty-three the second youngest President in the history of the Republic.

Eisenhower then escorted Kennedy into the Cabinet Room for a final meeting with senior advisers on both sides. On the Republican side: Secretary of State Christian Herter (successor to the deceased Dulles), Defense Secretary Thomas S. Gates, Treasury Secretary Robert B. Anderson, and Major General Wilton D. Persons; on the Democratic side, Dean Rusk, the incoming Secretary of State; Robert McNamara, Defense Secretary-designate; Douglas Dillon, the new Secretary of the Treasury; and Clark M. Clifford, former Truman aide, highly successful Washington lawyer, and Kennedy's chief adviser during the transition.

Although the old guard was yielding to the new, the men around the Cabinet table, including the new President, shared an essentially common view of the world, and of America's place in it. It was a view shaped in large part by twelve years of cold war. All believed in the existence of a supposedly monolithic Communist bloc that was determined to attack and defeat the forces of freedom, wherever they existed. All saw Russia and America locked in a struggle for the soul of man. True, Kennedy was to alter the Dulles vision of neutralism. To him, India was not a probable enemy but a possible friend. In his Inaugural Address, Kennedy was to speak of the Russians not as enemies but as adversaries. Yet he was soon to sanction a foredoomed invasion of Cuba and to raise the stakes in Southeast Asia.

No ideological barrier separated these men. In fact, of Kennedy's four-man team, two were Republicans; McNamara, recently appointed president of the Ford Motor Company; and Dillon, who had served as Eisenhower's ambassador to France and Under Secretary of State. There was, in short, no need for an interpreter. Persons and Clifford, who laid out the agenda, had agreed that the "deteriorating situation in Southeast Asia" would head the list of foreign-policy problems: not Cuba, not Berlin, not the celebrated "missile gap," but Laos and Southeast Asia, particularly Laos. Clifford took notes.

"President Eisenhower said, with considerable emotion," according to the Clifford account, which is accepted as accurate by most of the participants, "that Laos was the key to the entire area of Southeast Asia.

"He said that if we permitted Laos to fall, then we would have to write off all of the area. He stated that we must not permit a communist takeover. He reiterated that we should make every effort to persuade member nations of SEATO or the International Control Commission to accept the burden with us to defend the freedom of Laos.

"As he concluded these remarks, President Eisenhower stated that it was imperative that Laos be defended. He said that the United States should accept this task with our allies, if we could persuade them, and alone if we could not. He added, 'Our unilateral intervention would be our last desperate hope in the event we were unable to prevail upon the other signatories to join us.' "

Herter and Gates in turn also supported American intervention, if diplomacy should fail. Kennedy listened quietly, his demeanor suggesting neither approval nor disapproval. He asked Gates how long it would take to move a division of American troops into Laos. The outgoing Secretary of Defense replied that it would take about two weeks from the United States, less time if the troops happened to be in the Pacific area.

Kennedy offered no further comment. But, as Walt Rostow later recalled, he was "profoundly shaken" by "Ike's recommendation" that he might have to order American intervention in Laos. This was not at all what he had in mind for his Presidency. He had not yet taken the oath of office, nor yet delivered his stirring Inaugural Address, a copy of which was in his pocket. Already the problems of Southeast Asia were intruding into his dreams for the Presidency.

January 20, Inauguration Day, dawned cold and brilliantly clear; Kennedy weather, as reporters learned to call those miraculous changes from darkness to light. Some time before dawn the snow had stopped. By late morning the main arteries through downtown Washington had been cleared—the snow pushed back into glistening alpine foothills along the pavements. The Kennedy Presidency began, as Arthur Schlesinger has noted, "with incomparable dash" in the biting cold. The young President delivered his "splendid speech" and watched the parade coatless, often twiddling his top hat. That evening, after dining with his Cabinet, he made the round of inaugural balls and managed, well past midnight, to stop at the Georgetown home of Joseph Alsop, the columnist.

Business began the next day. He received a congratulatory message from Moscow. Khrushchev and Brezhnev expressed the hope that "by our joint efforts we shall succeed in achieving a fundamental improvement in relations between our countries and a normalization of the whole international situation." Kennedy answered immediately, saying he was "ready and anxious to cooperate with all who are prepared to join in genuine dedication to the assurance of a peaceful and more fruitful life for all mankind." A few days later Khrushchev took a concrete step. He released the crew of a downed American RB-47 reconnaissance plane, timing the release of the fliers to signal a desire for improved relations with the United States. Kennedy started his term, in short, with high hopes and soaring spirits, in spite of Eisenhower's gloomy warnings about Southeast Asia.

Kennedy had watched with some anxiety the remarkable rise of Soviet influence through the late 1950s. The Russians had launched the first successful artificial earth satellite, a sensational symbol of Russia's technological advance. The Soviet Union's rate of industrial growth surpassed America's. Khrushchev's very flamboyance, his un-Soviet style of behavior, suggested a "new" Russia—more tolerant, more open, less constrained by rigid dogma, less intimidated by the secret police. Revolutionary ferment seemed to be spreading round the world. Cuba belonged to Castro. The leftist Pathet Lao was on the attack in Laos. The Viet Cong were increasing their terrorism in South Vietnam. The N.L.F. was gaining the upper hand over the French in Algeria. Khrushchev believed that he was riding the crest of a revolutionary wave that would sweep capitalism off the face of the earth. More important, that he could accomplish this historic change, foretold by Marx and Lenin, without resorting to war. His Communist rival, Mao Tse-tung, discounted nuclear warfare, prophesying a "new civilization" would emerge from the ashes of such a holocaust. To Khrushchev, by his own description a "goulash Communist" who sincerely felt he had discovered an easier road to victory, this Maoist belief was "sheer madness." Khrushchev used to tell visitors that "the living would envy the dead" if statesmen were so foolish as to allow themselves to be drawn into nuclear war.

Still Khrushchev did not exclude all war from his calculation. On January 6, 1961, in a speech that deeply impressed the President-elect, Khrushchev analyzed the "world situation as it appeared at the beginning of the Sixties." He concluded that "there is no longer any force in the world capable of barring the road to socialism." He predicted that Castro's successful example would spread from Cuba throughout Latin America. On Berlin, he warned that "it is necessary to go ahead with bringing the aggressive-minded imperialists to their senses . . . and should they balk, then we will take resolute measures, we will sign a peace treaty with the German Democratic Republic." Then he talked of war. "World wars" and "local wars" (presumably Korea) were too dangerous in a nuclear age, he said. But "wars of liberation or popular uprisings" were not only sanctioned, they were blessed. "National liberation wars" begin, Khrushchev said, as "uprisings of colonial peoples against their oppressors" and then develop into "guerrilla wars." Khrushchev put the question: "What is the attitude of Marxists to such uprisings?" He gave the answer like a well-drilled catechist: "A most favorable attitude. . . . The Communists support just wars of this kind whole-heartedly and without reservation and they march in the van of the peoples fighting for liberation." He did not mention Laos, but he did mention Cuba, Algeria, and Vietnam as examples of this new, approved style of warfare.

Kennedy read the Khrushchev speech time and again—in his office, at Cabinet meetings, at dinners with friends, alone. At times he read it aloud and urged his colleagues to comment. Kennedy later came to believe that cooperation with Khrushchev was possible in some areas. Arms control was one area, and he succeeded in negotiating a limited test-ban treaty. Trade was a second area, and he relaxed some long-standing embargoes on Soviet goods. Exchanges were another, and he encouraged American artists, writers, and tourists to visit the Soviet Union. But on the big, neuralgic questions—Berlin, Cuba, and Southeast Asia—he saw little prospect of accommodation and much prospect of trouble.

Increasingly preoccupied with Communist insurgencies and guerrilla wars, Kennedy groped for an effective counter-strategy. Castro's rise in Cuba became a case study in successful guerrilla warfare at the U.S. Army's Special Warfare School at Fort Bragg. Mao and Che Guevara were required reading.

Dean Rusk, among other administration leaders, came to believe that the Communists were not likely to launch frontal attacks across established national borders; such attacks would be suicidal, since they could lead to nuclear war. Therefore, the Communists would try to exploit this new kind of warfare. Walt Rostow once described it as "this international disease

. . . guerrilla war designed, initiated, supplied, and led from outside an independent nation." Of the three testing grounds mentioned by Khrushchev, one, Algeria, was clearly outside the realm of American responsibility. Cuba was a *fait accompli.* That left Vietnam, an area of steadily deepening American concern since the Forties. Rusk did not think of himself as a confirmed believer in the domino theory. But he could see Eisenhower's point: If Laos or Vietnam fell to the Communists, "we would have to write off all of the area." Rusk often said that aggression (or subversion, or guerrilla war) must be stopped, not appeased; defeated, not rewarded. He saw Hanoi's drive into Laos, its terrorism in South Vietnam, as a restyled pattern of aggression by the totalitarian states. Since his Rhodes Scholar days at Oxford, Rusk had been a believer in collective security. He would remark to friends that if Mussolini had been stopped in Ethiopia, or Hitler in the Sudetenland, then perhaps World War II could have been avoided. He came to believe that if Ho could be stopped in Laos, or South Vietnam, perhaps World War III might be avoided. Rusk knew that there were profound differences between the Sudetenland and South Vietnam, between Hitler and Ho. "I am not the village idiot," he once exploded. But he profoundly believed that aggression by any other name was aggression still and that it must be checked. The case for stopping communism's advance in South Vietnam was, in his view, compelling.

In the early months of the Kennedy Administration the only sustained challenge to Rusk's vision of the world came from Averell Harriman and Chester Bowles, who argued for a more conciliatory line toward the Communists. But there was broad agreement on the overriding need to confront Communist expansion. To the President it seemed right and natural that the United States should use its power—if that became necessary—to stop Communist-backed insurgencies in Southeast Asia. In Vienna, during the grim Berlin-focused encounter with Kennedy in June, 1961, Khrushchev showed some willingness to arrange a coalition government in Laos, which in any case was the aim of Soviet policy; but he refused to discuss the Communist insurgency in South Vietnam, and he threatened war over Berlin

unless it were turned into a "free city." In fact, he rather de-
fiantly wished the Viet Cong success. When Kennedy returned
to Washington, Berlin very much on his mind, he ordered a
limited call-up of reservists, boosted the defense budget, flew
several thousand U.S. troops into West Berlin, and went a long
way toward deciding that he would probably have to make a
stand in Southeast Asia. If not, Khrushchev might get the notion
that this new President, humiliated at the Bay of Pigs and bullied
in Vienna, was truly vulnerable.

By an act of omission, Truman had not opposed, or
questioned the French return to Indochina; later, he helped
them fight the Viet Minh with arms and money. By acts of commission, Eisenhower had increased the flow of aid to the
French; and, after refusing to intervene militarily to save French
colonialism in Indochina, he willingly accepted the dual burden
of providing economic assistance to the Diem regime and bolstering its defenses against renewed Viet Cong terrorism, after
he had determined that nothing less than the "national interest"
of the United States was at stake. Kennedy appears to have
acted out of a complex of factors: First, historical necessity, as
he saw it. There was Khrushchev's threat to support all wars of
national liberation, which in Kennedy's view required a tough,
unflinching response. Second, as a Democrat, his party already
saddled with the "loss of China," Kennedy felt the need to prevent, if he could, the loss of Vietnam and, should the domino
theory prove valid, the loss of all Southeast Asia. (Oddly, no
Democrat ever accused Eisenhower of having lost Cuba to
communism. Eisenhower was a national hero; his reputation
perhaps conferred a kind of immunity.) Third, the grip of the
past was not easily broken. The United States had for fifteen
years funneled increasing amounts of military assistance, economic succor, and blasts of high-powered official rhetoric into
the effort to defeat communism in Indochina. It would have
taken a supreme act of conviction for any new President to shut
off the flow at a moment when the Viet Cong threat was rising.
There is no solid unpartisan evidence that Kennedy ever considered a reversal of policy toward South Vietnam. Instead he
raised the ante by ordering several thousand American advisers

into Vietnam. Before the new President had completed his first year in office, one of the advisers had been killed. The spilling of American blood made it harder than ever to turn back.

Eisenhower's somber warnings about Laos almost totally preoccupied Kennedy during the first months of his administration. He had inherited an uncomfortable though by no means hopeless situation. Under Eisenhower, the United States had invested some $300,000,000 in Laos to convert this unlikely little Asian kingdom into a "bastion of freedom." It was an impossible task, but few of Eisenhower's advisers would admit it. The bulk of the money was administered by the Pentagon, which meant that the Royal Loatian Army got the lion's share. Although Laos had no all-weather roads, the Pentagon outfitted Laos with tanks, trucks, half-tracks, and Jeeps. Everyone was preparing for conventional warfare, except the Pathet Lao guerrillas. Only $7,000,000 was earmarked for economic development, a clear indication of how dimly the administration perceived the problems of Laos.

In November, 1957, the two main political forces in Laos had agreed to set up a two-headed coalition government headed by Prince Souvanna Phouma, a neutralist, and his half-brother, Prince Souphanouvong, a Communist, much against the urgings of J. Graham Parsons, the American ambassador. The coalition was viewed by many Washington officials in the State Department and the CIA as nothing but a way station on the road to Communist rule. The Vientiane agreements horrified the Dulles brothers in particular, as well as Robertson and Parsons. If Souvanna was so foolish as to strike a deal with a known Communist, so childishly naïve as to consider coalition a workable proposition, then Washington had to write him off as unreliable. Ambassador Parsons favored replacing Souvanna with a Laotian politician named Phoui Sananikoune. The CIA had its own candidate, an ambitious right-wing general named Phoumi Nosavan, who had been living in Paris. The CIA prevailed, as it came to prevail more and more in Laotian affairs. Souvanna was ousted. Phoui briefly replaced him and in turn was overthrown in 1959 by Phoumi.

In early 1960, however, an unknown paratroop captain,

Kong Le, seized power in Vientiane and promptly restored
Souvanna to the premiership. The new American ambassador,
Winthrop Brown, sensibly saw the Kong Le coup as an opportunity to achieve some measure of stability by bringing Souvanna
and Phoumi together in a united government. Washington was
divided. Without strong backing, the opportunity soon slipped
away. Phoumi established one government in Savannakhet;
Souvanna, another in Vientiane; and political chaos reigned.
Washington intervened—but in a bungling manner. It dispatched former Ambassador Parsons, now Assistant Secretary
of State, to Vientiane in a crash effort to persuade Souvanna to
abandon neutralism and join forces with Phoumi against the
Pathet Lao. Souvanna profoundly distrusted Parsons; besides, he
disagreed with Parsons's plan to convert Laos into an anti-
Communist bastion. Having failed in his mission, Parsons returned to Washington and recommended all-out support of
Phoumi.

In December, 1960, soon after the presidential elections but
without consulting Kennedy or his representatives, the Eisenhower Administration encouraged Phoumi to march on Vientiane
and oust Souvanna from power. Souvanna fled to Cambodia.
Utterly disgusted with the United States, Souvanna reluctantly
reached an informal arrangement with Souphanouvong and
urged the neutralist forces of Kong Le to join up with the leftist
Pathet Lao. Souvanna, believing the United States had engineered his downfall, then turned to the Russians for military aid.
They were pleased to provide it. In fact, over the next several
months, sensing a splendid opportunity to hurry the forces of
history, they instituted a top-priority airlift of weapons to the
pro-Communist forces in Laos.

By the time Kennedy was inaugurated, Laos was being
pushed in one direction by the United States and pulled in the
opposite direction by the Soviet Union. Laos was not a country
"worthy of engaging the attention of great powers," Kennedy
said pointedly. He nevertheless set up a task force to study the
problem, and within a month the Pentagon had persuaded the
President to "unleash" Phoumi. The generals assured him that
Phoumi could defeat Kong Le's forces and retake the strategic

Plain of Jars in north central Laos. The generals' advice, as so often in the past, turned out to be dead wrong. The Royal Lao Army was beaten in a quick series of skirmishes, retreating to the safe haven of Vientiane. Kennedy then began to think in terms of a negotiated solution leading to the formation of a coalition government: precisely the alternative the Dulles brothers had vetoed in the Eisenhower days. The old guard at the State Department, the Pentagon, and the CIA—knowing that coalition meant the return of Souvanna—strongly resisted the idea. The new guard, led by Harriman, argued that the Russians could perhaps be enticed into accepting a coalition formula for peace in Laos—if for no other reason than to outflank the Chinese in the political maneuvering for Southeast Asia.

Through February and early March it was an open question whether the Communists would settle for a coalition. Their forces advanced slowly on Vientiane as Soviet supplies poured in by air. Kennedy was clearly alarmed. He had made it clear, he thought, that he favored a coalition government in Laos. But the Communists seemed to be pressing for total victory. On March 9 the President's task force recommended stepped-up American military aid to Phoumi's beleaguered forces. On March 15, at a news conference, Kennedy said that "a small minority backed by personnel and supplies from outside" was trying to prevent the establishment of coalition rule. "We are determined," he said, "to support the government and the people of Laos in resisting this attempt." On March 15 Rusk appealed to Soviet Foreign Minister Andrei Gromyko to accept the "neutralization" of Laos. Gromyko seemed unimpressed. On March 20 Kennedy scheduled an emergency meeting of the National Security Council. Clearly, something had to be done.

At lunch that day, so Arthur Schlesinger recalls, the President said it was indispensable to prevent "an immediate Communist takeover." He talked of the necessity of somehow holding Vientiane in order to have a basis for negotiation. "We cannot and will not accept any visible humiliation over Laos," Kennedy said. The words *visible humiliation* strongly suggest that Kennedy was disposed to act if that was the only way to prevent a quick Communist victory; but they also suggest that he remained willing to take his chances on a coalition government, which might over a longer period produce the same result.

When the Security Council met after lunch, Rostow recommended a limited deployment of American ground forces; not, he said, to fight the Pathet Lao but, hopefully, to deter them from pressing their attack and, at the same time, to bolster Phoumi's morale. The Joint Chiefs of Staff opposed a limited deployment. They refused to recommend any United States troop commitment unless it were a sizable force of, say, 60,000 troops with air cover and with advance authorization to use tactical nuclear weapons, just in case the Chinese Communists should intervene in strength. The council met the next day. Again no decision was reached.

On March 23, Kennedy held another news conference. On the platform behind him three maps of Laos were set up on easels. Pointing to one of the maps, rather nervously, he disclosed that Russia had flown more than 1000 sorties into the Pathet Lao areas since December. He appealed for a negotiated solution. "If in the past," he emphasized, "there has been any possible ground for misunderstanding of our desire for a truly neutral Laos, there should be none now." Then he issued a clear warning to Moscow. "The security of all of Southeast Asia will be endangered," he said, "if Laos loses its neutral independence. *Its own safety runs with the safety of us all*. I know that every American will want its country to *honor its obligations* to the point that *freedom and security of the free world* and ourselves may be achieved." *

Only two months in office, Kennedy was already extending membership in the "free world" to Laos; underscoring America's "obligations" to support Phoumi's government; and all but identifying Laos as another vital interest of the United States by saying that its "safety" runs with the "safety of us all." From private conversations it was clear that Kennedy knew better. But he obviously felt he could do no better.

As he spoke, his aides took certain military and diplomatic actions. The Seventh Fleet moved into the South China Sea;

* (Italics by M. K. and E. A.)

U.S. combat troops were alerted; Midway Island became an emergency base; 500 Marines were airlifted to hastily improvised positions in Thailand across the Mekong River from the Laotian capital, Vientiane.

At the same time, the White House dispatched a top-secret cable to British Prime Minister Macmillan. It had an explosive effect at No. 10 Downing Street and the Foreign Office. It recommended the quick implementation of *Plan Five*—a Rostow euphemism for an allied military landing in Laos. The landing would be made by United States Marines, supported by the mobile Commonwealth Brigade, which consisted of troops from Great Britain, New Zealand, and Australia. Sir Alec Douglas Home, the foreign secretary, and Edward Heath, then a minister of state, now prime minister, joined Macmillan in flatly rejecting the Kennedy proposal. Macmillan asked for an urgent meeting with the President. It took place on March 26 at a U.S. naval base at Key West, Florida. Macmillan informed Kennedy that the Commonwealth Brigade would not take part in any Laos operation, and he implored the young President not to dispatch U.S. troops to Laos but to rely upon a diplomatic solution.

The communiqué summing up their talks put maximum pressure on Moscow to join in a big-power effort to create a "truly neutral" Laos, but the communiqué revealed nothing about Kennedy's continuing tinkering with the notion of sending troops into Laos. On March 27 Rusk invoked the SEATO treaty at a ministerial meeting in Bangkok and succeeded in getting troop pledges from Thailand, Pakistan, and the Philippines. Kennedy readied himself for tougher decisions, though he was disappointed with Macmillan's uncompromising rejection.

They proved to be unnecessary, at least in Laos. On April 1, Khrushchev accepted in principle a British proposal to reactivate the International Control Commission for Laos and to convene a new Geneva conference. But the Russians were in no hurry. Three weeks passed—weeks of tension and tumult in Washington. Apart from his anguish over Laos, Kennedy was trying to decide just then whether an Eisenhower-initiated plan to support the landing of a U.S.-armed Cuban exile brigade in Cuba should be allowed to go ahead, as planned before he took office.

After days of hesitation, Kennedy agreed to the landing attempt. But, at the last possible moment, he refused to sanction American air support over the bridgehead. This half-hearted, half-baked action all but guaranteed the defeat of the exile brigade at the Bay of Pigs. It was Kennedy's first great blunder as President. He insisted upon shouldering full personal responsibility for the disaster. In Laos he felt the need to show more determination.

On April 20, coincident with the Bay of Pigs, Kennedy ordered American military advisers in Laos, who had been operating in mufti, to put on their uniforms and transform themselves into a Military Assistance and Advisory Group. He further ordered them to accompany the Royal Lao forces into battle. It was a major decision. On April 24 Khrushchev again said he was ready for Laos peace talks. But in Laos the Communist offensive continued. Kennedy felt he was being euchred—and he did not like it. On April 26 the National Security Council met once again to consider military intervention in Laos. Rostow again recommended limited deployment of American troops to the Mekong Valley. The White House task force agreed. Even Harriman said "yes" this time. But the Joint Chiefs balked. They said they could not guarantee a successful outcome, even if all 60,000 troops were committed to the Mekong operation. When the NSC met again the next day, there was still no decision. The service chiefs left the impression that only if the President would approve an initial deployment of 140,000 American troops, authorized to use tactical nuclear weapons if necessary, would they guarantee that Laos would not fall to the Communists.

Kennedy was perilously close to a decision to send some American troops to Laos. "I can't take a 1954 defeat today," he told Rostow. In 1954, Kennedy explained, Eisenhower could ride out the French defeat for two reasons: first, he could blame these setbacks on the French and take shelter behind America's traditional distaste for colonialism; and second, as a victorious military leader, Ike could draw on his vast personal popularity and political strength. Kennedy knew he did not possess comparable assets.

Fortunately, for him, the warring factions in Laos accepted a cease-fire arrangement on May 1. The new Geneva Conference opened on May 12. It took more than a year before a "declaration on the neutrality of Laos" could be successfully negotiated. This neutrality was based on a sharing of power through a three-headed coalition government. Prince Souvanna Phouma, the neutralist prime minister, was to be flanked by Prince Boun Oum on the right and Prince Souphanouvong on the left. Kennedy entrusted the negotiation to Harriman. In Geneva at the time few reporters or diplomats felt the deal could last. Most believed that Kennedy had settled for a slow, less visible humiliation as the coalition government inevitably gave way to a totally Communist regime. Harriman refused to be so pessimistic. The deal was, after all, his handiwork. Harriman continues to believe it was the best possible bargain under the circumstances, buying time for both sides while imposing no humiliation on either.

Years later Rusk charged that the Communists had violated the Geneva Accords of 1962 even "before the ink was dry." He pointed to the continuing North Vietnamese traffic along the Ho Chi Minh Trails in eastern Laos. Rostow told a friend in 1969 that the "greatest single mistake" of the Democrats during their eight years in office was "not making a federal case out of it" as soon as there was evidence that the Communists were not living up to the Geneva Accords on Laos. "When you make a deal with the Communists," Rostow said, "hold them to the letter of it scrupulously from the first day. We have gotten into more trouble in the postwar world by being soft about this, because in the end we do react. We are a nation like any other, and in the end we will fight for our vital interests."

The Republicans had worried about the Laos Agreements from the beginning. On March 30, 1970, the Republican National Committee recalled in its *Newsletter* that Congressman Melvin R. Laird of Wisconsin, later Secretary of Defense, had written Dean Rusk immediately after the Laos Agreements were announced that he thought they could not last and would fail to hold back the Communist advance. "I strongly believe," Laird wrote, "that the net effect of this agreement on Laos will be the intensification of the war in Southeast Asia and a weakening of the confidence of free Asians in the value of close cooperation with the United States." A week later, another Republican Congressman, Clark MacGregor of Minnesota, labeled the "Kennedy Administration–Averell Harriman-constructed coalition government a 'communist Trojan horse in the heart of Southeast Asia.' " MacGregor likened Laos, the G.O.P. *Newsletter* of August 10, 1962 said, "to the hub of a wheel and noted the critical supply lines that radiate from there": from China into Laos, from North Vietnam into Laos, and from North Vietnam through Laos into South Vietnam. Kennedy fully understood the strategic importance of Laos. But he was bearish about committing American ground troops, particularly in light of persistent reservations by the Joint Chiefs of Staff. The 1962 agreements satisfied Kennedy's needs at the time. They satisfied Hanoi's too.

Rostow's hard-line advice notwithstanding, the Geneva Accords implicitly recognized Communist control over the north-south supply routes through eastern Laos. Pathet Lao forces had for years past controlled the eastern provinces. Not once in the course of the Geneva negotiations was there any indication they would relinquish that control. From Hanoi's point of view, Geneva cooled the crisis in the rest of Laos. At the same time it assured the Communists of continued control over the vital supply route, allowing them to concentrate on their long-range program for controlling South Vietnam.

It took several more months before the Kennedy Administration was able to focus on Vietnam, so preoccupied had the President become with the never-decisive Laos fighting. Although the long and inconclusive deliberations of the National Security Council in April had focused primarily on Laos, Vietnam was not wholly ignored. At one point, the Joint Chiefs recommended that if troops were to be sent into Laos they ought also to be sent to Vietnam—not only for counterinsurgency purposes but also to provide logistical support for U.S. operations in Laos. The President had not decided what kind of additional military assistance he would send to Vietnam, or in what quantity. But he believed that something would have to be done before long. General Edward G. Lansdale helped to make up his mind.

On December 16, 1960, Lansdale completed a gloomy report on Vietnam. A veteran of guerrilla action against the Communist-led Hukbalahaps in the Philippines, Lansdale had just completed another trip up country in his capacity as Deputy Assistant for Special Operations to the Secretary of Defense. He was depressed. In March, 1960, the Viet Cong had formed the National Liberation Front and, in September, Ho had given his blessing, promising even more military equipment, advice, and troops, several thousand a year by 1960. The Viet Cong meant business. They killed about a half dozen village chiefs a day, burned and terrorized villages, planted booby traps along trails and mines on the roads. Lansdale examined the Communist challenge and the anti-Communist response. Then on the plane ride from Saigon to Pearl Harbor, he jotted down his unhappy impressions. The U.S. military establishment—in Vietnam as in Laos—was preparing to fight a conventional war, when in Lansdale's opinion it should have been preparing for guerrilla warfare. Diem, who had crushed an attempted military coup in November, now cracked down mercilessly on his political opposition, thus becoming even more aloof from the people and more ineffectual against the VC. Friction between the United States Embassy and the Presidential Palace was increasing. Unless there were a radical reorientation of the anti-Communist effort in South Vietnam, Lansdale felt, it was doomed to failure.

Between Pearl Harbor and Washington, he wrote a second memo. It described his visit to a small village in the marshy southeast corner of Camau Province south of Saigon. The village was run by Father Hoa, an impressive and resourceful Chinese priest who had led his parishioners in a Mao-like "long march" out of China, through Laos and Cambodia, and into South Vietnam to escape Communist rule. Diem probably suspected they were Communist agents. He assigned them to a remote village, surrounded by Viet Cong. The refugees chose to resist the Communists, using the tested methods of Chinese guerrilla warfare. At first they had no guns—only knives and wooden spears. But, after a time the Chinese immigrants acquired a considerable arsenal of weapons, most of them captured from the VC. To

Lansdale, their program represented the ideal form of counter-insurgency—so pathetically absent from all of the other areas he had visited.

When Lansdale returned to Washington, he submitted his report and his memo to Defense Secretary Gates. Neither produced immediate action. It was transition time. But Gates made a point of telling McNamara about them. The new Defense Secretary read the Lansdale memoranda and instantly passed them on to Walt Rostow in the White House. On February 2 Rostow handed the Lansdale reports to President Kennedy. "Look," the President said, "I've only got a half-hour today. Do I have to read it all?" Rostow nodded. Kennedy, a speed reader, flipped through the twenty-odd pages, then looked up at Rostow. "Walt," he said, "this is going to be the worst one yet." He paused. "I'll tell you something," the President resumed. "Eisenhower never mentioned the word Vietnam to me." Another pause. "Get to work on this, Walt," he said. Walt got to work.

It was the Lansdale reports that started the President thinking earnestly and prayerfully about Vietnam. Eisenhower's briefing, the day before Kennedy's inaugural, had put all the stress on Laos. It was an order of priorities somehow typical of the Washington bureaucracy; one crisis at a time was enough for any administration. Kennedy himself was no stranger to the intricacies of Vietnamese politics. In the House of Representatives and later in the Senate he had criticized United States policy, arguing that it underestimated the force of nationalism in Asian affairs and was far too engrossed in anti-communism. As a Senator he had complained that America was wrongly committed in Southeast Asia. Arthur Schlesinger has written that Kennedy had no choice as President but to work "within the situation he had inherited." Schlesinger contends: "Ironically, the collapse of the Dulles policy in Laos had created the possibility of a neutralist solution there; but the survival of that policy in South Vietnam, where the government was stronger and the army more willing to fight, left us in 1961 no alternative but to continue the effort of 1954." Other historians, less committed, may be less charitable. Kennedy, of all Presidents, might have been expected to take a critical look at the old, bi-

partisan assumptions. But the grip of the past and the new responsibilities of power came to outweigh and overpower his
own convictions as a Senator that American policy in Southeast
Asia was disastrously wrong-headed.

The Lansdale reports, which so greatly impressed Kennedy,
sharply undercut the official optimism in Saigon that the anti-
Communist effort there was going well. Lansdale, on the contrary, found it was going badly; that it lacked scope, audacity,
originality, direction, and, most important, any coherent concept.
By December, 1960, there may have been no more than 15,000
disciplined Viet Cong troops in South Vietnam. But they were
overrunning half the country by day and a good bit more by
night. The Lansdale reports focused on the problem of guerrilla
warfare.

Ever since Kennedy had read Khrushchev's January 6
speech, this problem had been on his mind. As he dwelt upon
it, the President became more and more convinced that guerrilla
insurgency war an entirely new form of warfare, requiring an
entirely new kind of response. The Communists would exploit
it; anti-Communists had to learn how to resist it. In fact, guerrilla warfare was precisely what had confronted American troops
for twenty years in the Philippines at the turn of the century. It
had confounded Chiang Kai-shek during the Chinese civil war;
it had baffled the Greek government in the late 1940s, the British in Malaya and Magsaysay in the Philippines in the 1950s.
It was not Khrushchev's invention. Kennedy nonetheless was so
impressed with Lansdale's story about Father Hoa that he personally telephoned the author and urged that the memo be published. It was, in an April, 1961, issue of *The Saturday Evening
Post.*

Middle-level officials in the Defense and State departments
agreed with Lansdale's emphasis upon guerrilla warfare. But
they could not get their superiors to reorient their thinking until the President gave the counterinsurgency idea new thrust. Inspired partly by Lansdale, partly by Khrushchev, Kennedy approved a counterinsurgency plan for Vietnam consisting of forty
separate projects of social and military reform. Rostow soon was
saying the war could be won in eighteen months, if those proj-

ects were successfully undertaken. Kennedy appointed a new
ambassador to Saigon, the career diplomat Frederick Nolting,
and instructed him to concentrate on reform and counterinsurgency. He also decided to send his Vice-President, Lyndon Johnson, on a good-will tour of South and Southeast Asia. Johnson's
mission was to reassure allies and friends that Kennedy's readiness to accept a coalition government in Laos (if he could get
one) should not be read as the start of an American policy of
withdrawal from Asia. The Vice-President also was instructed to
urge social and political reform as one way of stimulating an
awareness of counterinsurgency. The hybrid word became a
passkey to the inner councils of government, to the trust of the
President. If a high official expressed skepticism about the significance or newness ascribed to this style of warfare, it was
said, he risked shortening his tenure in office. McNamara, Taylor, and Rostow became early converts, and their White House
standing soared. Rusk never converted.

On his Asian trip, Johnson was accompanied by Jean and
Stephen Smith, the President's sister and brother-in-law. In Taiwan they talked with Chiang Kai-shek and Madame Chiang; in
Saigon, with President Diem; in Bangkok, with Marshal Sarit;
in New Delhi, with Prime Minister Nehru; in Karachi, with President Ayub Khan. Johnson's talks with Diem were the most important.

Diem struck the Vice-President as "remote from the people
. . . surrounded by persons less admirable and capable than he,"
so Johnson privately reported to Kennedy on May 23. In public,
however, Johnson unaccountably called Diem the "Winston
Churchill of Southeast Asia." And, in the May 13 communiqué,
summing up their official conversations, Johnson placed Diem
"in the vanguard of those leaders who stand for freedom on the
periphery of the Communist empire in Asia." On balance, Johnson was favorably impressed with Diem; the Vice-President
thought South Vietnam could be "saved—if we move quickly
and wisely." That involved better coordination of the U.S. "country team" and an "imaginative, creative American management
of our military aid program."

The Johnson-Diem communiqué, every word of which had
been cleared in advance by the State Department and the White

House, deserves special attention for two reasons: first, it reveals how far the U.S. had gone in publicly committing itself to the defense of South Vietnam, no matter what happened; and, second, it is the first major statement of Kennedy policy toward Vietnam. It suggests quite clearly that, if Kennedy was ready to take military action to forestall a quick Communist victory in Laos, he was no less ready to take similar action to prevent a Communist victory in South Vietnam.

The communiqué did not contain the word "commitment." But it underscored America's "responsibility" and "duty" to "assist a brave country . . . against unprovoked subversion and Communist terror." It linked the destiny of the two countries with such phrases as "a deep sense of common cause," "this recognition of mutual objectives," and "other free governments." The United States, moreover, pledged itself to "increase" and "accelerate" U.S. aid to South Vietnam, adding the open-ended promise that aid "may be followed by more far-reaching measures if the situation, in the opinion of both governments, warrants." The two governments agreed on eight steps.

First, to "extend and build upon existing programs of military and economic aid";

Second, to expand the "Regular Armed Forces of the Republic of Vietnam";

Third, the U.S. would provide military assistance to the "entire Vietnamese civil guard force";

Fourth, to "collaborate in the use of military specialists to assist and work with Vietnamese armed forces in health, welfare and public works activities in the villages of free Vietnam";

Fifth, an appeal for help from "other free governments" to the Republic of Vietnam.

Sixth, a "group of highly qualified economic and fiscal experts would meet in Vietnam to work out a financial plan on which joint efforts should be based";

Seventh, to "discuss new economic and social measures to be undertaken in the rural areas to accompany the anti-guerrilla effort";

Eighth, to "work together towards a longer range economic development program."

Johnson knew that the President faced a hard decision. In

1954, when he and Kennedy were both Senators, Johnson had been greatly troubled by the prospect of American military intervention in Indochina. He had told Dulles, back in April, 1954, that if he could not get strong allies, especially Great Britain, to join the United States in "united action" to help the French in Indochina, then he had better drop the project. But, just as Kennedy had apparently changed his position after becoming President, so too had Johnson as Vice-President. On May 23, 1961, shortly after his return from Asia, Johnson sent Kennedy a long private memorandum. It was, in some respects, a realistic appraisal of the tour. Johnson wrote: "Our mission arrested the decline of confidence in the United States. It did not—in my judgment—restore any confidence already lost. . . . We didn't buy time—we were given it. If these men I saw at your request were bankers, I would know—without bothering to ask—that there would be no further extension on my note." On the longer-range question of which way should America now turn, Johnson sensed that Kennedy and the nation were at a crossroads.

"The fundamental decision required by the United States— and time is of the greatest importance," Johnson emphasized, "is whether we are to attempt to meet the challenge of Communist expansion now in Southeast Asia by a major effort in support of the forces of freedom in the area or throw in the towel. This decision must be made in a full realization of the very heavy and continuing costs involved in terms of money, of effort, and of United States prestige. It must be made with the knowledge that at some point we may be faced with the further decision of whether we commit major United States forces to the area or cut our losses and withdraw should our other efforts fail. We must remain master of this decision."

Johnson could sense the slippery nature of a small commitment undertaken by a big power, the danger of becoming "a little bit pregnant," to borrow Robert McCloskey's apt phrase. He nevertheless recommended to Kennedy that "we proceed with a clear-cut and strong program of action." He explained his reasoning in apocalyptic terms:

"The battle against communism must be joined in Southeast Asia with strength and determination to achieve success there—

or the United States, inevitably, must surrender the Pacific and take up our defenses on our own shores. Asian communism is compromised and contained by the maintenance of free nations on the subcontinent. Without this inhibitory influence, the island outposts—Philippines, Japan, Taiwan—have no security, and the vast Pacific becomes a Red Sea.

"The struggle is far from lost in Southeast Asia and it is by no means inevitable that it must be lost. In each country it is possible to build a sound structure capable of withstanding and turning the Communist surge. The will to resist—while now the target of subversive attack—is there. The key to what is done by Asians in defense of Southeast Asian freedom is confidence in the United States."

It is hard to believe that so astute a politician as Lyndon Johnson, grand master in the fine art of splitting the difference when it came to domestic legislation, could discern no middle way between those stark either-or alternatives—to defeat communism in Asia or to fight the last battle for American freedom on the coast of California. His memorandum to Kennedy, short on facts and long on emotion, suggests that the Vice-President was somehow bewitched by the ghostly clack and rattle of falling dominoes, that his thinking was as sloppy as his language (Ngo Dinh Diem, "the Winston Churchill of Southeast Asia").

Building on Dulles's rhetoric of the Fifties, and anticipating his own as President, Johnson concluded in terms that might have impressed Kennedy as being overly dire. "The basic decision in Southeast Asia is here," he wrote. "We must decide whether to help these countries to the best of our ability or throw in the towel in the area and pull back to San Francisco and a 'Fortress America' concept. More important, we would say to the world in this case that we don't live up to treaties and don't stand by our friends. This is not my concept. I recommend that we move forward promptly with a major effort to help these countries defend themselves."

A month later the President sent Eugene Staley to South Vietnam to check on the economic situation. He returned with more recommendations. It was a yeasty time in Washington. Everyone seemed to have at least ten ideas a day, not all of

them realistic or feasible. For example, Chester Bowles had a
Vietnam proposal which appealed to the President—for a brief
time. Bowles believed that rather than deepen a unilateral "obligation" or "duty" to Vietnam and Thailand, the United States
ought to think about expanding the "Laos formula" to all of
Southeast Asia; that is, create a belt of "neutral and independent" states, including Burma, Thailand, South Vietnam, Cambodia, and Malaya, stretching in a big arc from the South China
Sea to India, that could eventually be guaranteed by Russia,
China, India, Japan, and the bigger SEATO powers, meaning
Britain, France, and the United States. Bowles thought that Russia might buy the proposal as one way of blocking China's southern expansion. He argued that if the Chinese tried to penetrate
these states and undermine their "genuine neutrality," then at
least the United States would have strong international backing
should it later be forced to intervene. Kennedy discarded this
proposal, in the final analysis, because it was too bold. It would
have required a fundamental policy reorientation not only in the
United States but also in South Vietnam, Thailand, and Malaya
—away from anti-communism toward an era of compromise and
cooperation with the Communists. Kennedy felt that, for him, at
that time, this was a politically unacceptable idea. Laird's and
MacGregor's objections to the Laos Agreements represented the
tip of the political iceberg. He could foresee endless trouble with
the Republicans. The White House, in short, felt it could risk
neutralism in Laos but not in all of Southeast Asia—certainly
not in South Vietnam.

So the Johnson view came to prevail. Early in October the
President decided to send Walt Rostow and General Maxwell D.
Taylor to South Vietnam to check on the situation and to
make their own recommendations for "action." The President's
instructions to Taylor, dated October 13, were quite specific. "I
would like your views," the President wrote, "on the courses of
action which our Government might take to avoid a further deterioration in South Vietnam and eventually to contain and elim-
inate the threat to its independence." Although Kennedy had
moved a long way toward a United States military commitment
for South Vietnam, he never wavered from his fundamental belief, shared by Vice-President Johnson, that the primary job

would have to be done by Vietnamese. "You should bear in mind," Kennedy continued, "that the initial responsibility for the effective maintenance of the independence of South Vietnam rests with the people and government of that country. While the military part of the problem is of great importance, its political, social, and economic elements are equally significant."

Taylor agreed fully with the President's view of the problem. So did Rostow. No program of counterinsurgency which ignored or discounted the nonmilitary components could possibly be successful, they believed. Kennedy wanted to be sure, for example, that there was an "authentic nationalism in South Vietnam."

The two-man fact-finding team worked hard. After crisscrossing the country and interviewing American and South Vietnamese officials, they retired to Baguio in the Philippines to write their report. Basically it was a military report, because both fact-finders perceived the problem in military terms: South Vietnam needed American military help in order to hold off a Communist military victory. Taylor and Rostow strongly recommended that this help be offered quickly; if not, they envisaged the collapse of South Vietnam and the subsequent collapse of Southeast Asia. They presented five basic recommendations to the President.

First, a "massive joint effort" to repel "Viet Cong aggression" and to handle the "ravages of the Delta flood." (South Vietnam was being swamped at the time by the biggest flood in a century. "Flying over it," Taylor recalled, "you couldn't see anything but a few little housetops sticking up . . . it was a major disaster.")

Second, they proposed that the United States assign military advisers "down to battalion level in ARVN"; and provide helicopter support, air reconnaissance, special intelligence activities, and air-ground support techniques; in addition to help in patrolling "coastal and inland waters."

Third, they urged the setting up of "joint GVN-USG survey" (Vietnam-U.S. Government) teams to examine the "social, political, intelligence, and military problems in the provinces." (Taylor was especially struck by official ignorance in Saigon about the ABC's of provincial life. "We were badly misled as to just what the basic facts were," Taylor told friends.) *

Fourth, the "USG should respond to Diem's request for U.S. ground forces by offering a Task Force to operate under U.S. control in providing logistical support to military operations or to flood relief." (Taylor later explained that he regarded this highly controversial recommendation as "rather narrow" in scope; specifically, that the United States ought to send an "engineer task force" to the Delta "with enough infantry just to give it local protection." Such a self-contained force, numbering about 9000 men, could be withdrawn after the floods subsided, or retained in Vietnam, as the President directed.)

Fifth, the U.S. should "review" its economic aid program in light of the floods, meaning increase aid.

Taylor and Rostow wrote a covering letter to President Kennedy, which stressed that the five recommendations did not "purport to be a final word as to the requirements for success." They realized that a great deal depended upon the outcome of developments in Laos and upon Hanoi's response to the new American program of military and economic aid to South Vietnam. "If Hanoi persisted in waging clandestine warfare across the frontiers of South Vietnam," they wrote, then "we would have to consider striking back by air across those frontiers at the source of the aggression."

This was largely Rostow's idea, prophetic of the air strikes that began in 1965, but Taylor accepted it. Earlier, in June, Rostow had delivered the commencement address at the U.S. Army Special Warfare School at Fort Bragg and, in menacing

---

* Recalling his 1961 visit to South Vietnam with Rostow, General Taylor said: "I was greatly impressed with what we didn't know about Vietnam, not in the sense that we lacked the kind of intelligence the CIA gets by listening at keyholes but we lacked the other kind: What kind of people are these Vietnamese? What is their background? What is the state of the economy?

"We had no experts on Vietnam, and Diem, up to that point, had resisted letting these foreigners run around the provinces and stick their noses into his business. If Washington asked for a complex report on the Vietnamese economy, let's say, our embassy people had to walk across the street to the Government and ask for the information. And usually one of two situations existed: One, the Vietnamese didn't have the information, and they were ashamed to say so, so they made it up; or, two, they had the information but it made them look bad so they changed it."

language checked and cleared by the President himself, he stated: "The sending of men and arms across international boundaries and the direction of guerrilla war from outside a sovereign nation is aggression; and this is a fact which the whole international community must confront and whose consequent responsibilities it must accept. Without such international action *those against whom aggression is mounted will be driven inevitably to seek out and engage the ultimate source of the aggression they confront.*"

In that June speech Rostow had deliberately left open the possibility (which he later discussed with East European ambassadors) of allied ground action against North Vietnam, unless Hanoi's aggression against the South ceased. In November he was less categorical. But he still argued forcefully for a limited air campaign against "the source of the aggression," at least as a contingency plan. Either way, it is significant and noteworthy that high administration officials were considering, and some were recommending, air attacks against North Vietnam back in 1961, four years before the bombing on a systematic basis began.

Before Kennedy acted on the Taylor-Rostow recommendations, he asked Ambassador John Kenneth Galbraith, then in Washington for consultations, to return to India by way of Saigon and to report his "dispassionate" impressions. Galbraith held that an anti-Communist success in South Vietnam was possible, if ARVN could be built up to a 250,000-man force ably led by a new Saigon government. But he predicted failure if Diem remained in power. "While no one can promise a safe transition," the ambassador reported, "we are now married to failure."

Kennedy respected Galbraith. But he ignored his recommendation just as, earlier in the year, he had rejected Bowles's neutral-belt proposals. Some New Left authors have suggested that Kennedy could not bring himself to move against Diem, a fellow Catholic. Others would have us believe that Kennedy harbored deep within himself a primitive hard-line attitude toward communism. His inner thoughts are—and must remain—a matter of conjecture. The fact is that he came down on Johnson's side of the Vietnam argument, although his admiration for

the Vice-President was so restrained as to be invisible. Kennedy
quickly accepted four of the five recommendations presented by
the Taylor-Rostow team. He refused at the time to send the
9000-man "engineer task force." But he specifically directed that
contingency plans be drawn up for the use of American ground
troops *either in accordance with the Task Force concept or for
broader purposes."* * One month later, in December, 1961, Kennedy took another one of those big steps deeper into the Vietnam bog. He approved a significant increase in the number of
American military advisers assigned to ARVN. The President,
moreover, put no ceiling on the number. At the time none was
considered necessary. Everyone was working on the blithe assumption that a little more American help, better managed and
directed, one more turn of the military screw, would save South
Vietnam. "Sink or swim with Ngo Dinh Diem" was Homer
Bigart's not-so-funny quip when he covered Vietnam for *The
New York Times* at that time. It was in fact a perfectly serious
description of U.S. policy. There had been about 1000 U.S. military advisers in South Vietnam in December, 1961. One year
later, there were 11,000.

Long after Kennedy was dead, Rostow volunteered this account of the President's strategic thinking at the time: "If we
ever had to fight, it would be better to fight in Vietnam than
Laos—for three reasons: One, the logistics were better. You
weren't up in that great arc of the Mekong. Two, you would
have the advantages of air and sea power. And three, which was
very interesting, you would have the cushion of North Vietnam
between you and China . . . so that you had a better chance of
doing what you had to do in Southeast Asia without triggering
a war with China. In any case, he [Kennedy] made that decision
in '61 with the knowledge that it might take him down a very
difficult road." Ten years later the explanation sounds unconvincing. Kennedy received no end of advice before making his crucial Vietnam decision. Vice-President Johnson urged better management of the military-assistance program. Taylor argued for
more aid. Rostow saw merit in air strikes against the North.
Lansdale favored an intelligent program of counterinsurgency

* (Italics by M. K. and E. A.)

(Father Hao on a national scale). Professor Galbraith wanted to get rid of Diem. Do these things, the President was urged, and the tide can be turned. Each of the counselors had his day. Every stratagem was considered. And the tide was an unconscionable time turning. Not one of the President's advisers, it appears, had gauged or even dimly anticipated the agony that Vietnam would become. None foretold the true cost, the antiwar movement at home, the torn national fabric, the sheer endlessness of this war.

Rostow insists the President himself was under no illusions: "He didn't go into this thinking, 'This is just a few more chips.' He went into this because he said: 'I got to hold Southeast Asia, come hell or high water.'" Ten years later the language still sounds more like Rostow than Kennedy.

In December, 1961, Presidents Diem and Kennedy exchanged letters. Diem's was dated December 7. The South Vietnamese leader catalogued the results of Communist aggression: In October alone, 1800 cases of "enemy-initiated" violence and more than 2000 casualties. "The Vietnamese nation," he wrote, "now faces . . . the gravest crisis in its long history." Diem promised total mobilization. "But Vietnam is not a great power, and the forces of International Communism now arrayed against us are more than we can meet with the resources at hand," Diem added. "We must have further assistance from the United States." Kennedy's response, which followed his decision to send thousands of military advisers to Vietnam, was dated December 14. He said the United States has been "deeply disturbed by the deliberate savagery of the Communist program of assassination, kidnapping, and wanton violence." This "campaign of force and terror," he said, was "supported and directed from the outside by the authorities in Hanoi." The President left no room for doubting his intentions: "We shall promptly increase our assistance to your defense effort. . . . I have already given the orders."

Thus, after one year of the Kennedy Administration, the United States stood ankle-deep in the Vietnam swamp.

In Washington, counterinsurgency was the rage. The President described it on January 18, 1962, as a "major form of po-

litico-military conflict equal in importance to conventional or
nuclear warfare." The administration talked of social and economic reforms. But it pressed an essentially military effort in
South Vietnam. This upset such Washington officials as Harriman, Bowles, and Roger Hilsman, sometimes the President himself. But counterinsurgency began to take on a life and momentum of its own.

In April, with loud fanfare, the counterinsurgency boosters
came up with an idea. They called it the strategic hamlet program, a scheme freely adapted from the British experience in
Malaya. Vietnamese peasants were to be removed from their
villages and resettled in fortified communities, surrounded by
barbed wire and bamboo spikes. In theory, such hamlets were
to give the peasants a new sense of security; in fact, they ended
up making them even more insecure. South Vietnamese troops
and their American advisers offered the peasants little choice.
Sometimes at bayonet point they were forced to leave their native villages (which to many constituted the only world they
had known) and move into ugly, unfamiliar, artificial hamlets.
The purpose was to show progress, using the western yardstick
of statistical measurement, and to dramatize an "imaginative"
allied response to the challenge of guerrilla warfare. By mid-
1963 Ngo Dinh Nhu, the president's highly arbitrary brother and
chief adviser, boasted that 7,000,000 South Vietnamese (half
the total population) had been herded into strategic hamlets. He
claimed further that the program was an "enormous success."
When some American reporters began to question that success,
Ambassador Nolting and General Paul Harkins, the new American military commander in South Vietnam, responded by questioning the honesty and ability of the reporters.

MAAC V, the American advisory mission, collected figures
on the number of "enemy-initiated incidents," enemy KIA's
(killed in action), defection rates, and, as Defense Secretary
McNamara reported to the President later in the year: "Every
quantitative measurement we have shows we're winning this
war." Taylor returned to Vietnam and thought he detected a
"great national movement" against the Viet Cong. Kennedy accepted the statistics. As 1962 turned into 1963, the President said,

in his State of the Union message: "The spearpoint of aggression has been blunted in South Vietnam." Everyone was feeling very hopeful.

In the beginning the Viet Cong were still baffled by the helicopter. Their casualties increased and they began to shrink into the jungle. In April, U. Alexis Johnson, a veteran State Department official, said that 30,000 VC had been killed in 1962— twice the estimated size of the enemy force. A Defense Department spokesman echoed this high-flying optimism. "We have turned the corner in Vietnam," he said. General Harkins told a skeptical reporter that the war would be won "within a year."

Kennedy checked with McNamara. Was all the optimism justified? he wanted to know. His loyal Defense Secretary said "yes," and the President returned to more pressing problems— his civil-rights battle with the Congress and the South, his irritation with de Gaulle, his wrangle with Harold Macmillan over the Skybolt, the test-ban negotiations. He had little time to listen to the rising doubts among some Washington officials: Harriman, who felt the United States was accenting the military side of the conflict and ignoring the civil-action side; Hilsman, who feared the U.S. was "over-Americanizing" the effort; Michael Forrestal, of McGeorge Bundy's White House staff, who began to doubt Diem's ability to stay the course. If he had little time for his own officials, Kennedy did have time to read the press; and he showed a certain unhappiness that some American newsmen in South Vietnam—above all David Halberstam of *The New York Times*—should be filing gloomy and downbeat dispatches, in sharp contrast to the upbeat reports coming out of MAAC V and the American Embassy.

All of this official optimism was jarred when, on May 22, 1963, the 2587th birthday of Buddha, a political crisis erupted in South Vietnam. The Buddhist uprising, as it came to be known, exposed the fragility of the Diem regime, the deep divisions in Vietnamese society, the shallowness of the claimed progress, the foolishness of the optimism and, perhaps for the first time, the true depth of the American problem in South Vietnam. Within several months Kennedy would have to make another of those wrenching decisions.

In Hué, the former Vietnamese capital, a group of Buddhists marched in protest against a government order forbidding them to fly their flags on Buddha's birthday. Diem's troops opened fire. They killed or wounded dozens of Buddhists—many of them young monks wearing their saffron robes. Popular indignation spread, lightning fashion, throughout the country. A majority of the people were in fact Buddhist although South Vietnam was ruled by northern Catholics. Several of the monks, or *bonzes*, burned themselves to death. Madame Nhu, Diem's sister-in-law, applauded these "barbecues," as she called them; but the fact is they undercut public morale and profoundly offended many American supporters. Filmed reports of these burning bonzes and street demonstrations, shown night after night on American television, were deeply upsetting to American viewers. Congressmen began to worry about the American investment—some, to question it. The President realized that he would have to take some kind of action. The Harriman group argued strongly that it was time to dump Diem. Harriman believed that Diem stood for repression and that the United States could not justify the spilling of American blood in behalf of a repressive government. Johnson, Rusk, and Taylor opposed dumping Diem, unless the President was sure he had a better replacement. Taylor, for one, thought that Harriman's recommendation to get rid of Diem was an example of "complete irresponsibility."

Kennedy limited himself to a tactical decision. He decided, in late June, to replace Ambassador Nolting. He hoped that Diem would get the message—that the United States was ready to change its seven-year-old policy of indiscriminate support for Diem, unless he stopped persecuting the Buddhists and started instituting some long overdue reforms. The President had in mind replacing Nolting with Edmund Gullion, another foreign-service officer who had befriended Kennedy in Saigon a decade before. But Rusk recommended Henry Cabot Lodge, Nixon's vice-presidential running mate in the 1960 campaign. Ordinarily, Kennedy might have overruled his usually diffident Secretary of State; he had done it many times. But Lodge presented him with a golden political opportunity. The appointment brought a major Republican into the Vietnam policy circle at a time when, as Kennedy knew, major decisions were only a few months off. It was one of the few times he yielded to Rusk's judgment.

Lodge was unable to leave for Saigon until late August. Nolting, who had been on vacation during the Buddhist crisis, thereby losing favor with the President, returned to Washington to plead Diem's case. He argued that many VC had infiltrated the Buddhist organizations and that Diem was trying to strike at them when he ordered his troops to attack the pagodas. The Buddhists, moreover, were a political force in South Vietnam, not merely a religious group. According to Nolting, they resented Diem's leadership not only because he was a Catholic but because his anti-communism was too virulent for their taste. They had heard about black demonstrations in the United States, and they had learned that one way to attract American attention, in hopes of loosening Washington's links with Diem, was to march and demonstrate. The explanation confirmed Harriman and Hilsman in their belief that Nolting was no longer capable of objectivity in assessing Vietnamese politics.

Rusk, who rarely took sides openly, advised Nolting to return to Saigon as quickly as possible. The ambassador arrived in the Vietnamese capital on July 11. After a quick check at the Palace and the Embassy, Nolting concluded that Diem had reason to be suspicious of growing Embassy sympathy for the Buddhists. In fact, the Palace feared that the Embassy was plotting a coup with certain anti-Diem generals. Nolting argued strenuously against this policy, predicting that it would only force Diem into greater repressions. He reported to the State Department that it was impossible to discard Nhu without also discarding Diem. That, he said, "would be like separating Siamese twins."

In mid-July, at a news conference, Kennedy sought to mollify Diem and ease his doubts. "Before we render too harsh a judgment on the people," Kennedy said, "we should realize that they are going through a harder time than we have had to go through." He stressed that the American goal remained a "stable government" and that the U.S. supported South Vietnam's "struggle to maintain its national independence." The President chose his words carefully. "We believe strongly in that [struggle]," he said. "In my opinion, for us to withdraw from this effort would mean a collapse not only of South Vietnam but Southeast Asia. So we are going to stay there."

The President's words should have eased Diem's doubts, but they did not. He continued to worry about the firmness of American support and about American understanding of Vietnamese politics. What Diem saw as a fundamental political challenge from the Buddhists Washington interpreted as the outcry of a persecuted religious majority. Diem tried without much conviction to negotiate a political compromise with the Buddhists, in part to ease his growing difficulties with Washington. But the Buddhist militants were not interested in a compromise; they wanted Diem's ouster, and they could see for themselves that the more spectacular their demonstrations, the more sympathy they aroused among Americans.

In late August, after he had promised departing Ambassador Nolting that he would never again attack the Buddhist pagodas, Diem ordered troops to ransack the Xa Loi Pagoda in Saigon and others throughout the country. Hundreds of Buddhists were arrested. Diem claimed many were VC activists or sympathizers. These army attacks—all in one long night of violence—stunned the U.S. Embassy, the CIA, and MAAC V. Not for the first time American officials had been completely in the dark about a major Diem move. They deeply resented it. Their subsequent cables to Washington stoked the fires of anti-Diem sentiment. White House officials believed that Diem and Nhu had timed their assaults on the pagodas for Lodge's arrival. The Boston patrician arrived in Saigon with the stench of tear gas still in the air. There were fresh traces of blood on the cobblestoned streets. Diem had tried to present Lodge with a *fait accompli*. But the tactic failed. Washington had lost confidence in Diem. His foreign minister resigned, shaving his head in sympathy with the bonzes. His Washington ambassador, who happened to be Madame Nhu's father, also resigned. And a group of generals quietly sent a message to the new ambassador, asking what his attitude would be if they moved against Diem. Lodge informed

Washington of the generals' approach, and requested instructions.

Washington's reply was drafted on August 24, 1962, a Saturday. It was a hot, sticky day with many of Washington's leaders out of town. CIA Director John McCone was in California. Defense Secretary McNamara was on vacation. Secretary of State Rusk was watching the Yankees, his favorite ball club, in New York. President Kennedy was at Hyannis Port for the weekend. The controversial cable was drafted by Harriman and Hilsman—with some help from Forrestal at the White House. Getting the cable cleared was a difficult task with so many senior officials away. Harriman and Hilsman found George Ball, then Under Secretary of State, playing golf at the Chevy Chase Club. The minute Ball read the cable he knew he would have to clear it with the President.

The three officials drove to Ball's home, where they made some minor changes in language. Then Ball called the President, who interrupted his predinner shower to hear a summary of the cable on the telephone. The President approved the summary. It is not clear whether he fully realized that not one of his Cabinet-level advisers had seen it.

Pentagon clearance came in a roundabout way. Forrestal called Vice Admiral Herbert D. Riley, director of the Joint Staff of the JCS, and read the cable to him. Sensing it was explosive stuff, Riley suggested that the cable be cleared by General Victor Krulak, the Pentagon's specialist on Vietnamese affairs. Krulak was also at the Chevy Chase Club. Forrestal caught up with him in the locker room. Krulak refused to clear the cable without reading it very carefully. He dressed and drove down to the White House, where he read it. This is dynamite, he thought. Krulak, therefore, recommended that Roswell Gilpatric, the Acting Secretary of Defense, clear it. Gilpatric was at his farm outside Washington. He had his doubts about clearing the cable, wondered why the rush. But when Forrestal assured him the cable had the "approval of the President," Gilpatric cleared it. Richard Helms, then Deputy Director of the CIA, also had initial doubts. But he, too, cleared the cable after being assured it had presidential approval. The cable was finally dispatched to Saigon late Saturday evening.

There can be little doubt that Harriman, Hilsman, and Forrestal were in a hurry to get that cable to Saigon. It instructed the U.S. Embassy to make a new effort to persuade Diem to fire his brother, release the Buddhist rebels, end press censorship, and restore other liberties suspended under the recently imposed martial law. Finally, the instruction to Lodge was that, while the United States would take no action to unseat Diem, if anything of the kind happened the United States would support a successor anti-Communist regime. As the late Marguerite Higgins noted: "'Rocking the boat' was no longer a U.S. taboo." With that cable of August 24, the U.S. signaled an end to its patience with Diem and an opening for the generals to move against him.

Diem was admittedly an uncertain ally in an unwanted war. Nevertheless, in opting for a coup the United States was storing up trouble for itself. Hilsman told Frank Conniff of the Hearst newspapers: "After the closing of the pagodas on August 21, the facts became irrelevant." A Hilsman associate at the State Department said: "What we have to do is divorce ourselves from the pagoda business and from Diem." The late Edward R. Murrow told Miss Higgins: "President Kennedy was very badly served on the issue of Vietnam. Feelings ran so high between the Diem-must-go school and the Diem-must-stay school that the processes of reason could not function." When a government loses its reason, it runs the risk of losing control.

It was midday Sunday, August 25, when the cable arrived in Saigon. At midday Sunday, Washington time, 13 hours later, Hilsman invited Stewart Hensley, the able and experienced correspondent of United Press International, into his office for an unusual briefing. Hilsman told Hensley, in effect, that official impatience with Diem was now so great that the Vietnamese president had become expendable. When Hensley left his office, Hilsman called a duty officer at the Voice of America to inform him that the UPI ticker would soon be moving a story which accurately reflected administration policy. The duty officer took the hint. When Hensley's dispatch ran on the "A" wire, he picked it up and broadcast it round the world, little realizing its explosive character. Hensley wrote:

> High American officials blame police, headed by President Diem's brother, Ngo Dinh Nhu, for anti-Buddhist actions in the Vietnam Republic. The officials say Vietnam military leaders are not responsible for last week's attacks against pagodas and the mass arrest of monks and students.
>
> Washington officials say that Vietnam secret police carried out the raids and arrests and that some of them were disguised as army troops or members of the Youth Corps.
>
> They say the military leaders agreed to martial law in the hope that it would lead to a peaceful settlement. But, they say, the military men were not advised of secret police plans to attack Buddhists.
>
> The officials indicate that the U.S. may sharply reduce its aid to Vietnam unless President Diem gets rid of secret police officials responsible for the attacks.

Clearly Hilsman was following through on the secret cable of August 24 by indulging in some fancy news management. His evident purpose was to signal the Vietnamese generals that the United States considered them innocent of any wrongdoing against the Buddhists and expected them to step up the pressure on Diem. In Saigon, Lodge asked his most trusted embassy advisers to run a discreet check on the generals. Lodge wanted to find out whether they were in fact ready, willing, or able to stage a coup. The surreptitious poll of seven coup minded generals took two days. It turned up the surprising fact (surprising to Hilsman, Harriman, and Forrestal at any rate) that the generals were not then prepared to move against Diem. Later General Duong Van Minh explained to a United States official: "After all those years of being told not to rock the boat in the middle of a war, it was hard for us to really convince ourselves that this was precisely what the United States wanted us to do."

A coup in Saigon was not precisely what the United States had bargained for, though General Minh had every reason for believing it was. The truth is, the United States Government did not know what it wanted. It was still divided. The President seemed to lean toward the Diem-must-go school. But, in

those critical days after the Harriman-Hilsman-Forrestal cable
went out, he remained undecided. On Monday, August 26,
when most top officials returned to their desks, they were astonished to discover what had happened. General Taylor was
furious. McNamara shared his anger. McCone was appalled.
So was Vice-President Johnson, who called several friends
at the State Department and warned them the United States
had opened a Pandora's box in Saigon which could only hurt
the war effort.

President Kennedy was annoyed. He felt he had been
stampeded into a possibly unwise decision. He discussed the
problem with Robert Kennedy, who in turn took it up with
McNamara and Taylor. They told him they disagreed with the
Harriman-Hilsman-Forrestal stratagem. And they had no idea
what was going to happen next.

On Wednesday, August 28, the President called a meeting
of the National Security Council to discuss Vietnam. Former
Ambassador Nolting was invited. He presented a reasoned case
for keeping Diem, adding that the United States should not
jump unless it knew where it was going to land. Other meetings
and cables followed. Lodge was informed that the policy of
unleashing the generals was being "reviewed"; a day later he
received instructions that Diem should be pressured to dump
his brother; the following day, that the United States would not
stand in the way of an "indigenous revolt." If Lodge was confused, so was everyone else.

Kennedy still refused to make a firm decision. He would
have preferred, of course, that Diem drop his brother, Nhu, ease
his pressure on the Buddhists, and get on with the war. But he
would not say so. The President's indecision at this decisive
moment inevitably added to official bewilderment and Diem's
own deepening suspicions of America. His silence, however,
heartened the anti-Diem forces in Washington and Saigon. They
came to believe that, despite the President's annoyance over
the August 24 cable, his sympathies were with them.

On September 2 the President appeared on the CBS Evening News; on September 9, on the Huntley-Brinkley Report.
The TV news programs were just inaugurating their new, half-

hour format. His comments reflected both Kennedy's impatience with Diem and his unshaken belief in the war.

To Walter Cronkite the President said:

"In the final analysis, it is their war. They are the ones who have to win it or lose it. We can help them, we can give them equipment, we can send our men out there as advisers, but they have to win it—the people of Vietnam—against the Communists. We are prepared to continue to assist them, but I don't think that the war can be won unless the people support the effort, and, in my opinion, in the last two months the government has gotten out of touch with the people. . . .

"With changes in policy and perhaps in personnel, I think it [Saigon] can [regain the support of the people]. If it doesn't make those changes, I would think that the chances of winning it would not be very good. . . .

"If [President Diem] does not change [his policy], of course that is his decision. He has been there ten years, and, as I say, he has carried this burden when he has been counted out on a number of occasions.

"Our best judgment is that he can't be successful on this basis. We hope that he comes to see that; but in the final analysis it is the people and the government itself who have to win or lose this struggle. All we can do is help, and we are making it very clear. But I don't agree with those who say we should withdraw. That would be a great mistake. That would be a great mistake. I know people don't like Americans to be engaged in this kind of an effort. Forty-seven Americans have been killed in combat with the enemy, but this is a very important struggle even though it is far away.

"We took all this—made this effort to defend Europe. Now Europe is quite secure. We also have to participate—we may not like it—in the defense of Asia."

Like Dulles before him, Kennedy saw American participation in the defense of Asia against communism as a logical outgrowth of the American defense role in Europe. It was logical and, in his view, it was necessary.

To Chet Huntley, a week later, the President said:

"I don't think [a reduction in U.S. aid to South Vietnam]

would be helpful at this time. If you reduce your aid, it is possible you could have some effect upon the government structure there. On the other hand, you might have a situation which could bring about a collapse. Strongly in our mind is what happened in the case of China at the end of World War II, where China was lost—a weak government became increasingly unable to control events. We don't want that. . . ."

Huntley asked if the President believed in the domino theory. "I believe it. I believe it," he replied. "I think that the struggle is close enough. China is so large, looms so high just beyond the frontiers, that if South Vietnam went, it would not only give them an improved geographic position for a guerrilla assault on Malaya but would also give the impression that the wave of the future in Southeast Asia was China and the Communists. So I believe it. . . .

"The fact of this matter is that with the assistance of the United States and SEATO, Southeast Asia and indeed all of Asia have been maintained independent against a powerful force, the Chinese Communists. What I am concerned about is that Americans will get impatient and say, because they don't like events in Southeast Asia and they don't like the Government in Saigon, that we should withdraw. That only makes it easy for the Communists. I think we should stay. We should use our influence in as effective a way as we can, but we should not withdraw."

The interviews with Huntley and Cronkite are particularly interesting for the light they cast on the President's thinking. Kennedy obviously wanted Diem to reform his regime, believing that if he did not the people would lose confidence in him and the war would be lost, as well. Lost to whom? Kennedy, it appears, gave little thought to the Vietnamese Communists, North or South. He had a fixation about the Chinese. China was to him the principal enemy. Vietnam was incidental. It just happened to be the battleground. He ignored the fact that not a single Chinese soldier was fighting in Vietnam. He also ignored the age-old bred-in-the-bone hostility of all Vietnamese throughout their long history to Chinese overlordship. All told, the President said little that would not have earned John Foster

Dulles's enthusiastic endorsement ten years earlier.

Another moment of decision had come and gone. The President could have found a competent successor to Diem, ordered the coup, and then hoped for the best. He could have "thrown in the towel," to use Johnson's expression, and ordered an American withdrawal from South Vietnam. He could have taken Nolting's advice and supported Diem against the Buddhists. None of these choices satisfied him. So he rejected them all and decided, in effect, to muddle through.

When a President decides not to decide, he generally sets up a presidential fact-finding team. In early September, Kennedy picked General Krulak of the Pentagon and Joseph Mendenhall of the State Department, a somewhat incongruous pair, and sent them to South Vietnam. Mendenhall's assignment was to roam the countryside; Krulak's to check on the military establishment. A USIA officer who accompanied them said: "The General and the FSO [Foreign Service Officer] not only appeared to dislike each other but also disagreed on what should be done about Vietnam." When they returned to Washington, they reported to a special session of the National Security Council. Krulak said the war was going well and the people were rallying to Diem's support. Mendenhall said the war was being lost and the people were becoming more disenchanted with Diem every day. The President listened to their sharply contrasting reports and asked: "Were you two gentlemen in the same country?"

A few days later he decided to send McNamara and Taylor on another inspection tour. Like so many Presidents before him, Kennedy learned to trust certain of his advisers more than others. On the issue of Vietnam he leaned toward McNamara and Taylor. They were to check on military progress and to find out whether Lodge's recommendation—that the United States immediately cut back economic aid to the Diem regime—made any sense. As Kennedy had told Huntley on September 9, the aid-cutting idea did not appeal to him. He feared that such drastic action might weaken Saigon and thus hasten its collapse, giving the Communists a victory, as in China during the late Forties.

McNamara and Taylor went through the usual Saigon briefing sessions and the mandatory VIP tours of the country-side. General Harkins showed them new and intricate charts designed to prove that enemy losses exceeded government losses, that more and more the countryside was coming under central control, and that ARVN was showing steady improvement. In other words, the military situation was good, and since Vietnam was viewed as a military problem, the overall situation was good. Senior United States officials, excluding Ambassador Lodge, felt that the "Buddhist affair" had been enormously exaggerated by the American press and that the American people had been "overly impressed" by the pictures of burning bonzes.

Lodge had another view in those days, a minority view. He had come to believe that Vietnam was primarily a political problem, not a military one, and that only a political recourse could be effective. One suggestion was cutting aid. Lodge strongly argued for this course of action. General Harkins opposed it.

McNamara felt more at home with Harkins's charts and statistical tables. But Lodge, fighting for the Secretary's ear and his support, managed to persuade him that Diem was getting to be so exasperating that the United States had to "get some leverage on that little fellow" to "shake him up." Taylor admired Diem. He considered him a courageous man of principle. But even Taylor acknowledged that he was becoming a "hard colleague" and that Lodge might possibly be right. The fact-finders returned to Washington on October 1. The following morning they reported to President Kennedy and that afternoon to the National Security Council.

Their joint recommendation was that aid be cut on a highly selective basis. Their hope was that Diem would react constructively and reform his regime. Their fear was that it might be too late. Cutting aid was one way of putting pressure on Diem. Another was to withdraw American advisers. This would demonstrate to Diem (or so the Washington strategists believed) that he could not lean on American military support indefinitely. Taylor did not consider the idea of possible troop withdrawals a gimmick. He sincerely believed, at the time, that "if the political situation holds," then the military side of the Vietnam problem could be wrapped up within a couple of years.

Later that afternoon the White House put out a policy statement. It affirmed that McNamara and Taylor had made a number of recommendations of a "classified" nature which would "be the subject of further review and action" [cutting aid] but that their "basic presentation," consisting of five points, had been unanimously "endorsed" by the NSC and "approved" by the President. The first point focused on the "security of South Vietnam," describing it for the first time as a "major interest of the United States." There was a pledge that the United States would work with the people and government of South Vietnam "to deny this country to communism and to suppress the externally stimulated and supported insurgency of the Viet Cong as promptly as possible."

Point two, inspired by the Harkins's briefings, stated that the "military program in South Vietnam has made progress and is sound in principle."

Point three sounded hauntingly like a new Navarre plan: major United States assistance, it said, would be needed only until the insurgency has been suppressed or until ARVN was capable of suppressing it. In this context, "Secretary McNamara and General Taylor reported their judgment that the major part of the U.S. military task can be completed by the end of 1965, although there may be a continuing requirement for a limited number of U.S. training personnel. They reported that by the end of this year the U.S. program for training Vietnamese should have progressed to the point where 1000 U.S. military personnel assigned to South Vietnam can be withdrawn." (One of Harriman's assistants, William Sullivan, accompanied McNamara and Taylor. He strongly objected to this kind of timetable pressure. But, in the administration's eagerness to suggest the American military involvement in Vietnam would not be endless, he was overruled.)

Point Four was a sop to Lodge. It called the "political situation" in South Vietnam "deeply serious," stressing that the United States continued to oppose "any repressive actions" in

the country. "While such actions have not yet significantly
affected the military effort," the statement continued, "they
could do so in the future."

The final point was rhetorical. It made known all over
again that the policy of the United States was "to support the
efforts of the people" of South Vietnam to "defeat aggression."

The exuberant statement of McNamara and Taylor that by
1965 the military job would be done overshadowed all else in
the newspaper accounts. Few readers noticed a carefully drafted
speech by McGeorge Bundy, the President's Adviser on National
Security Affairs. In the long history of Washington's escalating
rhetoric about Vietnam, that Bundy speech was highly significant. For the first time Bundy spoke of a United States "commitment" toward South Vietnam. What to McNamara and Taylor
had been a "major interest" became, in Bundy's word, a "commitment." He put it pointedly: "The commitment of the United
States to the independence of South Vietnam goes back many
years." Thus, even in the Kennedy years, when Vietnam pressures began to build-up, the administration was more than
willing to share the burden and the misery with past administrations.

In early October the United States began to pull the rug
from under Diem. Quietly the administration inaugurated a
selective suspension of aid. Diem kept his anger under control.
But his brother, Nhu, reportedly made some secret overtures
to Hanoi while Madame Nhu tried to rally sympathy and support among hard-line conservatives on a highly publicized trip
to the United States. She did not have Madame Chiang's good
fortune. At the beginning Madame Nhu managed to get several
southern Senators to make speeches in support of Diem. But
she oversold her case and in the end failed to make a dent in
Washington's policy.

Toward the end of the month the Washington-Saigon battle
reached a climax. It seemed, for a moment, that Diem might
yield under pressure. As he privately explained at the time, "I
can handle the Viet Cong if I get some American help. But I
cannot handle the Viet Cong and the United States at the same
time." On the last day of October Diem asked for Lodge's advice

after the two men, cool but correct antagonists, had dedicated an experimental nuclear reactor at Dalat. The ambassador replied that Diem ought to give Nhu a diplomatic assignment—in any case, get him out of the country—and then institute a broad program of reform. Much to Lodge's surprise, Diem did not reject the advice; he said he needed a little time to think about it.

Lodge was delighted. He cabled the dramatic news to Washington. But it was too late for Diem to save himself by sacrificing his widely detested brother. The following day Diem and Nhu were murdered. The story of American–South Vietnamese relations entered a new phase.

Schlesinger notes toward the end of *A Thousand Days* that there had been rumors of a possible anti-Diem coup in the last few days of October. The President believed that the pro- and anti-Diem forces in Saigon were about equal, and he saw no benefit in American action at that time. Lodge evidently did not take much stock in the coup rumors. In fact, he escorted Admiral Felt to the Presidential Palace in the early morning of November 1 for a meeting with Diem. The coup took place in the early afternoon. Schlesinger writes:

I saw the President soon after he heard that Diem and Nhu were dead. He was somber and shaken. I had not seen him so depressed since the Bay of Pigs. No doubt he realized that Vietnam was his great failure in foreign policy, and that he had never really given it his full attention. But the fact that the Vietnamese seemed ready to fight had made him feel that there was a reasonable chance of making a go of it; and then the optimism of 1962 had carried him along. Yet, with the memory of the French in Indochina in 1951, he had always believed there was a point at which our intervention might turn Vietnamese nationalism against us and transform an Asian civil conflict into a white man's war. When he came into office, 2000 American troops were in Vietnam [there were, in fact, fewer than 1000]. Now there were 16,000. How many more could there be before we passed the point? By 1961, choices had already fatally narrowed; but still, if Vietnam had been handled as a political rather than a military problem, if Washington had not listened to General Harkins for so long, if Diem had been subjected to tactful pressure rather than treated with uncritical respect, if a Lodge had gone to Saigon in 1961 instead of a Nolting, if, if, if—and now it was all past, and Diem miserably dead. The Saigon generals were claiming that he had killed himself; but the President, shaking his head, doubted that, as a Catholic, he would have taken this way out. He said that Diem had fought for his country for twenty years and that it should not have ended like this.

Even if John F. Kennedy from that day forward had planned to devote himself much more energetically and thoughtfully to the Vietnam problem, he did not get the chance. On November 22 he also was murdered in Dallas. His legacy to Lyndon Johnson, the new President, included a range of Vietnam options far narrower than those he had inherited from Dwight Eisenhower. An uncertain military junta, headed by General Minh, had just come to power. Because he was so tall for a Vietnamese, the Saigon press dubbed him "Big Minh." It was perhaps the most durable contribution by a newsman to recent Vietnamese history. Diem's supporters, who had run the government, and Nhu's followers, who had governed the secret police, were killed, exiled, or drummed out of the bureaucracy. Their successors were inexperienced and frequently inept. Administrative morale and efficiency (low in any case) fell disastrously. The strategic hamlet program withered and died in the confusion of the immediate post-Diem period. General Harkins's talk of steady "progress" was exposed within a month or two of Diem's death. The Viet Cong had seized control of most of the countryside. They appeared on the verge of striking for control of the whole country, but they held back and lost their chance. Had Kennedy lived, notes Theodore Sorensen, another sympathetic chronicler of JFK's Administration, he probably would have surveyed the bleak landscape and concluded that the U.S. had no choice but "to weather it out, a nasty, untidy mess to which there was no other acceptable solution." He had rejected withdrawal. That, he had said, "only makes it easy for the Communists"; i.e., the Chinese Communists. He seemed to have been much more preoccupied with the Chinese than with the Vietnamese Communists.* Like many another Western statesman scarred by

* On August 7, 1970, Life magazine published an eye-catching excerpt from Kenneth O'Donnell's book about LBJ and the Kennedys. It stated flatly that Kennedy had told O'Donnell during the Buddhist uprising in 1963 that he would order a "complete military withdrawal from Vietnam" after his 1964 re-election. "In 1965," Kennedy is quoted as having told O'Donnell, "I'll be damned everywhere as a communist appeaser. But I don't care.

World War II and the cold-war experience, Kennedy could not free himself of the idea that it was his "obligation" and "duty" to confront Communist aggression. He sent the first sizable numbers of American troops to Vietnam. In 1961, in April and again in May, he seriously considered a major commitment of ground troops to both Laos and South Vietnam. Always, while considering his next step in Vietnam, he was conscious of his political weakness at home, his tenuous grip on the Congress, his inability to move important legislation.

Sorensen has speculated that "if asked why he had increased this nation's commitment, he might have summed up his stand with the words used by William Pitt when asked in the House of Commons in 1805 what was gained by the war against France: 'We have gained everything that we would have lost if we had not fought this war.'"

It is hardly a sufficient answer.

If I tried to pull out completely now, we would have another Joe McCarthy red scare on our hands, but I can do it after I'm re-elected. So we had better make damned sure that I am elected."

O'Donnell wrote that Kennedy began to have his doubts about Vietnam in 1961 after listening to President de Gaulle's warnings about the pitfalls of American military participation in Vietnam. General Douglas MacArthur also had urged him to avoid an American military buildup in Vietnam. And he had listened to Senator Mansfield, the chronic doubter, tell him that the U.S. would be infinitely better off cutting military aid to Vietnam, rather than increasing it.

O'Donnell concluded that Kennedy had made up his mind to cut and run in Vietnam—but not then. He had to be re-elected first.

Kennedy, like so many of his top advisers, was clearly fed up with the frustrations of Vietnam. And, in the late spring of 1963, after reading the latest reports of Buddhist burnings in Saigon and Hué, sensing the utter hopelessness of the situation, he may well have considered withdrawing from Vietnam after the 1964 elections. But none of his advisers, O'Donnell excepted, believed that he would. Mansfield had his doubts too.

Throughout the summer of 1963, Kennedy agonized about Vietnam. By the early fall, he seemed to have concluded that the United States could not turn away from Vietnam. It could try to influence Saigon and Diem to move in a more profitable direction, but it could not pack up and leave. Moreover, assuming Kennedy's re-election, we doubt that he would have walked away from South Vietnam, when it was crumbling under Communist pressure. Kennedy's preoccupation with a China on the march would (we believe) have ruled out a total withdrawal—at least until South Vietnam could "stand on its own feet." That, in time, also became Johnson's preoccupation; and Nixon's as well.

SIX

"Let Us Continue"

NOVEMBER 24, 1963, was a Sunday. Henry Cabot Lodge, just
returned from Saigon by way of Honolulu, had been invited to
luncheon with President Kennedy at his new country home on
Rattlesnake Mountain in the hunt country of Virginia. Now
Kennedy was dead, and Lodge found himself briefing his old
friend, Lyndon Johnson of Texas, instead.

Shortly after Diem's assassination, at the beginning of that
bloody November, Kennedy had summoned Lodge home for
consultation. On the way, Lodge had conferred in Honolulu
with several of Kennedy's senior advisers: Rusk, McNamara,
Bundy, Harkins, and Felt. They met on November 20. Late the
next day, Rusk and McNamara, with several other Cabinet
officers, had flown off to Tokyo for a meeting with their Japanese
counterparts. Lodge flew to San Francisco, a rest stop. On
November 22, in his San Francisco hotel room, Lodge heard
that Kennedy had been shot in Dallas. The Cabinet officers were
high over the Pacific when they got the word by radio. Rusk
ordered the plane into a sharp turn: "We're returning to Washington," he told his shocked colleagues. From San Francisco,
Lodge called the White House for guidance. No one could tell
him anything. A few hours later an aide called to say that the
new President wanted him back in Washington immediately.

Lodge arrived in the shrouded capital on Saturday and went
to the East Room of the White House, where Kennedy's body
lay in state. He paid his respects to Mrs. Kennedy and to the
the fallen President's two living brothers: Attorney General
Robert Kennedy and Massachusetts Senator Edward Kennedy.
On Sunday morning, early by Washington standards, Lodge

went to Johnson's vice-presidential suite in the Executive Office Building. The new President, worried about a possible "Communist conspiracy" but even more worried about the need to rally a shocked and grieving nation, was already there. Within minutes the others arrived—Rusk and Ball from State, McNamara from the Pentagon, McCone from the CIA, Bundy from the White House basement. Johnson wanted to hear what Lodge had planned to tell Kennedy.

Lodge told him. The new government of South Vietnam was weak, shaky, chaotic, Lodge said. Ministers were being arrested, bureaucrats killed; the country was threatened with total disruption. The Communists were on the offensive. ARVN was intact, but Lodge feared it could splinter under heavy Communist pressure. Moreover, he emphasized, since Diem's generals had engineered the coup, they all seemed more interested in politics than in war.

According to Tom Wicker's reliable account, Lodge then told the "emotionally drained Texan" that if Vietnam were to be saved, some very hard decisions would have to be made. "Unfortunately, Mr. President," Lodge concluded, "you will have to make them."

The new President "scarcely hesitated," Wicker reported. "I am not going to lose Vietnam," he said firmly. "I am not going to be the President who saw Southeast Asia go the way China went."

"What kind of political support will you have?" Lodge asked.

"I don't think the Congress wants us to let the Communists take over South Vietnam," the President replied.

Nobody in the room could question Johnson's skill as a political operator, above all his grasp of congressional thinking. Yet, Lyndon Johnson, President less than forty-eight hours, had just made a major decision on Vietnam and a worrisome one. It was a decision by reflex: He was not going to be the President who lost Southeast Asia to communism, period. Without time for reflection or study, he had simply ruled out any decision but continued war. Other decisions would flow from that first, seemingly offhand statement.

Johnson, a middle-aged man from middle America, wanted
desperately to succeed, to be acknowledged a great President by
all those who had sniffed at his credentials and manners while
Kennedy lived: the money men from New York; the Ivy League
intellectuals Kennedy had recruited for the White House; the
Eastern Establishment. In those first hours, Johnson felt he had
to win them over, to demonstrate his strength and purpose.

"I wasn't sure how successful I would be in pulling the
divergent factions in the country together and trying to unify
them and unite them in order to get the confidence of the people
and secure the respect of the world," Johnson later told reporters.
"That's why I met with the Cabinet, or those of them there, and
the leaders that night. That's why I talked with my individual
counselors beginning at eight in the morning, and eighty-three
heads of government, to the leaders of Congress, by television to
the country . . . I tried to appeal to the best in everybody, but
not with my hat in hand . . . I tried to anticipate everything
that could happen. I tried to pull labor and business, the ex-
Presidents, Congress, even spiritual leaders together. People
don't know it, but Billy Graham spent two or three nights in the
White House. He got up at three in the morning and got down
on his knees and prayed for me. At six he'd have coffee with me
and we'd talk over the problems facing the country."

In the early weeks of his accidental Presidency, as Hugh
Sidey once put it, Lyndon Johnson performed prodigiously. No
one who lived through those days of foreboding could fail to
have been impressed by the tact with which he handled the
Kennedy family, or the skill with which he took charge of the
Government. The theme of continuity ran like a bright thread
through this tragic transition. He believed it was no time for
change—not in the palace guard, not in domestic policy, not in
foreign affairs. In solemn tones the accidental President appealed to a nation in tears: "Let us continue!"

Johnson had traveled far but, in a sense, he never left
Texas. "Know the difference between a Texas Ranger and a
sheriff?" he once asked some reporters. They were walking
through his boyhood home, a rickety frame house in the Hill
Country of Texas less than one hundred miles from the Alamo.

"When you shoot a Ranger, he just keeps comin' on," the President explained. LBJ was raised on the Alamo legend. Texas Rangers never knew fear. When Johnson visited Cam Ranh Bay in October, 1966, his first visit to the war zone as President, he urged the troops to "nail the coonskin" to the wall.

As a young man, rattling around Johnson City, learning to hunt and shoot and fish, LBJ must have listened to countless yarns of Ranger manliness and ingenuity. He told so many himself. He learned that life was no picnic. The soil in the Hill Country was always hard, and the odds against success in farming were high. Everyone knew that a man had to stand tall and fight for what he thought was right. Lyndon Johnson's grandfather was such a man. He earned his keep by driving cattle from Texas to Kansas. He was reliable, sturdy, a "good man to go to the well with." His grandmother had to be resourceful and wise. She was often left alone. Once she spotted a Comanche party heading for her house. She grabbed both her young children and ducked into the fruit cellar. Johnson's eyes would narrow as he told the story. She waited in the cellar for hours until the Indians left. Then she emerged unscalped. In those days, Johnson would say, people had to be crafty and endure many hardships. A man did not "turn tail" and run. A real man "hunkered down" and waited for the trouble to pass. And it always did.

Sam Ealy Johnson was his father, and, to judge from a family photograph, he was a tall, clear-eyed man in a four-button jacket and a ten-gallon hat. He was a politician, a state legislator, who spent more time in Austin than in Johnson City, a town of about 500 people in LBJ's youth, about 1000 now. His father's frequent absences left his mother, Rebekah Baines Johnson, chiefly responsible for the upbringing of five Johnson children. Lyndon was her first-born. Rebekah Johnson was a remarkable woman, a college graduate, publisher and editor of the *News*, the only newspaper in town. There was no one like her in Blanco County, Texas.

Growing up in her shadow, Lyndon developed a reverence for education and a drive to be somebody. He was clearly Johnson City's best, a small-town whiz. Thanks to his mother's

constant encouragement, he never believed that his own ambitions had to be limited by the boundaries of that little Texas
town. As a boy, he would often visit his father's office in Austin
and listen to stories about the great Sam Rayburn, who had been
Speaker of the Texas legislature before moving on to the Congress of the United States. Lyndon was an outstanding young
man; always first in his class. Yet, as he grew older, he seemed
to develop a chip on his shoulder about coming from Texas.
Why did others, clearly less able than he, have it so much
easier? Why did non-Texans—above all, Easterners—seem to
look down their noses at him? Why did they treat him as if he
were less deserving of power than others?

It was an attitude that Johnson carried with him long after
he had become a large national figure. Succeeding where his
maternal grandfather had failed, Johnson was elected to the
House of Representatives in 1937, running as a 100 percent supporter of Roosevelt's decision to pack the Supreme Court. He
got twice as many votes as his nearest rival, and FDR never
forgot the gangling young Texan, the protégé of Sam Rayburn.
LBJ's Tenth District soon was receiving Federal largesse on an
unaccustomed grand scale. Federal Housing Project No. 1 was
constructed in Austin. The Rural Electrification Administration
established the Pedernales River Electric Cooperative, one of
the largest of its kind, to provide cheap electricity for Johnson
City and the outlying farms. Hospitals, schools, recreational
centers were built. The young Congressman clearly knew how
to operate in Washington. He listened to Rayburn and, when
he felt the need, he turned to the White House.

It was good politics, of course; but it was more than that.
Johnson never forgot his origins—the merciless sun and the dry
land, the desperate need for water and electricity, the back-break-
ing toil. "When the rains came and the waters collected,"
Johnson once recalled, sounding almost Biblical, "the water
holes filled up and the rivers were full and there was happiness.
We could use the water on the land to make crops grow, and
the animals could drink. But when there was drought, or the
floods came, then things were horrible." He wanted to help
those Hill Country farmers who were so pathetically vulnerable
to the cruel vagaries of nature. When he entered Congress, he

devoted himself to building dams and stringing electric power lines across the flat, dry plains of the Southwest.

For Lyndon Johnson, as Vice-President, it was the most natural thing in the world to suggest to President Diem in 1961 that a major electrification program on the Mekong River could bring prosperity and peace to the troubled lands of Southeast Asia. Or, as President, to propose in 1965, after he had started to bomb North Vietnam, that Hanoi should receive economic aid after the war and share in a regional plan for economic development. Hanoi may have considered Johnson a charlatan for offering aid with one hand while bombing with the other. But Johnson was being himself in both roles. He was bombing the North because he wanted peace and could think of no better way to bring the Communists to the peace table; he offered aid because he had always believed in the healing force of economic improvement. It had worked in the Texas Hill Country. Why not in Southeast Asia?

In 1948 Johnson ran for the Senate and, after a hotly contested race, followed by a court challenge, he was declared the winner. In the Senate, his organizational skills flourished and his importance grew. Within just a few years Johnson had become Majority Leader, one of the youngest and most powerful in recent history. His strength and his reputation were founded upon an uncanny ability to persuade and manipulate powerful men, to deal for votes, balance pluses and minuses in legislation and thus assure passage. Lyndon Johnson made things work.

By the late Fifties many politicians were saying that Johnson was the second most important man in the United States Government, second only to Eisenhower.

Johnson naturally thought of himself as a potential President. John Kennedy, his chief rival for the Democratic nomination, had the money and glamour. Johnson believed that he had the power. He miscalculated badly. Kennedy won the nomination at Los Angeles, but he was persuaded to choose LBJ for his running mate because he himself appeared to be unpopular in the South.* Johnson understood the politics of this

---

* Kennedy reportedly told Kenneth O'Donnell that he had one other important reason for selecting LBJ. He did not want Johnson to remain as Majority Leader while he was President. "If we win," Kennedy said, "it

decision. Once in office, he carried out an assortment of tasks
for the new President, more or less cheerfully. But he knew that
he was forever an outsider in the Kennedy White House.

Never intimate with the President, ignored by much of the
Washington press corps, Johnson nursed his bitterness. He felt
snubbed, a victim of social discrimination by reason of his Hill
Country origins, his accent, his schooling. The hurt was still
there when he left the Presidency.

In May, 1970, he said to Walter Cronkite; "Very important
and influential molders of opinion" were forever drawing un-
flattering comparisons between himself and Kennedy—"my manner of dealing with things and his manner, my accent and his
accent, my background and his background." To many of the
Harvard men who had served Kennedy, Johnson did seem a
vulgar yokel. He was not their kind of man and they were not
his kind of people.

Yet he yearned to be accepted by this Ivy League crowd.
His brother, Sam Houston Johnson, records that "bright scholarly
men like McNamara, Bundy, and Abe Fortas had a lot of influence on [Lyndon's] thinking because he regarded them as part
of an intellectual elite. There was a hint of awe in his attitude
towards them." Sam Houston adds: "He had known plenty of
book-loving ignoramuses with Phi Beta Kappa keys from fancy
colleges, and seen them pull damn-fool boners on the simplest
matters, yet he could suddenly be self-conscious about his own
limited schooling at a small Texas college."

As President, Johnson felt that it was his duty and destiny
to unify the nation. He wanted to bridge the gaps between
generations and regions. He truly wanted to build a Great Society. That is why, in those anxious, early days of power, he kept
talking about continuity. He determined early to take no action
that could be interpreted as a break from Kennedy's policies or
that could have served as a pretext for the New Englanders and
New Yorkers to break with him. He knew that some of Ken-

---

will be by a small margin and I won't be able to live with Lyndon Johnson
as the leader of a small Senate majority. Did it occur to you that if Lyndon
becomes Vice-President, I'll have Mike Mansfield as the Senate leader, somebody I can trust and depend on?"

nedy's aides in the "Irish Mafia" disliked and distrusted him, but he suffered their calculated slights. He did not need them as much as he felt he needed McNamara, Taylor, Bundy, Rusk, Sorensen and, of course, Bobby Kennedy. He was determined not to damage the façade of national unity.*

If, at the time, so heavy an emphasis upon continuity reduced the possibility of re-examining the Vietnam policy, then that seemed a small price to pay for keeping the nation's body and soul together. No one in executive authority at that time had proposed a change of policy. In practical terms, continuity meant paralysis. It meant no changes in personnel, no questioning of assumptions, no tinkering with the system. In the context of the times—the national trauma caused by a presidential assassination—continuity made comforting sense.

Another presidential campaign was less than twelve months off. This factor tended to color the President's attitude toward every major issue—whether it was the quest for equal voting rights in the South, a workable majority in the House, or a viable anti-Communist regime in South Vietnam. Lyndon Johnson was a thoroughly political President. He could not help but see the nation's problems and opportunities through a political prism. Soon after taking office, Johnson began to shape the contours of his own campaign, in which the Vietnam War was to play its inevitable part.

It appeared that the Republican Party was split down the middle—Goldwater on the right, Rockfeller on the left. And Goldwater, a loose-talking, sometimes hair-raising, conservative from Arizona, would probably capture the G.O.P. nomination,

* One warm spring evening in 1964, the Kennedy clan threw a cocktail party for Jacqueline at the F Street Club, her first "public appearance" since the assassination. Johnson was invited. "Almost plaintively," O'Donnell recalls, "he asked Larry O'Brien and me to go to the party" with him. Johnson was virtually ignored. He was in a business suit. Everyone else was in evening clothes, swarming around Jackie, who looked radiant. Johnson and O'Donnell were standing to one side, each nursing a drink. "I guess they are all going someplace to a dinner," Johnson observed. "Are you going with them?" O'Donnell said no, he had to go back to work. "Would you mind coming back to the White House and having another drink?" asked the President. Both men were silent in the car. Later Johnson exclaimed rather pathetically: "Despite what they think, I am still the President of the United States. But I didn't want it this way."

talking the language of extremism and brandishing the bomb. Johnson calculated that he could win a landslide victory by contrasting his restrained and responsible conduct with Goldwater's flamboyant, occasionally frightening words. Every time Goldwater spoke out, he seemed to be playing into Johnson's hands. For example, when Goldwater proposed defoliating the Vietnamese countryside, Johnson called for peace talks with the Communists. When Goldwater suggested that individual commanders be given the right to use tactical nuclear weapons in defense of Western Europe, Johnson reasserted the concept of absolute civilian control. When Goldwater appeared to support McKinley-era policies in domestic affairs, Johnson pressed his programs for racial harmony and social uplift.

Johnson believed that after the calamity of assassination, the American people would overwhelmingly reject Goldwater's jingoist appeals and embrace his own calming, healing leadership. He instructed his advisers to prepare for the worst in Vietnam but to take no dramatic action that could possibly upset his campaign plans. On the domestic side, he urged them, in effect, to do nothing: just to sit back and enjoy the fireworks. Johnson rolled up his sleeves and, in one of the most breathtaking displays of energy, guile, and cajolery seen in decades, broke the legislative logjam on Capitol Hill. It was his finest hour.

Michael Davie of the London *Observer* wrote: "He is one of the most fascinating human beings ever to become President of the United States. He is more interesting, because he is infinitely more alien and complex than President Kennedy. To meet him is to be awed and excited. He is purely and aggressively American—the first uninhibited product of the American frontier to take over since Andrew Jackson. Washington is obsessed by him. No one is sure what kind of animal he is dealing with, but under the anxieties the feeling is beginning to grow that he may be a great President."

Over drinks in Georgetown or Cleveland Park, reporters and politicians marveled at his political techniques. Soon after the assassination, they recalled, he had leaned on three former Presidents—Hoover, Truman, and Eisenhower; mostly, on Eisenhower. "President Eisenhower got in his car and drove down from Gettysburg," Johnson recounted, "and sat in my office, borrowed a yellow note pad and pencil and sat there for a good while and wrote out his views." Ike recommended first, that Robert Anderson, his own trusted financial adviser, be invited to the White House to help with the tax bill; second, that Johnson quickly ease the anxieties of many farmers, intellectuals, labor leaders, and businessmen by telling a joint meeting of Congress (and the people, by television) that he would be friendly with everyone and play favorites with no one; and, third, that he appeal to the Congress to start clearing the logjam of legislative proposals left over from Kennedy's time.

Johnson soon established a warm working relationship with the former President, who happened to be the most popular and respected Republican in the land, a detail that had never escaped LBJ's attention. Whenever he had a problem requiring bipartisan support, Johnson would discuss it first with Eisenhower, then with the congressional leadership. It eased his problems considerably to have Ike's approval. Johnson always played the game of bipartisanship. When Eisenhower had been President, Johnson helped him; now Johnson needed help, and Ike gave it freely.

The Johnson-Eisenhower combination proved to be, in Johnson's words, a "formidable bulldozer." He said later: "We started moving forward, and legislation started moving, and the tax bill started moving, and the civil-rights bill started moving. And we enacted practically all of President Kennedy's program. And while they didn't go as far in some instances as I wanted them to go on my program, they enacted practically all of the Johnson program."

It was a formidable program. Johnson, the Texan, did more to advance equal rights for black Americans than any President before him. He pushed back the horizons of social legislation. He poured the foundations for his Great Society. For a time, it seemed, Johnson could do no wrong in domestic affairs. His political touch was sure and unfailing. But for Vietnam, he would certainly have gone into the history books as the "great

President" he craved to be. But Vietnam would not yield to his political magic. The war dragged on and it began to crowd him, to narrow his options.

Johnson's knowledge of the world was limited. As Vice-President he had traveled considerably; as a Senator and Congressman, seldom. The trouble with foreigners, he once said, was that "they're not like folks you were reared with." He spoke no foreign language. He read pitifully little about foreign affairs, or other subjects for that matter. "Don't remember readin' six books all the way through since college," he once told a friend. His Washington cronies were not diplomats; they were other politicians.

Of course, during the thousand days of his Vice-Presidency, Johnson had been forced to take a kind of cram course in foreign affairs. He had to read State Department briefing books on Vietnam, Berlin, Cuba, and de Gaulle. He sat in on many secret, high-level meetings during the Cuban missile crisis. He made few recommendations—partly because he was not asked, but also because he was not sure he had anything of value to contribute. He listened and, inevitably, he learned. But he was picking up his education in a very unusual university. There were no rebellious professors or dissident students. Everyone tended to accept the same hypotheses, having been schooled together in the wartime fight against fascism and the cold-war conflict with Russia. The nearest thing to a skeptic was George Ball; and Ball's views were not all that far out.

Thus Johnson's vision of the world was conventional: like ancient Gaul, the world was divided into three parts—the Communist bloc; the underdeveloped world, which the United States must help in order to keep it from slipping into the Communist camp; and the free world, including South Vietnam. Ever since the early days of containment, the United States had been helping small countries to resist Communist inroads. That policy had been successful in Europe, so it was being applied in Asia. Within this framework, the United States had been helping South Vietnam, and Johnson could see no reason why this help should not be maintained until the Communist insurgency, as Kennedy put it, had been suppressed. When LBJ told Lodge on

November 24, 1963, that he was not going to be the "President who saw Southeast Asia go the way China went," he was proclaiming the obvious. He was going to do what had to be done to defeat the Communist insurgency. He talked accommodation, of course. But it was not until 1968 that he earnestly tried and failed to make peace.

If it was natural for Johnson to pursue established policy in Vietnam, it was also natural for him to lean for advice upon the Establishment, especially the Kennedy Establishment. As he later explained: "I said to all the Cabinet: I want you to stay in. Just as you served President Kennedy, serve me—because, after all, it's not something you serve one individual; you're serving the country. This is your country, and you're peculiarly equipped by your experience and his trust." When LBJ spoke to *all the Cabinet,* he was speaking specifically to Robert Kennedy, the Attorney General, the one man in the world who conceivably could still deprive Johnson of his party's nomination. It was unlikely but possible. When he talked to the Cabinet, he stressed his right to the nomination. "I constantly had the picture in front of me," LBJ said, "that President Kennedy had selected me as his executor, his trustee, to stand in for him. He couldn't be there. He'd selected these men. How would I feel if I'd selected a group of men and left them in trust with certain responsibilities, and the first thing my successor did, he came in and started eliminating them and firing them and so forth?"

It was understandable that Johnson should have failed to persuade Robert Kennedy that he was President Kennedy's "executor" and "trustee." He had less trouble persuading other members of the Kennedy Cabinet. Dean Rusk was happier working for LBJ than for JFK. Robert McNamara was loyal, hardworking, conscientious. Other Kennedy appointees decided to stay on: John McCone, a hard-nosed California Republican, who ran the CIA; Ambassador Lodge, a closer friend of Johnson than of Kennedy; McGeorge Bundy, a moderate Republican and a former Harvard dean. These were the same men who had advised Kennedy to hold the line against the Chinese Communists in South Vietnam. They had all made what Harvard Professor James Thomson has called a "human ego investment."

Each had a personal stake in the earlier Vietnam decisions. As time passed, it became harder and harder for them to change their minds—in effect, to repudiate their earlier positions. They had consistently underestimated Viet Cong strength; repeatedly yielded to the idea of a military solution; and often simply fumbled opportunities to disengage from Vietnam. Thomson, a White House aide to both Kennedy and Johnson, remembered an appropriate story about Henry Stimson, Secretary of War under President Roosevelt.

"Mr. Secretary," a questioner asked, "how on earth can we ever bring peace to the world?" Stimson pondered the question, then responded: "You begin by bringing to Washington a small handful of able men who believe that the achievement of peace is possible. You work them to the bone until they no longer believe that it is possible. And then you throw them out—and bring in a new bunch who believe that it is possible."

Johnson had no intention of bringing in a new bunch; besides, the old bunch still thought it was possible to win in South Vietnam. The new President, who wanted to win an election and then a war, in that order, was perfectly happy with the advice of Kennedy's old bunch.

By mid-December, 1963, the reports from South Vietnam were bad. Viet Cong incidents had increased. The Communists controlled considerably more than half of the country. The strategic hamlet program was in deep trouble. There were disturbing signs of increasing defections from ARVN. Johnson sent McNamara and McCone to Saigon for another two-day swing through MAAC V's wonderland of charts and quick helicopter excursions through "secure" villages. The rot was not easily apparent, but the political situation *was* alarming. When McNamara returned, he urged the President to rescind his earlier recommendation that 1000 American advisers be withdrawn by the end of the year. It was a formality. They were not going to be withdrawn anyway. He also urged the President to bolster the sagging spirits of General Minh's military regime in Saigon. On December 31 Johnson sent Minh a New Year's message— notable for the ease with which the United States could shift its "wholehearted support" from a civilian government (President

Diem had run elections of sorts) to a military government (elections were suspended) without a tremor. (Over the next year or so, as one military regime succeeded another, Washington became more practiced in shifting allegiance from one general to another.)

Johnson sought to reassure Minh: "The United States will continue to furnish you and your people with the *fullest measure of support* in this bitter fight. *We shall maintain* in Vietnam *American personnel and material as needed* to assist you in achieving *victory*." * Strong words, and again the suggestion of an open-ended American obligation to support Saigon generals until victory. This was not the language of compromise. In fact, Johnson ruled out a political deal. "The United States Government shares the view of your government," the President wrote, "that 'neutralization' of South Vietnam is unacceptable. As long as the Communist regime in North Vietnam persists in its aggressive policy, neutralization of South Vietnam would only be another name for a Communist takeover. Peace will return to your country just as soon as the authorities in Hanoi cease and desist from their terrorist aggression."

McNamara, more than any other high official, set the tone and direction of United States policy in Indochina. Dean Rusk, characteristically cautious, believed in McNamara's policy. On January 27, 1964, in a statement before the House Armed Services Committee, McNamara acknowledged that the situation was grave. But, he added, in a plea for more U.S. military aid, "the survival of an independent government in South Vietnam is so important to the security of Southeast Asia and to the free world that *I can conceive of no alternative other than to take all necessary measures within our capability to prevent a Communist victory*." †

Three days later Major General Nguyen Khanh staged a lightning *coup d'état*, the second in a bewildering series of military coups after Diem's assassination. General Minh was demoted to the nominal job of chief of state. On February 7 Secretary Rusk pledged United States support of the Khanh regime. One

---

* (Italics by M. K. and E. A.)
† (Italics by M. K. and E. A.)

month later McNamara and Taylor left for another four-day
swing through South Vietnam. Johnson asked McNamara, now
Washington's No. 1 expert on Vietnam, to size up the new
Vietnamese leader. It was symptomatic of Washington's state of
mind that McNamara, not Rusk, was sent on a mission of this
kind. The problem was still perceived as chiefly military. Rusk,
who knew better, never argued. For four days McNamara,
Khanh, and Taylor fluttered through the Vietnamese countryside,
visiting one secure military base after another. Often they would
stop to pose for pictures and chat with officers, women, and
children—almost as though they were politicians on the stump.

On March 15 McNamara and Taylor returned to Washington. They reported to the President the following day and, on
March 17, to the National Security Council. The White House
then issued another of those informative statements, praising
Saigon and its leadership. The apparent purpose of the exercise
was to build up General Khanh personally, to endorse his promises about a vast, new mobilization of the Vietnamese people and
the creation of a "highly trained guerrilla force that can beat the
Viet Cong on its own ground." (This was supposed to have been
accomplished two and a half years earlier, but no one cited
this embarrassing detail.) If McNamara or Taylor had any
doubts about Khanh, there was no trace of them in the statement. The White House statement also came down hard on the
side of those officials in Saigon and Washington who believed
Hanoi was running the insurrection in the South. McNamara and
Taylor, it said, had "clear and unmistakable" evidence that
North Vietnam "controlled" the Viet Cong and that the Communists were taking "maximum advantage" of Saigon's coup-
caused political weakness.

Some initial criticism of policy began to be heard, anyway.
A handful of newsmen questioned the contention that Hanoi
"controlled" the VC insurgency. Nonsense, they said, it's a civil
war. In Western Europe, such allies as de Gaulle hinted—at first
discreetly, later loudly—that the only solution was political, not
military, a coalition government. De Gaulle also argued that
everyone's interests would be served by "neutralizing" all of
Southeast Asia. Chester Bowles, by then exiled to India, sent

cables to Rusk and Johnson from his embassy in New Delhi, arguing strenuously for a "neutralist" solution. But just as President Kennedy had ignored him in 1961, so Johnson ignored him in 1964. The President disliked criticism. It offended his sense of national unity. So he asked McNamara to deliver a major speech, titled "Response to Aggression," on March 26 before the James Forrestal Memorial Awards Dinner. It was a major statement of policy.

McNamara was blunt. Aid to South Vietnam, he said, is in "our own clear self-interest." He depicted Vietnam as an area of "great strategic significance in the forward defense of the United States." Moreover, it was a "test case" of the Communist doctrine of "wars of national liberation . . . the prime aggressor is North Vietnam, whose leadership has explicitly undertaken to destroy the independence of the South."

While McNamara acknowledged that the situation in South Vietnam had "unquestionably worsened" since the death of Diem, he ruled out any thought of American withdrawal or of neutralization. A neutralized South Vietnam, he contended, would be "an interim device to permit Communist consolidation and eventual takeover." The Secretary of Defense mentioned one more presidential option—the "initiation of military actions outside South Vietnam, particularly against North Vietnam." This option, he said, was being carefully studied, to be acted upon only if it was "forced upon us by the other side." Finally, as a Kennedy man in a Johnson Administration, McNamara borrowed a line or two from the dead President.

"It will take courage, imagination, and—perhaps more than anything else—patience to bear the burden of what President Kennedy has called the 'long twilight struggle,'" McNamara declaimed. "In Vietnam, it has not been finished in the first hundred days of President Johnson's Administration, and it may not be finished in the first 1,000 days [it wasn't]; but, in cooperation with General Khanh's government we have made a beginning."

So the first clear warning of possible American "military actions against North Vietnam" had been issued. Although few high officials, perhaps not even McNamara and Johnson, believed it would be necessary. North Vietnam, they felt, would get the message. "They're not ten feet tall, you know," a State Department official stated—as much, it seemed, to reassure himself as to persuade a skeptical reporter. The Communists "will back off," he predicted. "You can count on it." The State Department passed the word to Hanoi, through East European diplomats, that the U.S. "meant business." Some of these diplomats, who had had personal experience of the North Vietnamese, cautioned their American colleagues that they were underestimating the Communists' will to resist. The same caution was given to American reporters. When one of them mentioned this to Dean Rusk, the Secretary smiled, Mona Lisa style, and said, as he pressed his forefinger forcefully against his desk: "When the United States applies pressure on something, anything, it gives."

Harriman, Hilsman, and Michael Forrestal, whose combined efforts had initiated the move against Diem, questioned the conventional wisdom of the hour. They believed that "more of the same" would not do the job. In private sessions with George Ball, occasionally with Rusk and Bundy, they stressed that the United States must forget about a conventional military solution and concentrate instead on a sophisticated program of counterinsurgency—by which they meant a heavy emphasis upon economic and social reforms, backed by about 100,000 Green Berets. They tried to persuade McNamara and Taylor to their viewpoint. The effort failed. McNamara understood that the President was not then interested in controversial new initiatives. His own political battle plan against Goldwater did not allow for a 100,000-man troop commitment to South Vietnam—before the elections.

Hilsman promptly resigned as Assistant Secretary of State and retreated to Columbia University. Forrestal resigned to join a New York law firm. Harriman was eased out of his job as Under Secretary of State and appointed a roving ambassador. The lesson was not lost on the other Johnson bureaucrats.

A temporary silence fell upon the executive branch of government. Once the word got out that "tough decisions" should be kept away from the White House, fresh ideas withered on the vine. There was, as Philip Geyelin has noted, an "absence of decision-making," which could "amount to a decision in itself."

But, because all bureaucrats like to create the impression of change and movement, basically to hold off criticism, the President decided to shake up the U.S. command in South Vietnam. On April 25 Johnson announced that General William Westmoreland would replace General Harkins. On June 23 he announced that General Taylor would replace Lodge as ambassador to South Vietnam. A career diplomat, U. Alexis Johnson, was appointed Deputy Ambassador. Between the two announcements, McNamara and Taylor had raced in and out of South Vietnam on another of their inspection tours. Westmoreland's orders were to "hold the line"; Taylor's were to "bolster Saigon's will" and to serve as McNamara's (and the President's) man in Saigon. And Alex Johnson was to help on the diplomatic and political side, since Taylor would be devoting much of his time to the military side of the problem.

In the summer of 1964, as the American presidential campaign warmed up, the Communists vastly improved their military and political situation in Vietnam. In Laos they began a new offensive, overrunning neutralist forces in the Plain of Jars and threatening to lay siege to Vientiane. Very quietly, on May 21, the United States began to fly reconnaissance missions over enemy positions in Laos—in part to check on their infiltration of men and supplies into South Vietnam; in part to check on enemy buildups in Laos. A week later several T-26 fighter-bombers were sent to Laos. A week after that, two United States reconnaissance planes were shot down by Pathet Lao forces. The Pentagon then ordered air cover for the reconnaissance planes. From then on, American war planes began to fly combat missions over Laos, but it took years before the American public learned what was going on.

The increased activity in Laos was connected with Hanoi's "exploitation," according to a Taylor dispatch to Washington, of Saigon's weakened political position. Things went from bad to worse. Khanh could not cope with the chaos. Corruption was everywhere. The Viet Cong infiltrated the capital. Terrorists planted bombs in market places. American advisers were ordered to walk in pairs when in uniform. ARVN, which had been intact through the spring, began to come apart. Unit commanders

were obviously more interested in politics and profit-taking than
in fighting. So bleak was the overall situation that a veteran
American diplomat predicted: "Within six months, at most, the
VC will have the country." General Taylor later recalled: "We
damn near lost out" in 1964.

In Washington, the public word was that the situation was
grave but manageable. There was no visible alarm at the top
of Johnson's Administration. Goldwater advocated strong action,
but LBJ continued to present his unflappable front to the elec-
torate. Behind this contrived exterior, however, the President's
advisers were desperately worried. They had contingency plans
for everything, including, as McNamara had publicly warned,
direct American military action against North Vietnam. U.S.
warships were ordered to patrol the Gulf of Tonkin. A plan was
drafted, calling for the introduction of a limited number of
United States ground troops. But McNamara and the Joint
Chiefs of Staff, knowing the President would not buy it before
the election, scrubbed the plan. If any dramatic action had to
be taken, it would be, as one JCS officer put it, "an Air Force
and Navy show." By mid-July the rot in Saigon had gone so
deep that Hilsman's successor, William Bundy, McGeorge's elder
brother, began to tinker with a draft of a congressional resolution that would have sanctioned American military action against
North Vietnam. One high official said: "The President knew he
would have to take some kind of action against North Vietnam,
enough to suggest that the ground rules governing the war up
to that point might be changed; but he needed a reason, one
he knew would be politically palatable."

The reason, or the pretext, presented itself, obligingly, on
August 2. That day North Vietnamese gunboats fired on the U.S.
destroyer *Maddox*, patrolling international waters in the Gulf
of Tonkin. Whether the attack was premeditated—a naval Dienbienphu designed in the heat of a presidential campaign to
shatter morale in the United States—or whether it was provoked
by recent South Vietnamese commando raids north of the 17th
parallel, which had been carried out under the protective wing
of *Maddox* and other American warships in the area, was not
clear. In any case, although the incident served to rally those

hawks who had been advocating an air strike against the North
Vietnamese, the President decided not to retaliate. It did not suit
his political purpose.

First news of the *Maddox* incident reached Washington before dawn. It was a Sunday morning. The duty officer at the
State Department tried to reach Rusk at home, but no one
answered. It later turned out that Rusk was home but did not
hear the phone because his air conditioner was on. Rusk refused
to keep the phone on his night table; he kept it in an adjoining
room so that he would be forced to get out of bed when it rang
and wide-awake by the time he lifted the receiver. It was past
6 A.M. before General Earle Wheeler, Taylor's successor as
Chairman of the Joint Chiefs, Deputy Defense Secretary Cyrus
Vance, and Thomas Hughes, the State Department's Director of
Intelligence and Research, arrived at Rusk's home to brief him
on the *Maddox* attack. At eight o'clock they were in the White
House, briefing the President. He did not seem overly upset.
He was more interested in the postal bill and, for more than an
hour, treated his advisers to a lecture on the problems of moving
such a bill through the Congress. There was not another word
about the *Maddox*.

Two days later, on August 4, the North Vietnamese struck
again—or, so it appeared to officials in Washington. Flash reports reached the Pentagon indicating that enemy gunboats had
attacked not only *Maddox* but also *C. Turner Joy*, another destroyer which had been ordered to "cover" *Maddox* in the event
of further trouble. According to senior Pentagon officials, one of
the first reports said that more than twenty torpedoes had been
fired at both *Maddox* and *C. Turner Joy*. This report infuriated
the President, who wanted to show restraint but felt he dared
not show weakness. He immediately ordered a retaliatory strike
against several gunboat docks and "certain supporting facilities"
in North Vietnam. His twofold purpose was to teach Ho a lesson and deprive Goldwater of a campaign issue. He also decided to explain his actions on nationwide television late that
night, timing his appearance for the start of the air attacks. In
addition, sensing a political opportunity, he ordered Bundy to
present his draft resolution to Senator J. W. Fulbright's Foreign

Relations Committee for immediate passage. An air of crisis suddenly swept Washington. As Rusk, McNamara, Wheeler, and Bundy buzzed between their offices and the White House, a few hours before the broadcast, the Pentagon received late reports from the Gulf of Tonkin that cast considerable doubt upon the accuracy of the earlier reports, especially the one which had described an attack by "more than twenty torpedoes." Among these late reports was one suggesting that the skipper of *Maddox* might have exaggerated the scope of the "enemy attack." Another late report indicated that the sonar man, reading blips on the radar screen, had mistakenly assumed that some of the blips were approaching torpedoes when they might have been nothing more than the waves kicked up by the fast approaching *C. Turner Joy*. These late reports got through to McNamara and the President in time to call off the raids. But they chose to go ahead. At the time it seemed more important to retaliate against North Vietnam—and thus pick up several political chips—than to scrub the mission and double-check the facts.

That night the President spoke to the nation. The next day he sent a message to Congress, asking for immediate passage of a resolution "to promote the maintenance of international peace and security in Southeast Asia." The message was characteristically oversimplified. Johnson spoke about American commitments to South Vietnam, "first made in 1954 by President Eisenhower." United States policy, he said, had been "consistent" and "unchanged" since 1954. Johnson then revealed some though not all the details of United States military activity in Laos, noting cryptically that the enemy attack on *Maddox* was "not the first direct attack on Armed Forces of the United States." There had also been attacks on American reconnaissance planes over Laos, which required the President to furnish them with "escort fighters with instructions to fire when fired upon." The enemy attacks in Laos and the Gulf of Tonkin led him to conclude, Johnson said, "that I should now ask the Congress on its part to join in affirming the national determination that all such attacks will be met." He asked for a resolution "expressing the support of the Congress for all necessary action to protect our Armed Forces and to assist nations covered by the SEATO treaty."

The language of the resolution was more specific. It read: "The Congress approves and supports the determination of the President, as Commander-in-Chief, to take all necessary measures to repel any armed attack against the forces of the United States and to prevent further aggression." Section Two stated: The "United States is prepared . . . to take all necessary steps, including the use of armed force, to assist any member or protocol state" of SEATO. This language was explained to congressional leaders that afternoon at the White House. The next day Rusk and McNamara appeared before the appropriate congressional committees. The following day, August 7, Congress overwhelmingly endorsed the resolution. The Senate vote was 88 to 2—with Senator Fulbright dutifully sponsoring the resolution. The House vote was 416 to 0. "The President of the United States," Johnson later explained, "is not about to commit forces and undertake actions to deter aggression in South Vietnam to prevent this Communist conspiracy, unless and until the American people through their Congress sign on to go in. If the President's going in, as he may be required to do, he wants the Congress to go in right by the side of him. Why? Because that's the course of action I'd recommended for President Eisenhower when I was a Senator, when I was the Leader and he wanted the commitment for Formosa. That was the action I recommended in the Middle East Resolution."

Years later Johnson recalled that Senator Morse of Oregon had voted against the resolution, because he considered it the "equivalent of a declaration of war." Quite deliberately, Johnson had not asked for a declaration of war because "I didn't know what treaty China might have with North Vietnam, or Russia might have with North Vietnam." He did not want to run the risk of war with Russia or China by declaring war against North Vietnam. So he settled for the resolution.

Some reports have suggested that Johnson carried a draft of the Tonkin Gulf resolution in his hip pocket through most of July and that Bundy, too, carried one in his coat pocket. These are details, colorful but of no great significance. Clearly, both men were determined to move quickly for passage of a congressional resolution just as soon as the opportunity presented itself. For reasons of his own, the President chose to play down

the August 2 attack on *Maddox*. Perhaps he was too absorbed
with the postal bill. But, once informed of the August 4 incident,
he acted. The distinct possibility that his information might have
been faulty did not deter him.

Johnson felt that he needed the resolution for two reasons:
First, he could not be certain that the Communists were not
about to fire upon other American ships, troops, and planes; he
wanted congressional authority to strike back, if need be. Second, if events forced him to shoot from the hip, a policy then
being passionately advocated by Goldwater and opposed by
Johnson himself, he wanted to be certain that Congress was
behind him.

Senator Gaylord Nelson of Wisconsin, an early dove, wanted
to amend the Tonkin Gulf resolution to put the Congress on
record as opposing any "extension of the present conflict." Fulbright called the Nelson amendment superfluous. Two years
later, Fulbright was to confess that he had been "grossly and
sadly mistaken" in sponsoring the Tonkin resolution and in opposing the Nelson amendment.

At the time, most Senators and all Congressmen believed
that the resolution was a sensible precaution. But Hanoi was not
impressed by it. The Communists were intent upon gaining political power in South Vietnam. They pursued that objective
doggedly.

As the weeks slipped by, Senator Nelson's apprehensions
about the resolution began to seem unnecessary. The campaign
was by then in full swing, and Johnson reverted to his dove
line. Over and over again he said he would not widen the war,
he would not send American boys to fight in Asian wars, he
would not bomb North Vietnam, he would not fight China. This
was Johnson's consistent theme. If the North Vietnamese dis-
believed his peace rhetoric after Johnson had started bombing
the North and sending combat troops to South Vietnam, the
roots of that disbelief could be traced back to his own misleading speeches in the 1964 campaign. The President, in later years,
argued that there was nothing misleading or confusing about his
campaign posture. He contended that the Tonkin resolution and
McNamara's public warnings should have constituted ample

warnings to Hanoi. But this was an *ex post facto* justification. At the time, as the campaign speeches clearly show, he portrayed himself as a sensible, responsible statesman who would not dream of sending American boys to fight in a war that Asian boys should be fighting. He portrayed Goldwater, by contrast, as a wild Strangelove character, who could not wait to bomb China back to the stone age. The contrast made political sense at home but was of dubious value overseas.

The President's manner on the stump gave the voters no inkling that by late September Ambassador Taylor had filed a series of thoroughly alarming secret dispatches, saying that the tide of battle had now turned "unmistakably" against Saigon. The Communists, he believed, were fast approaching total victory in South Vietnam. Taylor told of sinking morale in the South, a high and rising defection rate in the army, and greatly increased Communist infiltration. Wealthy Saigonese were buying exit visas at exorbitant prices and fleeing the country. Washington officials knew the President would oppose any sustained new military action against North Vietnam until the elections were over. Their fear was that South Vietnam might not hold together till then. In the final weeks of the presidential campaign, an Alice-in-Wonderland quality crept into the policy deliberations.

Taylor kept recommending air strikes against the North. General Westmoreland kept agreeing. And McNamara, who knew Johnson would say no, kept arguing back that bombing the North would not win the war in the South, nor would it stop enemy infiltration. He contended the first essential requirement was "stability" in South Vietnam—then the bombing could begin. Taylor thought this was cockeyed reasoning. In his view, "stability" in South Vietnam might be the product of a systematic air campaign against the North, not the other way around.

This argument between Taylor and McNamara raged through October. There is some reason to believe Johnson sided with Taylor, but he refused to go against his Defense Secretary —not while the campaign was underway. He told Charles Roberts of *Newsweek* in May, 1965, that he had decided to initiate a bombing campaign against North Vietnam in October.

Clearly, however, he had not decided exactly when. On November 2, the day before the elections, the Viet Cong launched a surprise attack against the United States air base at Bien Hoa, killing five Americans, wounding seventy-six, and destroying six B-57 bombers. This was a frontal challenge. Taylor fired off a dispatch recommending an immediate start to the bombing of the North. He said the Communists must not be allowed to get away with the deliberate targeting of Americans. McNamara rejected his recommendation. He did not have to remind the ambassador that November 3 was Election Day.

Johnson won a landslide victory over Goldwater. His campaign tactics had been fully vindicated. Republican ranks were decimated, and the columnists wrote their premature obituaries. LBJ was "Big Daddy" in every way. His powers were so great, his mandate so massive, that Johnson conceivably could have announced, on November 4, that the United States was leaving South Vietnam—just packing up and going home. Such a thought never entered Johnson's mind, however. To him, that would have meant going back on the nation's pledged commitment; handing South Vietnam to the Communists and turning the Pacific Ocean into a Red lake. As he hoped he had made clear during the campaign, he was simply going to stay in Vietnam and see it through. He was determined to be the nation's Pacific President.

After the election Johnson opened a major policy review. He urged all his advisers to come up with new ideas—new approaches to this lingering, awful problem. But he imposed one condition, which made this top-secret exercise rather academic. He told them that he was not going to lose Vietnam. That eliminated the possibility of a quick exit, although he kept saying that he was open-minded about how to save South Vietnam. George Ball had sent a memo to Rusk, McNamara, and McGeorge Bundy, which became a basis for the review. It argued for a "neutralist" settlement in South Vietnam along the lines of the Laos agreement; there was to be no direct military involvement, no bombing of the North, no massive landing of United States ground troops. At the same time, Ball argued, the United States should provide maximum protection to Thailand,

Malaysia, and the rest of Southeast Asia. Ball had come to believe that the Saigon regime, as then constituted and so often reconstituted, offered no base on which to build a viable government.

The Ball memo produced some heated exchanges but no conclusions. Rusk counterargued that South Korea had been in desperate shape in 1953. But that as soon as the Communists decided to "leave their neighbors alone," progress toward a viable state had been remarkably rapid. McNamara also rejected the "neutralist" solution. It struck him as a disguised defeat. McGeorge Bundy felt the situation was dreadful, but that Saigon could be salvaged if the United States was willing to pay a higher price over a longer haul. The President listened but said nothing.

For several weeks this argument continued. In South Vietnam the rot continued, too. Communist harassment increased and grew bolder. On December 24, the Viet Cong attacked GI barracks in Saigon, killing two Americans and wounding fifty-two others and thirteen Vietnamese. Taylor again urged an immediate air attack. McNamara against rejected his recommendation. Not on Christmas Eve, he said, much to Taylor's disgruntlement. The ambassador was tired of excuses — first the elections, then the policy review, now Christmas. Taylor's impatience was reflected in his increasingly frequent cables to Washington. A number of the President's advisers thought that "the boss" was swinging around to the view that decisive American military action was needed to save South Vietnam. But Johnson was an extraordinarily secretive President, whose decision-making followed no set pattern. This had the effect of confusing some of his closest advisers.

In this period, Johnson was pondering many questions. Nikita Khrushchev had been ousted in October and his successors were a lackluster group of Party hacks—or were they? It was an important question. The Chinese Communists had just exploded their first atomic bomb. What would they do next? Move into North Vietnam or into Laos as they had moved into North Korea eighteen years before? Finally, Secretary General U Thant had an idea about direct United States–North Viet-

namese talks in Burma. Thant was not one of Rusk's favorite
people, so the idea generated no great interest in the Johnson-
era State Department. There is one well-founded report that
McNamara himself killed this initiative, though, at the time,
the Defense Secretary denied it. In any case, there was little
overall enthusiasm for peace talks in Washington. Almost everyone, Fulbright included, felt this was not the time for peace
talks. The United States had little bargaining strength; the South
Vietnamese had none; and the North Vietnamese held most of
the chips. No one, not even Ball, urged Rusk or the President
to seize the diplomatic opportunity to negotiate an "honorable"
American withdrawal.

The policy review continued, without major decisions. But
there were several minor ones which suggested the probable
direction of Johnson's ultimate policy. Ambassador Taylor had
returned to Washington for consultations. He painted a very
bleak picture of political decay and military disintegration in
South Vietnam. The President, Rusk, McNamara, and Wheeler
all listened carefully. Everyone agreed that the United States
had to send more economic and military aid to Saigon—much
more, in fact. Taylor returned to Saigon and told Prime Minister Tran Van Huong (the civilian figurehead of still another
military regime) that the United States intended to send more
men and more planes to South Vietnam. Huong expressed his
nation's thanks. Taylor added that the United States opposed
"neutralization" for South Vietnam. Huong expressed his personal gratitude. Taylor concluded that the United States and
South Vietnam saw eye-to-eye on the need to defeat the Communist insurgency. But, on the two big questions—whether the
U.S. would send large numbers of United States ground troops
to South Vietnam and would begin a systematic bombardment
of North Vietnam—Johnson had reached no final decisions. So
far as it went, Taylor's statement was technically accurate.

At roughly the same time, in late December, Ball flew to
Paris for a long talk with General de Gaulle. Though he was a
known dissenter on Vietnam policy, Ball, a skilled attorney,
argued Johnson's case. The timing of Ball's visit suggests that the
President had already made up his mind to escalate the war but

that he wanted de Gaulle's reaction in advance—one more factor to be thrown into the computation. Ball explained to de Gaulle that the United States wanted an independent South Vietnam, free of Communist control. The North Vietnamese, who were infiltrating men and arms into the South, appeared determined to unify all of Vietnam under their control. This presented Washington with two seeming alternatives: to go on, against heavy odds, trying to build a strong regime in the South that might one day prove capable of rallying popular support and thus defeating the Communists; or to launch a major military campaign against the North with the aim of forcing Hanoi to call off the insurrection in the South. (A third alternative— American withdrawal from South Vietnam—was never mentioned. It had been rejected by the President at the start of the late-1964 policy review.)

Ball then stressed that the United States would attack the North if the President should conclude that it was impossible to build up the South in time. Johnson realized that this course ran the risk of involving the Chinese. But, according to Ball, the President could see no reasonable alternative. Clearly, the President had blended the Taylor-McNamara argument into a single and, in his mind, coherent policy. He preferred, as McNamara did, to limit United States action to South Vietnam. But, if it proved impossible to control the Communist insurrection without going to the "source of the aggression," as Taylor had consistently recommended, then the United States, however reluctantly, would have to carry the war to the North.

De Gaulle argued against Johnson's policy, just as he had argued privately against Kennedy's. He believed that there was little chance of Chinese involvement in Indochina. He was, however, sympathetic with the President's problems in Vietnam and suggested that Johnson press for a cease-fire in South Vietnam and for negotiations leading to a political solution—*i.e.*, a coalition government. Later on, East and West could get together and agree to "neutralize" all of Southeast Asia.

Ball replied that such a course would be utterly unacceptable to the Saigon regime. A cease-fire would only help the Communists, and negotiations would facilitate the creation of a coalition government. The United States, Ball added, was committed to helping the South Vietnamese resist Communist aggression.

On this note of irreconcilability, Ball departed. When he returned to Washington and reported to Rusk and Johnson, he sensed that the President's attitude toward the war had hardened during his absence. Later Ball learned that the President had already instructed McNamara, as part of the Pentagon's contingency planning, to make logistical preparations for a massive American military buildup in and around South Vietnam. It was clear from Taylor's alarming cables that the Saigon regime could not last much longer, so the ground rules governing the war had to be changed. The North, so Taylor argued, would have to be attacked—if for no other reason than to bolster Saigon's vanishing will to resist. Taylor stressed that air attacks, on a sensible and systematic basis, could reduce enemy infiltration into the South and make life extremely difficult for the North. But, most important, they would give the South new hope. Ball came to realize that the President had made up his mind to bomb the North, although the official record showed no decision, not yet. No decision was final until the President announced it. It is therefore literally impossible to define the exact moment of Lyndon Johnson's 1965 decision to escalate the Vietnam war. It is possible to mark dates on a calendar that show the end products of his idiosyncratic method of decision-making, but they tell little about the process itself. McGeorge Bundy, an adviser to both Presidents Kennedy and Johnson, thought that both men protected their options up to the last possible moment but that Johnson was an "extreme case of guarding one's hand." Johnson said to one senior adviser that he would probably have to bomb the North, to another that he probably would not, and to a third that he had not made up his mind.

To clarify the President's choices, McNamara decided in mid-January to draft a memo outlining every possible course of action. Bundy helped with the drafting. The President had, they felt, three basic options. He could, first of all, decide for a political solution, based on the Laos agreements. That would almost certainly lead to a coalition government, and the total withdrawal of American power from the area. He could, second, start a limited air war against North Vietnam and, at the same time, modestly increase the number of American advisers in the South. That would seem to be a policy of "more of the same," which had not proved a shining success in the past. Finally, he could massively increase the number of American troops in South Vietnam; and, behind that shield of American power, on the ground and in the air, Saigon might be able to pull itself together and create a viable government. McNamara stressed that this course of action would be the most difficult. Neither he nor Bundy made any specific recommendation as they submitted the memo to the President on January 25.

Johnson made no immediate decisions of consequence—or so it seemed to his advisers. He sent McGeorge Bundy to Saigon for a quick indoctrination course. Bundy, though a senior adviser to both Presidents since 1961, had not visited South Vietnam. It was in his absence, late in January, that Washington officials began to "smell" a presidential decision. There were more than the usual number of secret meetings and "eyes only" cables. Reporters found old friends in the State and Defense departments remarkably uncommunicative. Early in February Soviet Premier Aleksei Kosygin arrived in Hanoi. Certain Washington experts speculated that the Russians, having reason to expect a Communist victory in South Vietnam, wanted to steal a march on the Chinese by getting to Ho Chi Minh first. India's Prime Minister Lal Bahadur Shastri proposed Soviet-American talks on Southeast Asia. Johnson politely declined. He obviously felt this was not the time for a "political solution." Within the context of the McNamara memorandum, which insiders began to call the "fork in the Y" memo, the President was eliminating Option 1. Neither Option 2 nor 3 especially pleased him. But he tended toward Option 2, perhaps because it was not as extreme or wrenching as No. 3.

This was his frame of mind on February 7, 1965. Kosygin was in Hanoi and Bundy was touring the South Vietnamese countryside when the Viet Cong attacked United States military installations in the provincial capital of Pleiku. It was the third time in recent months that the Communists had struck at American bases. This was interpreted in Washington as a major change in strategy, requiring a major change in American strategy. This time, Washington was prepared to move.

For several weeks before the attack at Pleiku, as the President's mind drifted unhappily toward Option 2, American and South Vietnamese commanders in Saigon had been preparing for an air campaign against North Vietnam. This was considered part of the contingency planning. The exercise heartened Saigon's squabbling politicians and generals. Some targets were recommended and approved. When the President received word of the Pleiku attack, he summoned an emergency meeting of the National Security Council. The contingency plan for an allied attack against "barracks and staging areas" in the southern part of North Vietnam only then received the President's final approval. Orders were flashed to Saigon, and within a couple of hours, American and South Vietnamese planes, their bomb bays fully loaded, were on their way. The allies bombed "military areas" only—areas that were "supplying men and arms for attacks in South Vietnam," so the White House promptly announced.

The announcement, confirming another step toward the "wider war" no one wanted, stated that the allied bombing response was both "appropriate" and "fitting." Although the White House, as customary, vowed that the United States "seeks no wider war," it added: "Whether or not this course can be maintained lies with the North Vietnamese aggressors." With the benefit of 20-20 hindsight, it is now clear that the United States was suggesting that American ground troops might be sent to Indochina, if the Communists persisted in their "course of aggression."

At the time, however, State and Defense department officials, who briefed reporters about the February 7 and 8 air attacks, strenuously denied any intention to send combat forces. They conveyed a different picture to newsmen and, through them, to the American people. The raid was described as limited in intent and scope—a "reprisal" attack, nothing more, similar to to the one-shot Tonkin reprisal. Most senior officials believed that a gradual buildup of American military pressure against

North Vietnam would slowly bring Hanoi to the realization that victory was impossible. A formal end to the conflict would be as unnecessary as a declaration of war; Hanoi would just "stop doing what it is doing," as Rusk so often put it.

The gradual buildup raised Saigon's morale, above all, though Rusk and McNamara, in public or privately, put the stress on three other factors. The bombing, they claimed, would reduce enemy infiltration of men and supplies; it would hurt the enemy; and it might persuade him to negotiate.

The adversary had his own plans. On February 10 the Viet Cong assaulted an American billet in the coastal town of Qui Nhon, killing at least twenty-three soldiers. Coming so soon after the first American and South Vietnamese bombings of the North, this looked like an act of calculated defiance. Hours after the billet assault, allied planes were flying north on a new bombing raid—that day and the next day too. The Communists seemed to defy intimidation. Their propaganda made much of the Qui Nhon attack and promised more of the same. As a precaution, the United States Embassy in Saigon, on Rusk's orders, began to evacuate American dependents. In Hanoi, Kosygin promised "all-out Soviet aid" to North Vietnam, if the Americans should invade the North. The Chinese, somewhat outflanked, went a step further. They promised to send troops into North Vietnam, should the Americans invade.

The world began to tremble. Indian diplomats called for reconvening of the Geneva Conference. Washington and Moscow responded ambiguously. Peking rejected the proposal. Hanoi said the war could end if the Americans went home; Washington said the war could end if the Communists would go home. The air was filled with charges—countercharges; proposals—counterproposals; propaganda—counterpropaganda. Step by step the United States moved deeper into a major military commitment. But Johnson insisted his purpose was peace. A week after Pleiku and Qui Nhon he told some visitors that he still believed in negotiations. Somewhat overstating the case, he said: "There's a small percentage that wants to bomb Hanoi and there's a small percentage that wants to get out. But I'm the ringleader of a peace settlement." In those days the President was easily upset,

particularly by reporters who took a grave view of the bombing.
Johnson ridiculed their talk of a crisis in South Vietnam. Nonsense, the President would shout; "They woke us up in the
middle of the night, and we woke them up in the middle of the
night. Then they did it again, and we did it again."

On February 28, after repeated enemy harassment of American and South Vietnamese bases, the President decided to maintain "continuous" though "limited" air strikes against North
Vietnam. United States officials explained that there was simply
no other way to bring Hanoi to its senses.

Although the bombing improved Saigon's morale, it did
nothing to improve the anti-Communist position through South
Vietnam. There was a special problem in I Corps, the northernmost province of the country. Communist troops roamed the
countryside at will. South Vietnamese forces, even with American advisers, were incapable of stopping them. General Westmoreland feared the Communists might move against Da Nang,
and warned that he did not have the manpower to stop them.
He felt the situation was so critical that the United States ought
quickly to send a couple of Marine battalions, roughly 3500 men,
to Da Nang, if only for limited duty. Otherwise, he could not
insure the security of I Corps. Johnson was still resisting the idea
of sending American ground troops into South Vietnam. Taylor
was also uneasy about this idea. "Once you put that first soldier
ashore," he later told friends, "you never know how many others
are going to have to follow him."

For a time, despite Westmoreland's pressure, Taylor managed to keep the Marines off the Asian mainland. They were to
be kept "afloat, just over the horizon" as a warning to the Communists. But the VC continued to tighten their noose around
Da Nang. Westmoreland again warned that Da Nang would
fall unless Taylor relented. He urged the President to allow an
impressive amphibious assault, Normandy-style, on the beaches
near Da Nang. This warning cracked the White House attitude
of calculated coolness toward any further military escalation.
In early March the President flashed the green light. On March
6, two combat-ready battalions of United States Marines waded
ashore unopposed near Da Nang. Taylor stressed that they were

there for "defensive purposes only," that their mission was "limited." The White House echoed this line. So did the State Department and the Pentagon. One presidential adviser soothed an anxious reporter: "Don't worry," he said softly, "this President is not about to get involved in a land war in Asia. He is just not going to do it."

Yet it was happening before everyone's eyes. "It was almost imperceptible, the way we got in," another presidential adviser told Philip Geyelin then of *The Wall Street Journal:* "There was no one move that you could call decisive, or irreversible, not even very many actions that you could argue against in isolation. Yet when you put it all together, there we were in a war on the Asian mainland, with nobody really putting up much of a squawk while we were doing it."

This creeping realization was a kind of monument to Johnson's method: his sad delusion that a carefully calibrated escalation of the war would surely convince Hanoi to "stop doing what it is doing" (over and over again one heard that "it worked in Cuba"); and his political sleight of hand in mounting a major escalation seemingly without public alarm or opposition. Not until a couple of years had passed, when the casualty lists lengthened and the war's cost became monumental, did Vietnam, as a political and economic issue, come home to roost.

In 1965, the year the escalation began, the United States was widening the war while denying that anything had changed. The contrast between word and deed produced the Johnson Administration's famous credibility gap. When the Marines landed at Da Nang, Rusk said their mission was to provide "local close-in security." McNamara said they would "patrol within narrow limits" and "should not tangle with the enemy." But, as their numbers grew and their activities broadened, they did tangle with the enemy. It was unavoidable. The tangling was officially defined as "combat-support," a step up from "close-in support." But Rusk, McNamara, and the rest all denied that this represented a change in the United States mission. When the State Department's spokesman, Robert McCloskey, bravely attempted to define "combat-support" and, in the process, acknowledged that U.S. troops had engaged in "combat," the

White House exploded. "There has been no change," the White House spokesman said, on Johnson's personal order, "in the mission of the U.S. ground combat units in Vietnam in recent days or weeks." When the dust settled, in early June, there were about 50,000 American troops in South Vietnam. But the White House continued to insist there had been no change in policy, no change in "mission."

It was a transparent lie. More and more American troops went into battle as more and more South Vietnamese troops left the battle. Defection rates were at an all-time high. Entire ARVN units were being cut up and destroyed. Nothing stood in the way of a smashing Communist victory in South Vietnam except that handful of American troops and advisers. By June 28 they were fighting the Communists on their own. They had no choice. It became painfully embarrassing for reporters to listen almost daily to repeated White House denials that United States troops were engaged in combat. The military situation had sharply deteriorated. If the Marines and GI's were not engaged in combat, their presence served no useful purpose. And if they *were* engaged in combat—leaving aside the morality of denying the obvious truth—they were too few to do the job.

By every indicator available to the White House, the war in Vietnam was being lost at a terrifying pace. The President, desperately anxious for peace but stubbornly sticking to his "commitments," tried to strike a peace theme as he led the nation into its most mistaken war. In his Johns Hopkins University speech of April 7, he offered North Vietnam a generous peace—one billion dollars in postwar economic aid to Southeast Asia, including North Vietnam. Hanoi scornfully rejected his Texas-scale offer. For six days in May, from the 13th to the 19th, he suspended air attacks against North Vietnam. This was to be the first in a series of long and short bombing "pauses," designed to produce some flexibility in Hanoi's apparently fixed policy aim of taking over the South. In late June he gave his reluctant blessing to a British Commonwealth peace mission. Johnson, in other words, made a demonstrative though unconvincing effort to explore the possibility of a settlement. Hanoi, in return, brushed aside the overtures and pressed its military advantage throughout South Vietnam. Johnson understood. If he had possessed Hanoi's advantage, he would almost certainly have pressed it too. In his mind, at the time, there was little doubt that Hanoi intended to "humiliate" and "humble" the United States. As President, a Texan raised on the legends of the Rangers, he simply would not have it.*

The President was in a foul mood, in any case. He had, just a month before, ordered thousands of American troops into the Dominican Republic in a shoot-from-the-hip reaction to the possibility of a leftist, though not necessarily Communist, takeover by followers of Juan Bosch. His explanation was that American citizens in the Dominican Republic might be in danger. The explanation helped stretch the President's credibility gap all the way from Southeast Asia to the Caribbean. A thousand American Marines could easily have insured the safe evacuation of all Americans from the Dominican Republic. When the President dispatched 28,000 troops, it was obvious he had a larger political purpose in mind, one he did not share with the American people. Again, the commentators criticized the President, and some began to question his judgment. It was his handling of the Dominican crisis—not Vietnam—that led to the President's first confrontation with his critics. He lost Senator Fulbright and part of the Eastern Establishment. It bothered him. For weeks he was moody, touchy, worried.

At the same time there was the distinct possibility that the

---

* In those days of all-but-total presidential preoccupation with war-or-peace decisions, Professor Henry Graff of Columbia University managed to see Johnson and certain of his aides. In his book, *The Tuesday Cabinet*, the historian recounts a conversation with the President, who had "one leg draped over the arm of his chair, a glass of root beer in his hand." He said to Graff: "The worst mistake we ever made was getting rid of Diem." As Vice-President, Johnson had opposed the anti-Diem movement within the administration. As President, he believed his crucial problem was how to stop the Chinese Communists, those "yellow hordes," from grabbing Southeast Asia. "What will be enough and not too much?" he said to Graff. "I know the other side is winning; so do they, too. No man wants to trade when he's winning. In this case, we have to apply the maximum deterrent till he sobers up and unloads his pistol."

Graff also reports a conversation with Dean Rusk to the effect that "dictatorships underestimate democracy's willingness to do what it had to do." Rusk conceded that "perhaps the Communist world misunderstood our presidential campaign." The President kept saying that he did not want a wider war, Rusk reflected, and yet the Communist side believed *it* could widen the war without penalty.

war in Southeast Asia was slipping out of his control. Were he another kind of President, more secure about his place in history, he might have decided, then and there, to let the war slip slowly, while he manufactured a face-saving political alternative. Nicholas deB. Katzenbach, then Attorney General, believes that Kennedy, had he lived and won re-election, might have chosen this sort of policy alternative. Kennedy had proved himself by his cool handling of the Cuban missile crisis. But Johnson, with no similar triumph in foreign affairs, was forever proving his manhood. Besides, he sincerely believed that a Communist victory in South Vietnam would be a calamity for the overall American position in Asia. He was determined to stamp himself a great President who had protected freedom abroad while assuring equality at home. In the end his vision of greatness became a casualty of his own decisions in Vietnam.

In late June Johnson received a gloomy report from Paul Nitze, then Secretary of the Navy, a cool and trusted veteran of many Korean War decisions. For one week, in mid-June, Nitze had traveled from Da Nang, to Saigon, to the Delta, checking not only on Navy installations but also on the general military situation. In Da Nang he saw that the Marines controlled a three-mile perimeter on one side of the air base and a half-mile perimeter on the other side. A small town north of the base was under Viet Cong control. The countryside was under Viet Cong control. In Da Nang itself, Viet Cong infiltration was considerable. In the Delta, ARVN was losing two or three army battalions every week. Security was virtually nonexistent. In Saigon the political decay was obvious. In Nitze's mind, it was China all over again: an unstable government in the capital, a dedicated Communist enemy spreading his control over the countryside.

When he returned to Washington, Nitze told McNamara that, in his judgment, the war was just about lost. It would take "an absolutely immense effort," he said, to salvage the crumbling Saigon government. Even if the President decided to make that effort—and if he were President, Nitze said, he would not —he "doubted very much" whether the United States could get a sufficiently large and effective fighting force into South Vietnam in time to prevent a Communist victory.

McNamara asked Nitze: "What do you think the effect will be if we let this whole thing collapse?" Nitze answered: "Very bad indeed!" He thought for a while, then added: "I just know it is going to be bad either way."

The President agonized over that July Fourth weekend. He frequently called the War Room in the White House basement for up-to-the-minute information. Just as frequently he called some of his old Capitol Hill cronies and asked for their advice. He took the Nitze report seriously, but he questioned whether the United States could or should allow a Communist victory in South Vietnam. He seemed constitutionally unable to accept so bleak an outcome to the "twilight struggle" in Southeast Asia.

On July 8 Johnson announced that Henry Cabot Lodge had agreed to return to Saigon as United States Ambassador, replacing Maxwell Taylor, who remained skeptical about the wisdom of a major American troop commitment. Old-time Johnson watchers might have known that Lodge's return meant the President had all but decided to send tens of thousands, perhaps hundreds of thousands, more troops to South Vietnam. Johnson's political instincts told him that the best way to make sure of broad bipartisan support, even as he so greatly increased the scale of America's commitment in a war that was going so badly, had to be through the appointment of a prominent Republican as ambassador to Saigon. At a news conference, two days later, Johnson pledged "our power and our honor" to the defense of South Vietnam. Coincidentally or not, thousands of fresh American troops started to arrive in Saigon on July 12. Soon there would be 70,000 American troops in Vietnam, one staff officer announced.

On July 13 McNamara accompanied Lodge to Saigon. McNamara had not been there in fourteen months. His private instructions from the President were to find out what more was needed to stave off a Communist victory; how many more troops, planes, guns, Jeeps. The public story was that Johnson had still not made up his mind.

The following day, McNamara met with Lodge, Taylor, General Westmoreland, and Nguyen Cao Ky, the flamboyant new leader of South Vietnam, to begin an urgent review of military problems. The review lasted the better part of a week. On his departure from Saigon, McNamara conceded the obvious. "In many respects," he said at the airport, "there has been a deterioration"; but the United States would live up to its obligations in South Vietnam.

When he returned to Washington, McNamara thought long and hard about his recommendations to the President. Then he proposed a massive inflow of American troops to save the country from Communist control. He believed that he could get the troops there in time, despite Nitze's reservations. The President asked: "How many men will you need?" Only then, it seems, did McNamara realize that the President had decided to take the plunge. McNamara replied that the President would have to send approximately 115,000 additional troops before the end of the year. He would also have to make ready another 115,000-man contingent to be sent early in 1966. In all, he recommended that, by the middle of 1966, American troop strength in South Vietnam should peak at about 380,000 men. It was McNamara's practice to plot current strategy on the basis of successful precedent. In late July, 1965, his precedent was Kennedy's handling of the Berlin summer crisis of 1961. Accordingly, he recommended that the President appear on television to explain the war to the people—and then announce the calling up of the reserves together with a tax increase. Such an approach had worked in 1961 with Khrushchev. It might work in 1965 with Ho. McNamara believed that only in this coordinated, dramatic fashion could Hanoi be made to understand that the United States had determined to pay the necessary price in order to get an acceptable peace in South Vietnam.

Paul Warnke, a top Pentagon planner in those days, believed that McNamara's rcommendations made good sense. Like most administration officials, Warnke had no doubt in 1965 that if the United States seriously applied its military power in South Vietnam it could defeat the Communists. Dean Rusk had his doubts—not about the commitment of troops but about the relative ease with which military victory could be won. Characteristically, he kept his doubts to himself. So overwhelming was this sense of official confidence in American power that the President's policy, when finally formulated, left little room for an improved war effort by the South. No one had much faith in ARVN; let the United States get on with the job. Ky argued against this slighting of his own forces, but he was ignored. Not until three years later, after the Tet offensive had shattered many illusions, did the United States conscientiously begin a modest program of Vietnamization, later to be adopted and extended by the Nixon Administration.

The President, as always in moments of high drama, listened quietly and carefully to McNamara's recommendations. He agreed that the United States could and should stop the Communists in South Vietnam. According to one account, he delivered a short speech about how the United States had fought back from Pearl Harbor to eventual victory over Japan and how it was not in the American character to accept defeat. He also agreed to send the 115,000 additional troops to South Vietnam before the end of the year and to ready an equal contingent to be sent early the following year. But he wondered whether the extra contingent would be needed. McNamara expressed the hope that it would not. Having accepted McNamara's military assessment, he refused unalterably to disturb his Great Society. He would not make a speech about the war. He would not call up the reserves or raise taxes. Johnson obviously underestimated his problems, just as McNamara consistently underestimated Hanoi's will to resist. This quality of underestimating difficulties plagued the Johnson Administration to the end. McNamara, to his credit, raised a *sotto voce* objection when the President refused to take the necessary steps to raise money for the expanding war in Vietnam. He cautioned that big wars require big money. Johnson concluded the meeting by complimenting McNamara in a jocular way on his genius for organization—implying that if anyone could raise an army and run a war without raising taxes and risking wild inflation, McNamara was that man.

In this way, Lyndon Johnson took his second major decision on Vietnam in 1965. It was a painful decision, in view of Johnson's campaign promise that he would not send American boys to fight Asian wars. Yet there he was, a peaceable Democrat pursuing a Goldwater policy. The contrast between word and deed rankled with the President. He kept insisting that his goal was peace, even though he had to wage war. And he underscored his fidelity to the Great Society programs by pressing on with them as though Vietnam did not exist. He was determined to have guns *and* butter.

For a time he appeared to succeed. General Westmoreland brilliantly organized a logistical system for the steadily expanding American military presence in South Vietnam. By October 23, 1965, there were 148,300 American troops there. By March 2, 1966, there were 215,000. By December 31 the head count was 389,000, exceeding McNamara's far-out estimate of July, 1965. By June 22, 1967, 463,000 Americans were bogged down in Vietnam. And, on August 3, after a drawn-out struggle between Westmoreland and McNamara, Johnson announced that he had fixed a "maximum limit" of 524,000 U.S. troops by early 1968— somewhere around Tet time.

Bill Moyers, who sat at the President's right hand through this period, was troubled by what he calls "the element of incremental policy-making," which made each step in the process of escalation appear inexorable. "With but rare exceptions," Moyers said, in a 1968 *Atlantic* interview, "we always seemed to be calculating the short-term consequences of each alternative at every step of the process, but not the long-term consequences. And with each succeeding short range consequence we became more deeply a prisoner of the process."

It was not only the "long-term consequences" that the President and his top advisers tended to ignore; it was also the very nature of the war that they consistently miscalculated. Many years later, in late 1970, shortly before his retirement, General Lewis Walt, a battle-toughened Deputy Commandant of the Marine Corps, confessed that he knew very little about guerrilla warfare when he led the Marines into Da Nang. Once, he recounted, he entered a village and talked with the chief, who struck him as a nice, cooperative old man. When Walt left, another villager informed him that the old man was the local leader of the Viet Cong. Walt was astonished. "He seemed so nice," he said. There were countless other examples of American naïveté, ignorance, guilelessness. Back in Washington, McNamara talked knowingly about guerrilla warfare; out in Vietnam, General Walt learned the hard way that before you could win a guerrilla war you had to learn the ABCs of it.

Nevertheless, within one year after this phenomenal escalation began, the United States had achieved its minimal military objective. On August 13, 1966, General Westmoreland, dressed in his most splendid dress uniform, returned to the United States for two days of Texas ranch talk with the President. Westmoreland proudly reported to his Commander-in-Chief that a Communist military victory in South Vietnam was, by then, "impossible." He did not predict an Allied victory. In fact, the President cautioned the American people not to expect a "quick victory." But his note of caution revealed that the United States, having sent a major expeditionary force to South Vietnam, had raised its military sights once again to contemplate defeating the Communists in South Vietnam, not quickly perhaps but in the fullness of time.

Over the next year and a half progress was reported throughout the country. When Westmoreland returned to Washington on November 15, 1967, for more consultations, he told newsmen: "I have never been more encouraged in my four years in Vietnam." In an appearance before the National Press Club, the bemedaled general was bursting with optimism. "We have reached an important point," he stated, "when the end begins to come into view." Westmoreland gave ARVN high grades. He predicted that he would soon be able to turn "a major share of front-line DMZ defense over to the Vietnamese Army." Within two years, he predicted, the President could begin to withdraw American forces from South Vietnam, as the GIs "became superfluous."

But the war was not going well in the United States. The national will to carry on the fight was failing. The enemy played on this crucial fact, determined to weary the United States, just as the French had wearied and lost their will to fight in 1954. "In evaluating the enemy strategy," Westmoreland declared on April 28, 1967, "it is evident to me that he believes our Achilles heel is our resolve." It took no special insight to arrive at that conclusion.

One could say the erosion began on August 19, 1965, when the Pentagon announced, for the first time, that 561 American troops had been killed in action in South Vietnam—most of them in the last few months. It may have begun on October 15, 1965, when David J. Miller, a twenty-two-year-old Catholic relief worker, burned his draft card. Or on November 2, 1965, when Norman R. Morrison, a thirty-two-year-old Quaker from Baltimore, committed suicide by fire on the steps of the Pentagon to express his concern over "the great loss of life and human suffering caused by the war in Vietnam."

Early in 1966, Chairman Fulbright's Senate Foreign Relations Committee opened its historic round of televised hearings on the Vietnam war. The Arkansas Democrat, who less than two years earlier had steered the Tonkin Resolution through the Senate, turned on the President and the war. His opposition became a rallying point for other dissidents and in time made antiwar sentiments respectable on Capitol Hill.

Lieutenant General James Gavin (retired) questioned the administration's "search and destroy" operations in South Vietnam. He advocated an "enclave" strategy. U.S. forces should pull back into fortified enclaves and, rather than pursue a military victory, build up the South Vietnamese forces and wait for the enemy to accept a political settlement.

Former Ambassador George Kennan questioned the administration's diplomatic strategy. He said that South Vietnam was not a "vital interest" of the United States, no matter how often high administration officials contended that it was. The war ought to be liquidated as quickly as possible, Kennan argued, so the United States could focus on "potentially more important" problem areas.

Senator Robert Kennedy, a constant threat to LBJ's political future, stimulated antiwar pressures on Capitol Hill by questioning the administration's priorities. Why spend billions on a questionable war?, Kennedy asked, when there were so many domestic needs being starved for lack of interest and money.

The more doubts were raised, the more did the Johnson Administration deny any reason for doubt. Those who "counsel retreat," Johnson exclaimed, "belong to a group that has always been blind to experience and deaf to hope." The doves, many of whom counseled retreat, thought the administration was being blind and deaf. Whenever the Communists would drop a hint, however insubstantial, that if the U.S. stopped the bombing they might consider peace talks, the doves fluttered wildly. The hawks considered every "peace feeler" a trap. The administration choked off some "feelers," checked out others. But the war dragged on and on.

The hopelessness and endlessness of it all, the total frustration of fighting a resourceful enemy whose strongest ally had always been the calendar, depressed many citizens and by summertime, 1967, began to depress some officials within the administration. Ironically, the germ of disaffection struck first at the Pentagon—more precisely, at the cool, composed Secretary of Defense. McNamara lost heart in his war and thus lost the confidence of his President. As disaffection spread, the President became more and more isolated, leaning on the optimists among his generals and diplomats in the field, listening less and less to those who felt there was something tragically wrong with the whole business.

SEVEN

Exit Robert McNamara

By THE LATE SUMMER OF 1967 the President and the country
were in deep trouble. Johnson's notion that America was rich
enough to fight a major war in Southeast Asia and, at the same
time, build a Great Society at home without raising taxes looked
more and more like a shabby politician's trick; or, at best, a case
of sloppy presidential management. The war was beginning to
distort and deform the national economy. Inflation in that hot,
muggy summer was racing, like an automobile with a jammed
throttle. The American dollar, the basic international currency,
suddenly looked vulnerable to European speculators. The notori-
ous gnomes of Zurich, according to the financial newspapers,
were unloading paper dollars for gold.

The war was taking its moral toll, too. Churchmen assembled in Washington to urge the President to stop the bombing. They saw a link between licensed killing by Americans in
Vietnam and the newly emerging pattern of unlicensed racial
violence, verging on urban guerrilla war, in the great cities of
the United States. More and more churchmen started sermon-
izing against the war and denouncing the President from their
pulpits.

Even in the President's official family there were stirrings of
psychological defection. The doves were anguished that the war
should drag on with no significant move to negotiate peace. The
hawks too were troubled because, in their view, the generals
were not being allowed to win by piling on more bombs. Robert
McNamara, chief architect of the Vietnam strategy, had more
reason than others to be torn by doubt. He had sincerely be-

lieved that a rational, measured application of American power would in time persuade Hanoi's stubborn leadership that negotiated peace was a better bargain than continued warfare. But, like many another Washington official, McNamara had consistently misread Hanoi's intentions, failing to understand its drive and dedication, its unwillingness to be measured by the charts and statistics in his own Pentagon office. The Defense Secretary—like Rusk and the President—constantly underestimated Hanoi's simple will to resist; he also grossly overestimated the capacity of a nuclear power, hypnotized by a vague "commitment," to influence political developments in a small and backward Asian country with bombs and bullets.

As the American casualty figures went up month by month, and the bombing continued to no conclusive effect, the Secretary of Defense began to question his own strategy. It was a painful business. The President would not hear of changing policy, and McNamara, deeply troubled by his own responsibility for the original policy, could not bring himself to consider resigning. Averell Harriman, a close friend, traces McNamara's disenchantment back to several months after the start of the bombing. "As early as late December, 1965," Harriman recalls, "McNamara was urging the President to extend the bombing halt beyond the thirty-seven-day period." Paul Warnke remembers that "the consistent voice for limiting the bombing and stopping the bombing was McNamara." Only his intense loyalty to the President kept McNamara from making known his doubts and hesitations for many an anguishing month. More than once during that stretch of self-enforced silence he discussed with Pentagon associates one plan or another for scaling down or halting the bombing. But nothing more would be heard of the plan after he had put it to the President. McNamara's rectitude about respecting presidential confidences was overpowering, a quality he shared to a degree with Dean Rusk.

A few close friends—the Harrimans, Robert and Ethel Kennedy, and others—sensed that he was under intolerable strain. But McNamara kept his silence, refusing to break with the President even when his most careful recommendations were rejected. Not until the summer of 1967 did McNamara make known his disenchantment in a resounding, public way. In August of that year, Senator John Stennis summoned eleven witnesses before the Preparedness Subcommittee of his Senate Armed Services Committee to answer questions about the war, specifically, why it was not being won. Ten of the witnesses were admirals and generals. Without exception they called for more and heavier bombing with fewer civilian-imposed targeting restrictions. Several argued passionately for permission to bomb the North Vietnamese port of Haiphong.

The eleventh witness, McNamara, patiently explained how he had come to believe that Hanoi could simply not be "bombed to the negotiating table": North Vietnam was a primitive, chiefly agricultural, country possessing few industrial or military targets. Its transport system was so diversified (the human back or the bicycle was used to move heavy loads considerable distances) that bombing could never knock it out. Carefully calculating the capacity of its ports and railroads, McNamara found that no more than 14,000 tons of goods a day could be landed in the country, although North Vietnam in fact was importing only 5800 tons. Of this total, it needed to shift no more than 100 tons a day to keep its men fighting in the South. He saw no way of cutting off this tiny trickle through bombing.

The tragic and long-drawn-out character of that conflict in the South [McNamara testified] makes very tempting the prospect of replacing it with some new kind of air campaign against the North. But, however tempting, such an alternative seems to me illusory. To pursue this objective would not only be futile but would involve risks to our personnel and to our nation that I am unable to recommend.

To the Senate hawks this was pure heresy; to the increasing flock of Senate doves, plain common sense. President Johnson, still dedicated to the proposition that continued bombing must bring Hanoi to the conference table, was not pleased by McNamara's testimony. He wrote it down to a loss of nerve caused by prolonged fatigue. On November 28, Washington was startled to learn that McNamara would be getting a new job as president of the International Bank for Reconstruction and Development. It was not that the bank lacked a president at the time. George Woods was in the job, and the directors had already voted to extend his term until December 31, 1968. The White House staff put out the story that Johnson had been moved by simple compassion to find a congenial job for his loyal, exhausted Secretary of Defense. The story convinced few people. It was clear that McNamara had been dumped, a victim of presidential disfavor. It was not that LBJ had ruled out any change in Vietnam policy. He was, at the time, dabbling with a number of possible alternatives, including a reduction in the bombing and his own withdrawal from the presidential contest. But he could not stomach the idea that McNamara, of all officials, should be venting his doubts in public, perhaps encouraging others in the administration to follow his example. Johnson, always insecure, felt comfortable only when every man in the orchestra followed his beat. And the administration line that fall was that the war was going very well; in fact, never better.

Like other Presidents, Johnson enjoyed being told that he was right, especially by the right people: for example, by the Senior Advisory Group on Vietnam, known less reverently as The Wise Men, The Old Men, or the Council of Elders. This was an informal assemblage of distinguished former officials, retired generals, ambassadors, and other Establishment figures who had been meeting with the President at his request once or twice a year since 1965.

These were big, successful men, the kind of men whose approval Lyndon Johnson craved: Clark Clifford, for example; Dean Acheson; former Under Secretary of State George W. Ball; General Omar Bradley; McGeorge Bundy, now president of the Ford Foundation; Douglas Dillon, former Secretary of the Treasury; Arthur H. Dean, law partner of the late John Foster Dulles and Korean armistice negotiator; Henry Cabot Lodge; John J. McCloy, former United States High Commissioner in Germany; Robert D. Murphy, retired career ambassador; General Matthew B. Ridgeway, former Army Chief of Staff; and General Maxwell Taylor.

The President was greatly reassured when this blue-ribbon panel met in November, found that the war was going well and, with the single exception of George Ball, endorsed the administration's Vietnam policy. Ball's dissent, being predictable, was easily dismissed. As Dean Rusk said of his former Under Secretary, who for years past had functioned as a kind of licensed gadfly within the foreign-policy establishment: "George started out as the devil's advocate and he wound up persuading himself." However, the President's confidence that he could see daylight at the end of the tunnel was not fully shared by the American people. In November, 1967, the Gallup Poll found that 57 percent disapproved of Johnson's handling of the war. Only 28 percent approved. As the casualties mounted, so also did the congressional mail reflecting unsuspected new depths of antiwar feeling across the land. Senator Thruston Morton, a Kentucky Republican who had never before criticized the war, joined Senators Clifford Case of New Jersey and John Sherman Cooper of Kentucky in denouncing the President's policies. They saw no hope for a negotiated settlement until the United States stopped the bombing. Senator Eugene McCarthy had spoken out against the war; also Senator Robert Kennedy. More and more conservative newspapers started publishing critical editorials.

The President, in those days, kept thinking of himself as George Washington at Valley Forge. He was fond of historical parallels. Walt Rostow, who understood this, could be relied upon to remind his chief that other great wartime leaders had been criticized and condemned for doing the right things, particularly Lincoln. Rostow used to recount Lincoln's sufferings during the Civil War, when casualties mounted, and popular anguish deepened, and the war seemed endless; and yet, in time, victory was won. In November, 1967, the President revealed the effect of Rostow's coaching, when he told reporters:

I don't need to remind you what happened in the Civil War. People were here in the White House begging Lincoln to concede and to work out a deal with the Confederacy when word came of his victories. . . . I think you know what Roosevelt went through, and President Wilson in World War I. . . . No one likes war. All people love peace. But you can't have freedom without defending it.

At this point Johnson decided to call home General Westmoreland and Ambassador Ellsworth Bunker by way of persuading an increasingly skeptical public that the war was going well.

Bunker, a quiet Vermont Democrat, sounded quietly optimistic. From him the public got no premature victory claims, just figures and more figures of steady progress on every front. General Westmoreland, far less restrained, reported to the National Press Club that the war had been turned around.

"Whereas in 1965 the enemy was winning," Westmoreland said, "today he is certainly losing." The White House passed the word to the television networks that Bunker and Westmoreland were available to tell their story. This official nudge resulted in a number of interviews, culminating in a joint Bunker-Westmoreland appearance on NBC's "Meet The Press."

The general, questioned by Warren Rogers, then of *Look* magazine, said: "We are winning a war of attrition now. . . . We have evidence through our intelligence that the enemy has very serious manpower problems in the South. He is unable to recruit the guerrillas that he needs. He is having destroyed on the battlefield literally thousands of guerrillas on a monthly basis. This manpower cannot be replaced. He has, therefore, had to resort to moving men down from North Vietnam, and we have intelligence that he is having manpower problems now in the North."

The evidence Westmoreland produced was the capture of a seventeen-year-old North Vietnamese in the battle of Loc Ninh and the capture of a thirty-eight-year-old. Rostow was to make a great deal of these two individuals in the weeks to come —proof, as he saw it, that North Vietnam was "scraping the bottom of the barrel."

When Seymour Topping of *The New York Times* asked Westmoreland whether he would need more troops, beyond the 525,000 scheduled for 1968, the general replied: "I believe that a force of 525,000 will put us in an excellent military posture. Based on the situation as I see it now, and as I project, we should continue to grind down the enemy so that he will be progressively weakened."

As for Ambassador Bunker, he reported excellent progress by the South Vietnamese toward democracy. "The will of the South Vietnamese people to continue the war effort is firm, is strong," Bunker said.

The President had no difficulty crediting the optimism of his commanding general and his ambassador in Vietnam. He appeared to believe that the American people would respond, giving him time and elbow room to see the fighting through to its proper conclusion. On the night of November 17, after a White House dinner, Johnson asked Westmoreland to stay behind for a private talk. It lasted more than two hours. Johnson confided to the general that he would probably not be a candidate for re-election in 1968. Westmoreland believed him. He was impressed with Johnson's gravity as he described the incapacity of Woodrow Wilson and Dwight Eisenhower during their second terms in office. The clear implication was that Johnson feared four more years in the White House might bring on a second heart attack. (He had suffered his first in 1955.) Westmoreland flew back to Saigon, saying nothing to any of his associates about that long, late-night conversation with the President.

The general had a war to win. The President left no room for doubt that a victory of sorts was still his goal, his policy "more of the same." A few days before Christmas, when the inevitable speculation started about one more bombing pause, he called a news conference to announce: "We are not going to be so softhearted and pudding-headed as to say that we will stop our half of the war and hope and pray that they stop theirs.'

Johnson's terms for halting the bombing had been stated in a speech at San Antonio, Texas, on September 30, 1967. The United States would stop the air war against the North, Johnson said, only if prompt and productive peace talks would follow. He was prepared to assume that the adversary would "not take advantage" of the cessation of bombing. There was some dispute about the meaning of that cryptic phrase, which may also have puzzled the North Vietnamese leadership. Clark Clifford, for one, designated to succeed McNamara as Defense Secretary on March 1, 1968, was disppointed by Hanoi's lack of response. His disappointment turned to dismay when he discovered what the administration meant by not taking advantage of the cessation.

"I found it was being quietly asserted," Clifford wrote in the July, 1969, issue of *Foreign Affairs*, "that, in return for a bombing cessation in the North, the North Vietnamese must stop sending men and matériel into South Vietnam. On the surface, this might have seemed a fair exchange. To me it was an unfortunate interpretation that—intentionally or not—rendered the San Antonio formula virtually meaningless. The North Vietnamese had more than 100,000 men in the South. It was totally unrealistic to expect them to abandon their men by not replacing casualties, and by failing to provide them with clothing, food, munitions, and other supplies. We could never expect them to accept an offer to negotiate on those conditions."

Clifford, a pillar of the Washington Establishment, had long been a friend and counselor to Johnson. Though in private law practice since the end of the Truman era, Clifford had done odd jobs for Kennedy as well as Johnson. As chairman of the Foreign Intelligence Advisory Board and a true believer in the necessity of substantially increasing the American commitment in Vietnam, he had visited Southeast Asia in 1965. The hopeful reports of American and Vietnamese officials confirmed his confidence in the essential correctness of Johnson's policy. He had opposed the thirty-seven-day bombing halt, considering that Hanoi might read it as a sign of weakness.

Yet Clifford was to surprise those in high places, Johnson particularly, who looked for a genuine hawk to replace the dovish McNamara. He too had experienced the first flutters of doubting in the late summer of 1967. Clifford at the President's request had flown to Vietnam with Maxwell Taylor, and on from there to other allied capitals. In South Vietnam Clifford and Taylor heard all over again how the enemy was hurting badly, thanks to the bombing and superior American firepower on the ground. From Saigon, they flew to Thailand, the Philippines, South Korea, New Zealand, and Australia. Clifford's mission was to persuade each of the Allies, with Taylor's help, that the time had come to send more of their own troops to Vietnam. Thailand had all of 2500 men in Vietnam, and, as Clifford and Taylor soon discovered, was in no hurry to commit more. The Philippines, so close and ostensibly so vulnerable (if there was any

substance in the domino theory), preferred that Clifford and
Taylor stay away from Manila. President Marcos warned Johnson that the public reaction might be unfavorable. South Korea
refused to send more troops because the North Koreans were
making trouble. In Australia, Prime Minister Holt presented a
long list of reasons why Australia could not increase its troop
commitment. New Zealand, which had raised 70,000 troops for
overseas service in World War II, had only 500 men in Vietnam
and was not about to send more.

"I returned home," Clifford wrote, "puzzled, troubled, concerned. Was it possible that our assessment of the danger to the
stability of Southeast Asia and the Western Pacific was exaggerated? Was it possible that those nations which were
neighbors of Vietnam had a clearer perception of the tides of
world events in 1967 than we? Was it possible that we were
continuing to be guided by judgments that might once have
had validity but were now obsolete? In short, although I still
counted myself a staunch supporter of our policies, there were
nagging, not-to-be-suppressed doubts in my mind."

The doubts were in the back of his mind, seldom surfacing.
To the public, certainly to the President, he remained a hawk, a
long-time believer in American power, a product of the containment psychology, an old-style anti-Communist, a Democrat who
tended to see many issues of foreign policy from the viewpoint
of domestic politics. Perhaps that was why his appearance before
Stennis's Armed Services Committee aroused so much attention
in the press, so much agitation in the administration. The date
was January 25, 1968; the purpose was to confirm the nomination
of the new Defense Secretary. Senator Symington, a hawk turned
dove, had heard that Clifford did not share Rusk's rigid interpretation of the San Antonio formula. He asked for Clifford's interpretation.

Clifford did not flinch. He gave the Senators his own understanding of what the President had in mind when he called
upon North Vietnam to "not take advantage" of a bombing cessation. It was his assumption, Clifford said, that the North Vietnamese would be free to "continue to transport the normal
amount of goods, munitions, and men to South Vietnam" at the

Exit Robert McNamara

205

same levels as before the bombing had stopped. This was a free-hand effort by the incoming Secretary of Defense to make the San Antonio formula more palatable to Hanoi by easing its rigidity. Behind the scenes at the State Department and the Pentagon there was considerable grumbling over Clifford's bold amendment. Dean Rusk was reported to be furious. But, significantly, the President allowed the Clifford interpretation to stand.

Five days later, on January 30, as tens of thousands of South Vietnamese troops trekked home to their villages for the Lunar New Year holiday, the Communists launched their Tet offensive. It burst like a thunderstorm on a sunny day. Suddenly the euphoria so carefully nurtured by the President, that famous gleam of light at the end of the tunnel, was snuffed out. Confident that he had the enemy on the run one day, Westmoreland found himself on the next fighting a bitter defensive battle the entire length of South Vietnam. "The Tet offensive," as Henry A. Kissinger has written, "overthrew the assumptions of American strategy." The jolt was felt round the world.

President Johnson was quick on February 2 to dismiss the enemy offensive as a "complete failure." In retrospect, admittedly, Tet does not look like a clear victory for the Viet Cong and the North Vietnamese, certainly not in the strict military sense. They suffered enormous casualties. But it was hardly the dismal failure the President tried to make it appear. An enemy supposedly deprived of the military initiative, supposedly incapable of replacing his losses, and supposedly being ground down by superior American firepower had somehow mustered the men and the courage to mount a brilliantly coordinated country-wide offensive that reached into the American Embassy compound itself. An Army spokesman in Saigon called it a "last, desperate push." Hardly. The enemy managed to attack thirty-six South Vietnamese cities and towns all at once. His forces entered Saigon by stealth, in civilian dress, several thousand strong; they captured Hué; seized a large section of Kontum in the Central Highlands; penetrated Ben Tre, Mytho, Cantho, and Soc Trang. United States forces were caught off guard. To protect the threatened cities, Westmoreland had to recall thousands of GI's from pacification duty in the countryside. The pacification program—as the National Liberation Front proclaimed with some justice—was a shambles.

In Saigon, heavy fighting continued for almost three weeks after the President had pronounced the offensive a failure, chiefly in the Cholon district. Artillery and air strikes had to be ordered against heavily populated districts of the capital, with heavy civilian casualties. To reconquer Hué, captured January 31 by North Vietnamese troops, took twenty-four days.

The demonstrable fact that the American command had been caught off guard by the scope and ferocity of the Tet attacks almost wrecked a quiet party on Dean Rusk's fifty-ninth birthday, February 9. A group of reporters, all regularly assigned to the State Department, met with Rusk late that afternoon in his eighth-floor reception room. They presented him with a small gift, then got down to discussing the effects of the enemy offensive.

John Scali of ABC News pressed the Secretary of State to admit there had been an intelligence failure. Rusk was in no mood to admit anything. Scali pressed harder, asking whether Rusk was satisfied with the American performance. Rusk responded in a flood of angry words:

"No. One is never satisfied. But the point is I don't quite see why you have to start from the dissatisfaction. There gets to be a point when the question is whose side are you on. Now I'm Secretary of State of the United States, and I'm on our side."

"You're not implying——" Scali protested, but Rusk swept on, his words edged with uncharacteristic bitterness:

"Now, during World War Two there was never a time when you couldn't find a reason to bitch at your allies or at intelligence or at the commander of the adjoining unit or the quartermaster who wasn't giving you your portable toilet seat at the right time. There wasn't a time when you couldn't find something to bitch about.

"But what do you talk about? Do you talk about how to win this thing? Or do you throw this thing in and say everything is lost?"

Scali again protested that wasn't the question he had put to the Secretary. Rusk was not to be stopped or diverted.

"I know," he resumed. "But on my fifty-ninth birthday forgive me if I express myself on these matters because none of your papers or your broadcasting apparatuses are worth a damn unless the United States succeeds. They are trivial compared to that question.

"So I don't know why, to win a Pulitzer Prize, people have to go probing for the things that one can bitch about when there are two thousand stories on the same day about things that are more constructive in character."

It was a speech Spiro Agnew would have been proud to deliver, off the cuff that way. The reporters, most of whom had developed a genuine affection for Rusk after watching him at close range for seven years, were astonished. They came away with the impression that Rusk, the beaming Buddha or, as he preferred to speak of himself, the "friendly bartender," was rattled as they had never seen him rattled before. He had lost control of himself, perhaps the most convincing proof that in spite of all those brave words, he knew—and could not bring himself to say—that Tet had been a disaster for the administration and the country.

On February 14, General Westmoreland estimated the enemy dead at 33,000, in addition to 6700 captured. He acknowledged allied losses of some 3400 dead and 12,000 captured. Of the dead, 1100 were Americans.

Kissinger, writing in the January, 1969, issue of *Foreign Affairs* offered his own analysis:

The Tet offensive brought to a head the compounded weaknesses . . . of the American position. To be sure, from a strictly military point of view, Tet was an American victory. Viet Cong casualties were very high; in many provinces, the Viet Cong infrastructure of guerrillas and shadow administrators surfaced and could be severely mauled by American forces. But in a guerrilla war, purely military considerations are not decisive: psychological and political factors loom at least as large.

On that level the Tet offensive was a political defeat in the countryside for Saigon and the United States. Two claims had been pressed on the villages. The United States and Saigon had promised that they would be able to protect an ever larger number of villages. The Viet Cong had never made such a claim; they merely asserted that they were the real power and presence in the villages and they threatened retribution upon those who collaborated with Saigon or the United States.

As happened so often in the past, the Viet Cong made their claim stick. . . . The words "secure area" never had the same significance for Vietnamese civilians as for Americans, but, if the term had any meaning, it applied to the provincial and district capitals. This was precisely where the Tet offensive took its most severe toll. The Viet Cong had made a point which far transcended military considerations in importance: there are no secure areas for Vietnamese civilians.

In the United States the effects of Tet were only slightly less devastating. Overnight the national pendulum swung from euphoria to deep depression. Walt Rostow did his best to comfort the President and, through the press, also the nation by setting out to prove that Tet was, if not a famous victory for the United States, then at least a famous defeat for the Communists. The enemy, after all, had failed to hold any of the province or district capitals; he had suffered terrible losses; moreover, he had failed to ignite a popular uprising against the South Vietnamese Government. All true enough but, as Kissinger has pointed out, all beside the point.

It may have been, as some "captured documents" seemed to indicate, that the Communists intended to hold the cities they penetrated and thus to touch off a revolutionary uprising. Such might have been their maximum aim, though it seems unlikely. But they had no reason to be dissatisfied with the results of their stunning offensive.

It was enough for them to discredit the claims of Saigon and Washington that all was going well, that victory was near, that (as President Johnson boasted in his State of the Union Message) Saigon was steadily extending its writ into the countryside and that 67 percent of the South Vietnamese population lived in relatively secure areas.

The loss of public confidence in the President and his war policies, so suddenly revealed in the aftermath of Tet, had been building since 1965. Townsend Hoopes, then Under Secretary of the Air Force, recalls that inside the Pentagon "the Tet offensive performed the curious service of fully revealing the doubters and dissenters to each other in a lightning flash." There had been doubters and dissenters all along: in the Pentagon, the State Department, Congress, and the Central Intelligence Agency. Tet showed them they were not alone and gave them courage to fight together in the open now for a new American strategy aimed at ending the war without victory, without glory.

Even LBJ later admitted: "I have never seen some of our stalwarts in our operation in Washington dealing with the Southeast Asia theater that were as depressed as they were after Tet."

Politically, the effect of Tet was stunning. Senator Eugene McCarthy entered the presidential primaries in New Hampshire and Wisconsin, seeking to deny the President his own party's renomination. "I am concerned," McCarthy said in his announcement, "that the administration seems to have set no limit on the price it is willing to pay for a military victory."

Soon after Tet, the price America was willing to pay moved to the top of the presidential agenda. General Westmoreland, with some 500,000 troops already in Vietnam and 25,000 more promised (under a Pentagon plan called Program Five), had not contemplated asking for more manpower. But President Johnson was worried. At a meeting with Rusk, McNamara, General Wheeler, Rostow and Clifford, the President instructed the Joint Chiefs of Staff to find out what more Westmoreland needed. Clifford was struck by the President's attitude: "It was to find out *what* Westy needed, not *whether* he needed more men. In this critical time, he wanted it clear that his field commander would not be in the posture later on of claiming he did not get what he needed." Thus, on the fourth day of the Tet offensive, February 3, 1968, Westmoreland received the first in a series of secret messages from General Wheeler:

> THE PRESIDENT ASKS ME IF THERE IS ANY REINFORCE-
> MENT OR HELP THAT WE CAN GIVE YOU.

Westmoreland, busy fighting to re-establish control of the threatened cities, did not respond immediately. On February 8 he heard again from Wheeler:

> QUERY: DO YOU NEED REINFORCEMENTS? OUR CA-
> PABILITIES ARE LIMITED. WE CAN PROVIDE 82ND AIR-
> BORNE DIVISION AND ABOUT ONE HALF A MARINE
> CORPS DIVISION, BOTH LOADED WITH VIETNAM VET-
> ERANS. HOWEVER, IF YOU CONSIDER REINFORCEMENTS
> IMPERATIVE, YOU SHOULD NOT BE BOUND BY EARLIER

AGREEMENTS. . . . UNITED STATES GOVERNMENT IS
NOT PREPARED TO ACCEPT DEFEAT IN VIETNAM. IN
SUMMARY, IF YOU NEED MORE TROOPS, ASK FOR THEM.

The President, in short, through General Wheeler, was
prompting Westmoreland to ask for more troops, offering specific
units and advising the Vietnam commander that he need not
be bound by the 525,000 troop ceiling, laid down in 1967.
Predictably, the general responded the same day with an interim
request. It was, Westmoreland said, "only prudent to plan for
the worst contingency, in which case I will definitely need reinforcements." He specifically requested the units General Wheeler
had offered—both the 82nd Airborne and half a Marine division.
Westmoreland also asked the President to authorize an amphibious landing by the Marines in the North, noting that "surf
conditions would permit the operation to start in April." The
next day, February 9, he sent a second message explaining why
and where the fresh troops were needed:

NEEDLESS TO SAY, I WOULD WELCOME REINFORCE-
MENTS AT ANY TIME THEY CAN BE MADE AVAILABLE.

A. TO PUT ME IN A STRONGER POSITION TO CONTAIN
THE ENEMY'S MAJOR CAMPAIGN IN THE DMZ-QUANG
TRI-THUA THIEN AREA AND TO GO ON THE OFFENSIVE AS
SOON AS HIS ATTACK IS SPENT.

B. TO PERMIT ME TO CARRY OUT MY CAMPAIGN PLANS
DESPITE THE ENEMY'S REINFORCEMENTS FROM NORTH
VIETNAM, WHICH HAVE INFLUENCED MY DEPLOY-
MENTS AND PLANS.

C. TO OFFSET THE WEAKENED [SOUTH] VIETNAMESE
FORCES RESULTING FROM CASUALTIES AND TET DESER-
TIONS. REALISTICALLY, WE MUST ASSUME THAT IT WILL
TAKE THEM AT LEAST 6 WEEKS TO REGAIN THE MILI-
TARY POSTURE OF SEVERAL WEEKS AGO. . . .

D. TO TAKE ADVANTAGE OF THE ENEMY'S WEAKENED
POSTURE BY TAKING THE OFFENSIVE AGAINST HIM.

General Westmoreland added that if he might have the
82nd Airborne and the Marines on a six-month loan it was
conceivable the tide could be turned "to the point where the
enemy might see the light or be so weakened that we could re-

turn them, particularly if the ARVN can rebuild itself following its recent battles and improve its fighting quality by virtue
of the modern weapons it is scheduled to receive."

The exchange of messages makes clear that both Wheeler
and Westmoreland were gravely concerned by the effects of
Tet, far more concerned than they—or the White House—were
letting the public know. Westmoreland, for example, admitted
in a message to Wheeler on February 12: "Our overall campaign
plan for 1968 has been disrupted." An earlier message, dated
February 9, detailed the heavy losses suffered by the South
Vietnamese forces:

. . . it is going to take some time to build ARVN back to strength.
I have emphasized this to President Thieu and urged that he proceed
immediately to draft 19-year-olds to be followed as needed by the
drafting of youths of 18. . . . From a realistic point of view, we must
accept the fact that the enemy has dealt the GVN [Government of
South Vietnam] a severe blow. He has brought the war to the towns
and the cities and has inflicted damage and casualties on the population . . . and the economy has been disrupted.

"At Tet," Westmoreland later recalled, "a lot of people were
on leave, they couldn't get back; a lot of them deserted, the
training centers were closed, conscription was stopped, so they
were taking a hell of a lot of casualties and nobody was coming in. It was not until the twenty-fourth of March that we were
able to get those training centers and schools going again."

Johnson tended to view the Tet attacks as an "all-out Kamikaze attack, an assault with everything they've got, with their
entire stack in for the purpose of trying to roll over us and have
another Dienbienphu." During those gloomy, tense days he kept
comparing Ho with Hitler, the Communists with the Nazis, the
Vietnam War with the Second World War. These comparisons
told a great deal about the administration's state of mind: So
deep in a guerrilla war, the President was still seeing it in conventional World War II terms.

Westmoreland saw a parallel between the Tet offensive
and the Battle of the Bulge because, as he put it, "the enemy
exposed himself, gave us a chance to inflict maximum casualties,
and he would ultimately be weakened."

Paul Nitze, a Navy man, preferred the analogy of the Battle

of Leyte Gulf, when the Japanese "put all their last cards into trying to destroy our forces in the Philippines and, you remember, almost succeeded." For Nitze, the question at issue was "who would pick themselves out of the dust first," the Americans or the Communist forces. The sense of urgency that Nitze reflected was fully shared by General Wheeler. Responding to Westmoreland's report on the sad state of South Vietnamese forces, Wheeler messaged back:

> . . . IT OCCURS TO ME THAT THE DEPLOYMENT OF
> THE 82ND AIRBORNE DIVISION AND MARINE ELEMENTS
> MIGHT BE DESIRABLE EARLIER THAN APRIL TO ASSIST
> IN DEFENSE AND PURSUIT OPERATIONS. . . .
> PLEASE UNDERSTAND THAT I AM NOT TRYING TO SELL
> YOU ON THE DEPLOYMENT OF ADDITIONAL FORCES
> WHICH IN ANY EVENT I CANNOT GUARANTEE. . . .
> HOWEVER, MY SENSING IS THAT THE CRITICAL PHASE
> OF THE WAR IS UPON US, AND I DO NOT BELIEVE THAT
> YOU SHOULD REFRAIN FROM ASKING FOR WHAT YOU
> BELIEVE IS REQUIRED UNDER THE CIRCUMSTANCES.

Only a general made of stone could have resisted such entreaties to ask for more troops. Westmoreland proved that he was made of flesh and blood. On February 12 he formally requested the immediate deployment of "a Marine Regiment package" and "a brigade package of the 82nd Airborne Division." He also requested that remaining elements of these two divisions be made ready to follow at a later date. (The need never arose.) The request, so carefully prompted by Wheeler, was granted the same day. Westmoreland felt called upon to reassure Washington that he wanted the additional troops "not because I fear defeat if I am not reinforced, but because I do not feel that I can fully grasp the initiative from the recently reinforced enemy without them." The two reinforcing units, Wheeler messaged back the same day, had been alerted by the Joint Chiefs of Staff to start moving out by February 26.

To the Joint Chiefs and to Admiral Ulysses S. Grant Sharp, the overall Pacific commander, the Tet emergency signaled a great opportunity. They sensed that the President was finally in a mood to consider sympathetically their long-standing but long-deferred requests for a major expansion of American military strength. Johnson later recalled his worries about "many other situations that were rather alarming at that time on the world scene." It was "not just . . . South Vietnam," he said. "There's always the possibility that the Communist world that's aligned against us would create other incidents that would require a beefing up of our forces elsewhere." *

There were plenty of worrying incidents at the time. The *Pueblo* and her crew had been captured by North Korea. A North Korean suicide squad had infiltrated the Blue House in Seoul in a clear attempt upon the life of South Korea's President, Park Chung Hee. Two and one-third South Korean divisions were fighting in Vietnam, and Seoul wanted them recalled to man the home front. On February 1, in fact, Admiral Sharp had urged General Wheeler to draft contingency plans for the return of South Korean forces from Vietnam. General Westmoreland, caught up in the first stages of the Tet battle, balked. The return of South Korean units at that moment, he warned, was "militarily unacceptable." Westmoreland added: "No surcease can be forecast for the near future." The upsurge of North Korean activities also worried Washington. Walt Rostow, in the President's behalf, had put an alarming question to Westmoreland in a separate cable: "Do you believe there is a relationship between activities in South Vietnam [the Tet offensive] and those in Korea?" Westmoreland and Bunker responded jointly: "It would seem to us that there is a relationship."

There was bad news elsewhere. Nam Bac, the easternmost Laotian outpost, had been captured by the Pathet Lao, and two Lao general reserve battalions were all but wiped out. At about the same time Russian planes started buzzing West Berlin. In these circumstances, the Joint Chiefs were asking themselves whether all these moves in Asia and Europe might be parts of a single, coordinated Communist thrust. "There was not a single division that was combat-ready outside of Vietnam," Westmoreland later recalled. "Even our troops in Europe were flat on their butts. Our troops in Korea were not combat-ready. There

* Interview with Walter Cronkite, broadcast February 6, 1970, on the CBS Television Network.

wasn't a single division in the United States that was ready. They were in absolutely pathetic shape."

From his headquarters in Hawaii, Admiral Sharp kept coaxing Westmoreland to ask for more troops in view of Washington's apparent readiness "to relax the military ceiling" of 525,000 troops. "I think it is in our long-range interest during the cur- "to get Washington to accept the premise that the 525,000 ceil- rent emergency buildup," he messaged Westmoreland in Saigon, ing no longer applies." General Wheeler had similar notions. He made clear to Westmoreland, in a message announcing he would visit Saigon February 23, that the Joint Chiefs had passed beyond the stage of merely seeking to assure an adequate flow of reinforcements to Vietnam. He wanted Westmoreland's views, Wheeler wrote, in connection with some "hard decisions" the administration was facing. There was, of course, the matter of "providing you with additional troops" but, in addition, the question of "recouping our strategic reserves in CONUS (Continental Command) and obtaining the necessary legislative support in terms of money and authorities."

In sum, the Joint Chiefs had a far more ambitious program in mind than merely to restore the pre-Tet stalemate in Vietnam. They wanted to rebuild the strategic reserve in the United States, step up the bombing, hit Haiphong—in short, "go for broke" in pursuit of the Vietnam victory they longed for. Westmoreland recalls the Wheeler visit to Saigon:

"The JCS were worried. Wheeler came over to me and we talked about this very frankly. We both agreed that this was a benchmark in the history of the war; that it was only logical that the Administration reassess their strategy and determine if they were going to make a change in policy and strategy. Wheeler faced me with this proposition: Assuming that there is a change of strategy which will inevitably involve a callup of reserves, and the [new] strategy of the war is one toward putting more pressure on the enemy to end this thing once and for all, to include step-up of the bombing, and to put maximum pressure throughout the whole of the structure with a possibility of lifting some of the political constraints, geographical-style

(I don't have to spell this out further); you develop a plan, a reinforcement plan, under those assumptions."

It was a clear case of the Joint Chiefs using a popular commander to help them sell the President and the incoming Secretary of Defense on a new strategic posture for the United States—one that would go far beyond the predicted needs in Vietnam alone. (It seems doubtful that Wheeler and the service chiefs would have dared to propose such far-reaching changes but for McNamara's impending departure. They had higher hopes for Clifford, the reputed hawk.)

Wheeler instructed Westmoreland to assume, in drawing up his plan, that the South Vietnamese Army had collapsed completely in the aftermath of Tet, that the North Vietnamese had sent five more divisions to fight in the South, and that the Koreans had withdrawn their two and one-third divisions. It was an exercise, directed from the Pentagon, based on the over-riding hypothesis that everything that could go wrong would go wrong—not only in Vietnam but everywhere.

Westmoreland hastily drew up an outline plan and General Wheeler carried it back to Washington, arriving at Andrews Air Force Base early on the morning of February 28, 1968.

It was General Wheeler who presented that sketchy plan to a breakfast meeting at the White House the same chilly morning. He used no specific figure for the number of additional troops required. Wheeler outlined the new, more aggressive strategy Westmoreland was said to have in mind: to go on the offensive throughout South Vietnam, seeking out and destroying the guerrilla and main-force units on the ground; to step up the bombing campaign in the North, including air strikes to close the port of Haiphong; to move troops into Laos in order to cut the Ho Chi Minh supply trail; to raid selected border sanctuaries in Laos and Cambodia; and to launch amphibious and joint amphibious-air mobile operations against enemy bases in North Vietnam, just beyond the Demilitarized Zone.

To carry out all these objectives, General Wheeler reported, Westmoreland would need many more troops. He outlined a three-phase plan:

• By May 1, one brigade from the 5th Mechanized Division, six battalions from the 5th Marine Division, one armored cavalry regiment, and eight tactical fighter squadrons.

• By September 1, the remainder of the 5th Mechanized Division and four more tactical fighter squadrons.

• By December 31, one infantry division (to be mobilized from the Army Reserve) and three additional tactical fighter squadrons.

The scope of the new plan, which Westmoreland to this day insists was not a request, staggered many of the President's advisers at that White House breakfast. It amounted to increasing the troop commitment in Vietnam by fifteen tactical fighter squadrons and the equivalent of three combat divisions.

Many of the advisers were shaken. They had expected a military judgment based upon Westmoreland's post-Tet needs in Vietnam. They got, instead, without explanation, a far-reaching, JCS-inspired request for a substantial military build-up far exceeding the immediate military needs in Vietnam.

President Johnson listened gloomily as General Wheeler, with murals of the American Revolutionary War at his back, stood there in the family dining room of the White House and called for these massive reinforcements. Not that Tet had been a defeat for Westmoreland's forces; far from it, Wheeler said. On the contrary, the enemy had been thrown back with heavy losses, there was no popular uprising against the Thieu-Ky regime, and fence-sitters in the South Vietnamese population were beginning to cooperate with the government in Saigon now that the Communists had "scared the living daylights" out of them. It was just that the South Vietnamese forces were off balance, vulnerable to another offensive, and General Westmoreland felt that with the reinforcements he had requested it would be possible to regain the initiative, exploit the enemy's losses, and end the war more quickly.

It was a presidential election year. The cost of the war was already running at some $30 billion a year. Inflation at home and a gold rush abroad were battering the American dollar. At the end of February, 1968, public support for the war was fast evaporating. Senator McCarthy, campaigning in New Hampshire against Johnson and the war, had drawn an astonishing response. Congress, for so many years willing and eager to vote whatever new legislation Lyndon Johnson asked for, was becoming recalcitrant. The Joint Chiefs could not have chosen a less auspicious time to demand, through Westmoreland, 206,000 more troops for Vietnam and many billions more dollars. Yet that was the improbable figure cranked out of the Pentagon computers when Westmoreland's hasty outline was processed in Washington. No way existed of finding the additional manpower without mobilizing the reserves, enlarging draft calls, or requiring Vietnam veterans to go back for a second tour of duty. The choices confronting the President, in short, ranged from the unappealing to the appalling. At that first White House breakfast, however, no one suggested scaling down the war instead of enlarging it. In a grim mood, the President and his advisers determined to consider the new plan most carefully and to examine how the need could be met, even in an election year.

Clifford has testified that the President's directive was to figure out *how* to satisfy "Westmoreland's request," not *whether* it ought to be satisfied. Johnson has insisted that he was merely asking for "recommendations"—not, as he later stressed, "implementations." "Former government officials," he said, naming no names, "can make errors."

Johnson's account of the February 28 directive was made public on February 6, 1970 during a TV interview with Walter Cronkite. In an effort to refute Clifford, Johnson declassified a top-secret memorandum.

"As I indicated at breakfast this morning," [LBJ] related, reading from his *Memorandum to Secretary of State and Secretary of Defense,*] "I wish you to develop by Monday morning, March 4, recommendations in response to the situation presented to us by General Wheeler and his preliminary proposal. I wish alternatives examined. In particular, I wish you to consider, among other things, the following specific issues: What military and other objectives in Vietnam are additional U.S. forces designed to advance? What specific dangers is their dispatch designed to avoid? What specific goals would the increment of force, if recommended, aim to achieve in the next six months or over the next year? What probable Communist reactions do you anticipate in connection with each of the alternatives you examine? What negotiating postures should we strike in general? And what modifications, if any, would you recommend with respect to the San Antonio formula? What major congressional problems can be anticipated? And how should they be met? What problems can we anticipate in U.S. public opinion? And how should they be dealt with? You should feel free in making this report to call on the best minds in this government to work on specific aspects of the problem, but you should assure the highest possible degree of security up to the moment when the President's decision on these matters is announced."

Johnson did not care for leaks. He was soon to suffer the one leak that helped "turn the war around."

Later that day, most of the President's breakfast guests reassembled in the gilded East Room at a farewell reception for Robert McNamara. The President spoke gravely of this "loyal, brilliant and good man," who had given seven years of his life to the Sisyphean task of running the vast defense establishment. Then he presented McNamara with the Medal of Freedom. McNamara, possibly for the first time in his public career, choked with emotion. Two or three times he tried to speak, gasping and clearing his throat. Finally, he excused himself: "Mr. President, I cannot find words to express what lies in my heart today. I think I had better respond on another occasion." It was not clear whether McNamara, outwardly so cool that people who didn't know him well spoke of him as a walking computer, was brought to the verge of tears by gratitude for the President's words of praise; or it may have been the haunting awareness that he had failed his country and his own convictions by not somehow reversing the war policy during his long term in office under two Presidents. If Wheeler and Westmoreland had their way, as he had reason to know, most of the careful restrictions he had fought so long to impose upon the professional military leaders would soon go overboard.

EIGHT

Who Poisoned the Well?

AT 10:30 A.M. ON FRIDAY, MARCH 1, Clark Clifford took the oath
of office as Secretary of Defense. It was to Clifford that the
President had entrusted the painfully difficult assignment of
presiding over a new task force to consider the Westmoreland-
Wheeler proposals. Clifford was so eager to get started on his
new responsibilities that he buttonholed his deputy, Paul Nitze,
at the swearing-in ceremony in the East Room of the White
House. "After this is over," Clifford said, "why don't you and I
meet back at the Pentagon and we'll have lunch."

Nitze had known Clifford since the Truman days and
thought of him as a "very impressive, very able fellow." He
knew Clifford as a private citizen frequently called upon to advise the President who had been "very much on the hawk side."
But Nitze saw no reason to temper his advice. "No matter who
the Secretary had been, I'd have laid it out exactly the same
way," he later recalled. Among the most experienced and inde-
pendent-minded public servants of his time, Nitze had never
gone along with the Administration's shibboleth about bombing
North Vietnam to the conference table. It did not seem to him
a feasible goal. "It didn't seem to me that the Russians and the
Chinese could permit that to happen," he used to say. "Just as
we couldn't permit the South Vietnamese to be overrun by forces
from across the border, they couldn't permit it either." As a
scarred veteran of the bureaucratic wars in Washington at the
time of Korea, Nitze saw a curious parallel: "Just as in Korea,
MacArthur's objective of defeating the Chinese—he wanted, in
fact, to overthrow the Mao Tse-tung government—seemed to

me wrong, so the idea of overthrowing the Hanoi government seemed to me excessive."

Nitze had long since concluded that the bombing would never succeed in cutting off the tiny trickle of men and supplies needed to sustain the war in the South. "You looked at the photographs of the Mui Gia Pass and it looked like Verdun," Nitze said. "It wasn't that the air attack wasn't effective. It was effective as hell. It knocked the beJesus out of the places they were trying to knock the beJesus out of. And yet, all the time you'd see little paths going through the jungle someplace else, where they'd been weaving between the craters." As for the psychological effect of the bombing in the North, Nitze felt that in the short run at least it was strengthening the will of the North Vietnamese to go on fighting.

At lunch with Clifford that first day, Nitze produced a memorandum he had written for McNamara on February 27, making essentially two bold new recommendations: First, the bombing should be stopped all the way down to the 17th parallel, the actual frontier between North and South Vietnam; second, Westmoreland should receive limited reinforcements, up to 50,000 men, not the full 206,000. It seemed to Nitze probable, perhaps unavoidable, that a complete bombing halt would lead to negotiations. And he was certain the United States would get no more out of those negotiations than it had earned by the strength of its position, military and political, in South Vietnam. All he looked for was an agreement to stabilize the Demilitarized Zone—"an agreement that if we were not going to use our forces north of the 17th parallel, they would not use the DMZ to move their forces south of the 17th parallel."

Nitze argued that the United States had little to lose—and might gain something—by ending the air war against the North. "The thing that was really hurting us was the concern—the legitimate concern—in this country and the world that the Vietnamese War could escalate to something larger," he said. "If you could get rid of that bombing, then from the domestic and world-wide point of view you would at least diminish that concern and you would have a better chance of concentrating on the battle that I thought was necessary to achieve an interim solution. This was the substance of what I was trying to get across to Clark."

Clifford gave no sign of agreement but he listened. That seemed to Nitze "a tremendous leg up." The battle for the mind of Clark Clifford had started earlier. Encouraged by the discovery that he was not alone in believing the current Johnson-Joint Chiefs policy was a disaster, Townsend Hoopes had written a letter to Clifford on February 13. The Under Secretary of the Air Force made three basic points:

First, the idea of a US victory in Viet Nam is a dangerous illusion (primarily because both the Russians and the Chicoms have the capacity to preclude it—probably by supply operations alone, but if necessary by intervening with their own forces); second, if events in Viet Nam are ever to take a turn toward settlement, definitive de-escalation is a prerequisite; And, third, admitting all the uncertainty and the risk, the most promising approach to negotiations and thus settlement continues to involve a cessation of the US bombing effort against North Viet Nam as one of the first steps.

Hoopes and Nitze were not of one mind, in spite of their agreement that the bombing must stop. To Hoopes the idea of military victory was sheer illusion. Nitze did not for a moment rule out the possibility of victory in the South. "I thought there was—and still think there is—the possibility of a political and military solution," he said in a 1970 interview. Hoopes, in his letter to Clifford, also attacked the established belief that an end of the bombing would necessarily increase American casualties on the ground—the heart of the President's argument. If Westmoreland were ordered to end search-and-destroy missions in uninhabited places, and to use his forces instead to protect populated areas, the casualties would go down, he contended.

Present US casualty levels [Hoopes wrote] are a function of the US ground strategy in the South; they are only distantly related to the bombing. Yet as we address the prospect of a bombing cessation, it becomes apparent that, however tenuous the military linkage, a political linkage has been allowed to develop. . . . From this I draw the conclusion that, if the President is to accept the consequences of a bombing halt, he must take a corollary decision to alter the ground strategy in ways that will reduce US casualties; otherwise, the domestic political risks may be too high.

There were other dissenters in the Pentagon, chiefly civilian officials, emboldened now to make known their dissent, at least to one another: Paul Warnke, for example; his deputy for Far Eastern Affairs, Richard Steadman; Alfred Fitt, assistant secretary of defense for manpower; David McGiffert, Under Secretary of the Army; Alain Enthoven, head of the Systems Analysis office; and Phil G. Goulding, assistant secretary of defense for public affairs.

Nitze, Warnke, and Goulding had the most direct access to their new boss. They saw him every morning, and it was there, in the Defense Secretary's morning meetings, that the battle to end the bombing and turn the war around was fought out, in the first stage. Clifford started with his own doubts about the domino theory, the product of his 1967 mission to the capitals of the troop-contributing countries. He had at the outset no fixed view on stopping the bombing. "He was putting himself in the President's shoes," Nitze recalled, "as chairman of a group working for the President. He was trying to get all the views without taking a strong position himself. He was trying to see where the analysis led."

"I don't know whether the Chiefs expected to get the 206,-000 men," Clifford recalls. "But the President was prepared to send them, if he thought they were needed. The question arose: Where would they come from?"

There was talk of borrowing helicopters from the British, of withdrawing more troops from Europe, of reducing the minimum force stationed in the United States, of calling up 300,000 reservists. Above all there was the question of cost. The task force heard offhand estimates that a troop increase on the order Wheeler and Westmoreland had proposed—40 percent—would add something like $10 billion to the already astronomic cost of the war.

Just as the first task-force memorandum was being prepared, Dean Rusk went to see the President alone on March 4. That was his way of doing business. For many months Rusk had toyed with the idea of a limited bombing halt. At a National Security Council meeting in the autumn of 1967, Rusk had passed a slip of paper to Paul Nitze, reading "What would you

think of calling off the bombing to the 19th parallel?" Nitze had
not heard the suggestion before. He remembers writing back:
"If you're going to do it, you really ought to do it all the way."
"All the way" meant to the 17th parallel. Rusk carried more
weight with President Johnson than any other Cabinet officer.
George Christian, White House news secretary in the final
months of the Johnson Administration, has written: "He listened to Clifford, McNamara, George Ball, and others who sometimes differed with Rusk on specifics, and he might blend these
views into a decision; but mainly it was Rusk's judgment he
wanted in the end, and Rusk's judgment he followed."

Rusk's judgment, confided to the President that day in
early March, was that perhaps the time had come for scaling
down the bombing; not a total halt all the way back to the 17th
parallel but perhaps to the 19th. Recalling his own state of
mind at the time, Rusk says: "We had to think of contingencies
in two directions: one towards war, the other towards peace. So
we came up with the bombing-halt proposal. It was my initiative."

The President, still keeping his options open, said: "Get on
your horses and get me a plan." Rusk assumed from that moment that the President was favorably disposed toward limiting
the bombing.

Rusk had been meeting secretly from time to time with
Rumania's first deputy foreign minister, Gheorghe Macovescu,
who had direct access to Hanoi. Macovescu, in fact, had come
to Washington for a meeting with Rusk on Friday, March 1.
They met a second time on Monday, March 4, and the word
the Rumanian carried was that the time might just be ripe for
arranging peace talks if the bombing could be stopped.

The Rumanian channel had been open for a good many
months, but the results till then had been disappointing. It was
opened on June 26, 1967, when Corneliu Manescu, Rumanian
foreign minister, and Ion Gheorghe Maurer, the prime minister,
who were in the United States for a special UN session on the
Middle East, called on President Johnson at the White House.
The President talked to them at length about his desire to stop
the steady escalation of the war and to start talking with the

Vietnamese Communists. The Rumanians came away somewhat impressed and, though Johnson had not asked for their help, they felt there was enough flexibility in his position to make a fresh peace effort worthwhile.*

After Maurer and Manescu had returned to Bucharest, the Rumanian Government decided to send Macovescu on a mission to Peking and Hanoi. He was fully briefed beforehand on the signs of Johnsonian flexibility: chiefly the President's readiness to stop the bombing if he could *assume* that Hanoi would not "take advantage" of the cessation. (In short, the San Antonio formula, yet to be announced.)

Macovescu returned to Bucharest after his talks in Hanoi, persuaded that if the bombing were stopped "meaningful negotiations" could then start. Macovescu passed on his impression to Richard Davis, the American ambassador in Bucharest, who promptly relayed it to Rusk in Washington. There was no immediate response from the United States. But when, on September 30, the President delivered his San Antonio speech, the Rumanians deemed it a move in the right direction and so informed Hanoi.

In November, Averell Harriman stopped in Bucharest on one of his overseas trips to see whether the Rumanians had any further information. He met President Nicolae Ceausescu and Premier Maurer, was briefed in detail on Macovescu's Hanoi contacts, and discussed the San Antonio formula. Harriman left Bucharest believing that Hanoi was interested.

Macovescu then returned to Hanoi. The Rumanians had been careful throughout the sounding process to make clear that

* Johnson had just met Soviet Premier Alexei Kosygin at Glassboro, New Jersey, an unusual location for an East-West summit meeting. Kosygin was at the UN, Johnson in Washington. Neither wished to journey to the other's headquarters. Glassboro was the equidistant compromise. According to Chester Cooper's *The Lost Crusade*, "Kosygin showed President Johnson a message he had just received from Hanoi which stated that the North Vietnamese would be ready to talk if the United States halted the bombing." A "cautious, tentative reply" was given to Kosygin. We understand that its wording was vague and its demands too excessive for Hanoi to meet. Nothing more was heard about this feeler. Nevertheless, the President wanted to build on its possibilities, and he deliberately demonstrated a flexible American attitude to the Rumanians on the central question of a bombing halt.

they were acting on their own initiative, not in behalf of the United States. Thus Macovescu told the North Vietnamese officials he met that, in his opinion, the United States was ready to take a step toward peace. He cited the rising volume of protest against the war, adding that in his opinion the President himself might be of a mind to turn down the war and start negotiating.

Conceivably in response to Macovescu's intimations, Hanoi moved on New Year's Day, 1968, to remove one ambiguity in its stated position. Foreign Minister Nguyen Duy Trinh had said in early 1967 that a bombing halt "could" lead to negotiations. In his New Year's statement, Trinh used much the same language but this time changed the "could" to "would." This diplomatic signal promptly brought Macovescu to Washington. Washington chose to deal with the development in split-level, bureaucratic fashion. For public consumption, William P. Bundy, Assistant Secretary of State for Far Eastern Affairs, was instructed to douse the could-would shift in plenty of cold water. He told reporters that he could not be sure Hanoi was "anywhere near the point" of yielding; the enemy, he thought, might use a bombing halt to strengthen his military position. Rusk, meanwhile, met secretly with Macovescu, heard from him some amplifications of Trinh's cryptic remarks, and gave the Rumanian his answer. Rusk asked for "assurance" that talks would begin "promptly," within a matter of days after the bombing was stopped. By way of demonstrating American good will, Rusk arranged that there should be no air attacks on Hanoi during Macovescu's return visit in late January. The Rumanians felt Rusk's reply was "in general, positive."

When Macovescu reached Hanoi, he found that the North Vietnamese had lost their ardor for peace talks, at least for the moment. They told him the time was "not yet ripe." Macovescu later concluded that Hanoi preferred not to get pinned down to a schedule for possible talks; with the Tet offensive then in preparation they expected soon to be in a more powerful bargaining position. Corneliu Bogdan, the Rumanian ambassador in Washington, delivered Macovescu's disappointing message to Rusk in the second week of the offensive. The message had its redeeming side, however. Bogdan told Rusk that, on the basis of information available to the Rumanians, the United States should not give up hope for talks. He expressed confidence that Rusk would find the wisdom and the flexibility to take the next step at the right time.

In the first week of March Macovescu flew again to Washington. He and Rusk agreed that perhaps the right moment had come for one more effort. They approached this conclusion from different directions: Macovescu, believing Hanoi had made its "point" during Tet and was now ready to talk from a "position of strength"; Rusk, believing, as the President later put it, that "they put their stack in . . . and found they didn't have the horsepower." In this frame of mind, Rusk encouraged Macovescu to try again. The Rumanian left Washington the very day that Rusk outlined his partial-bombing-halt scheme for the President and promptly passed on his "positive impression" to Hanoi.

The Secretary of State was not greatly interested in the Wheeler-Westmoreland proposal for a more aggressive strategy, requiring 206,000 more men. "There was not much likelihood that contingency would arise," Rusk said. "So I put the other alternative. And the President said: 'Get it ready.'"

Rusk's deputies, Under Secretary of State Nicholas deB. Katzenbach and Assistant Secretary Bundy, had been pressing him for a new diplomatic approach that might lead to negotiations rather than a wider war. Katzenbach recalls: "The idea of holding back the bombing to a designated parallel was an idea that Bob McNamara, to the best of my knowledge, originated. And it had for quite a long period of time always appealed somewhat to Dean Rusk, who thought it was a possibility at the right time to offer this kind of thing."

Katzenbach saw no prospect of getting peace talks started, however, unless all the bombing were stopped. "Frankly, I never thought it would work," Katzenbach said. "Because I thought they [the Hanoi leadership] had a principle involved in the bombing and that only a partial halt was not going to do it."

It was characteristic of Rusk that he did not go back to

the State Department on March 4 and tell Katzenbach that the President had instructed him to work up the bombing-halt idea. He discussed the idea freely enough with Katzenbach, as his own. But he gave no intimation of the President's attitude. Both Katzenbach and George Ball, his predecessor as Under Secretary, had been driven wild by Rusk's secretive attitude. He used to say: "The President is entitled to my advice, but it's only for him, not for others to know." During the Cuban missile crisis in 1962, Rusk had taken the same attitude, refusing to declare himself for or against a particular policy, in the presence of Cabinet and sub-Cabinet colleagues, until he knew that the President agreed with him. "In the State Department," Rusk said after his retirement, "I was determined that no blue sky would show between the President and myself."

President Johnson, in any case, had not committed himself to stop the bombing any more than he was committed to send Westmoreland 206,000 additional troops. Both contingencies were being studied. The President had his doubts about the value of a bombing halt. He remembered that back in the Christmas season of 1965 the Russians had assured him that if the bombing was stopped for fifteen days "something would happen." It was stopped for thirty-seven days and nothing happened, a point the President made over and over again to his critics. In March, 1968, he remained wary. But Rusk shrewdly argued that stopping the bombing just then would cost the United States little and might turn out to be an important move toward peace. At that season, he pointed out, bad weather would in any case have ruled out any major air attacks on North Vietnam. "We were proposing to stop only 5 percent of our sorties, in fact," Rusk explained. "Most of the sorties at that time of year were in the southern part of North Vietnam. So there was no military disadvantage to our side in cutting back."

Clifford's task force, meanwhile, met every day and every evening at the Pentagon. Rusk appeared at the first session, said little, and was not seen again. It was his first—and last—formal visit to Defense in eight years. Katzenbach thereafter sat in for Rusk, along with William Bundy and Philip Habib. Nitze, Warnke, and Goulding were there to assist Clifford. General

Wheeler represented the Joint Chiefs, Richard Helms, the CIA; Rostow, the White House; Henry Fowler, the Treasury Department; and Maxwell Taylor, as a special adviser. McNamara attended only the first session, held round an oval oaken table in the dining room provided for the Secretary of Defense.

The hard line, as expected, was voiced by Rostow, Taylor, and Wheeler. For them, there could be no question of turning down the troop request. All three saw the Tet offensive as a Heaven-sent opportunity: the enemy had suddenly exposed himself after years of avoiding battle; this was the moment to reinforce Westmoreland so he could clobber the enemy once and for all time. Wheeler contended that unless the still-secret request for 206,000 men were met, Westmoreland would see the decision as a lack of confidence in his leadership. Taylor doubted that even the 206,000-man increase would be enough to do the job Westy had in mind. McNamara, that first day, argued that the time had come for a compromise settlement through negotiations. Military power alone, he said, could not assure America's political objectives in Vietnam, not even if it were vastly increased. Nitze, Paul Warnke, and Katzenbach saw no convincing evidence that the Tet offensive had been a desperation tactic or that the enemy had anything so ambitious in mind as wholesale uprisings against Saigon. To them it seemed more likely that the enemy's purpose was psychological: to create panic among Vietnamese civilians, wreck the pacification program in the countryside, and jolt American public opinion by demonstrating that victory was not possible. After seven days of inconclusive argument, the task force sent an unsigned memorandum to the President that begged the question of a strategic change without answering it. It recommended an initial deployment of some 50,000 more troops to Vietnam, the rest to be provided in a year. Clifford knew it could not end there.

"By the time of the delivery of our report," he said, "it was something of a formality. The President was conscious of what was going on. He knew we were involved in a basic, agonizing review of the war."

So the debate continued, with Clifford more and more

deeply troubled, always conscious of "the enormity of the request." A 40 percent troop increase would have tied down more than 730,000 American troops in Vietnam. Clifford kept thinking: "While I'm in this building, someone is going to want to round it off at a million."

Like the President himself, Clifford was a political animal. Under Harry Truman's tutelage at the time of the Marshall Plan, he had learned something about the indispensable need for any President to assure himself of broad public support. His antennae told him that if the President went along with the Joint Chiefs and Rostow in a strategy of piling on more men and bombs, the country would "come close to civil war." Thousands of students had burned their draft cards. In New Hampshire on March 12, Senator McCarthy had polled 42.2 percent of the vote against a write-in vote for President Johnson of 49.4 percent. Overnight McCarthy had made himself a national figure, proving even in a highly conservative state that there was political profit in opposing the war. On March 16 Robert Kennedy entered the presidential campaign. Johnson and his supporters were badly shaken by both events. Clifford, moreover, knew something the public could not know. To meet the 206,-000-man request would certainly mean calling up reserves, a move the President had carefully avoided even before his leadership of the Democratic Party had been challenged by McCarthy and Kennedy. It would mean raising the monthly draft call. The cost of all this could only be roughly estimated. But preliminary calculations showed that the cost of Vietnam was likely to rise from $30 billion to something like $42 billion in 1969. In the precarious state of the dollar, still being buffeted on European exchanges in the flight to gold, Clifford had reason to believe that wage and price controls would have to be imposed. In this frame of mind, Clifford suggested that the task force keep working. The President, fully aware of the awful choices confronting him, agreed, even though he had occasion to wonder whatever had happened to Clifford, the hawk. "The irony was," Clifford recalls, "that he chose me to replace McNamara because he wanted a good, staunch, stalwart supporter of his policy in the Pentagon. Then this Judas appeared!"

The President was willing to hold off the decision briefly while Clifford and others sorted out their doubts. But he soon demonstrated, in a thunderous way, that he had not been persuaded the bombing was wrong. On March 15, the day before Robert Kennedy entered the race, Arthur J. Goldberg, the American ambassador to the United Nations, had sent the President an eight-page memo urging that he stop the bombing in order to get negotiations started. Goldberg's suggestion was that all the bombing be stopped, down to the 17th parallel. He had no knowledge at the time of Dean Rusk's partial-halt proposal. Goldberg had particular reason to feel frustrated. He had given up his seat on the Supreme Court to accept the ambassadorship because, more than anything else, he wanted to help achieve peace in Vietnam. The President had led him to believe that he would not be just another ambassador; no, indeed, he would have a great deal to say about American foreign policy. Other distinguished men have been led up the same garden path, Adlai Stevenson for one. In the end, both discovered that American foreign policy was made in Washington, not New York; that an ambassador's job was to carry out instructions, not to draft them. For the better part of two years, Goldberg had been a good soldier. But even the best soldier has his breaking point. Thus, Goldberg, in his frustration, finally dared to recommend a complete reversal of the bombing strategy in a memorandum marked "For the President's Eyes Only." Copies were sent by the White House to Rusk and Clifford, although Goldberg had not consulted either of them.

The President was meeting with his senior advisers the day after the Goldberg memorandum reached Washington. When someone brought up the matter of a bombing halt, Johnson exploded with rage:

"Let's get one thing clear," he said. "I'm telling you now I'm not going to stop the bombing. Now I don't want to hear any more about it. Goldberg has written to me about the whole thing, and I've heard every argument. I'm not going to stop it. Now is there anybody here who doesn't understand that?"

The President's burst of indignation could have been calculated, his own Johnsonian way of protecting his options and the elaborate secrecy that he and Rusk always favored. It could have been an expression of pique: the President had a low threshold of tolerance for the badgering of subordinates. It could also have revealed his own deep-seated skepticism toward all proposals for scaling down or stopping the bombing. No one will know for sure.

One thing was certain. During Rusk's ten hours of public testimony that month before the largely hostile Senate Foreign Relations Committee—theoretically, the subject was foreign aid —he did reveal that the administration was engaged in an "A to Z" review of its Vietnam policy. While holding to his overall strategic view that "abandoning [South Vietnam] is catastrophic, not just for Southeast Asia but for the United States" too, Rusk dropped a significant hint that unfortunately was ignored in most news reports. He said the "A to Z" review included "all of the alternatives," including the one of "de-escalation," or "limiting" the bombing, while stressing that the President had not yet made his "final decision." Rusk did not tell the Senators that he had been receiving diplomatic reports which suggested Hanoi might be preparing a peace offering of its own. It had invited a few foreign reporters, including Charles Collingwood of CBS News, so that they could be present in the North Vietnamese capital in late March "for the news." What news? the reporters asked. Hanoi provided only enticement, no enlightenment. For their part, the Senators were so intent on heading off another troop increase that they did not catch or follow up Rusk's hint. Neither did the press.

Clifford, too, had been called before the Foreign Relations Committee. He begged off with the excuse that he was so new in office, so preoccupied with Vietnam, that he had little to offer by way of mature judgments on the military assistance program. Clifford and Johnson then agreed that if the Senators had no objection, Paul Nitze should testify in place of his chief. Nitze was fully aware that the committee had only a marginal interest in the aid program. As their treatment of Rusk had demonstrated, many of the Senators were determined to bear down on Vietnam, taking advantage of the television cameras to let the country know how deeply they opposed the war. Clifford

was horrified when Nitze refused to testify on the ground that
he was not in a position to defend the administration's Vietnam
policy. He coupled the refusal with a letter for President Johnson, saying he could well understand that in view of his position the President might want his resignation. He was prepared
to offer it.

Nitze's personal attitude toward the war had already been
made clear to Clifford. To him, going along with the 206,000-
man troop request was a plain case of "reinforcing weakness."
He had urged Clifford to fight for a total bombing halt on the
new Secretary's very first day in office. Nitze felt the task force,
at the time of Senator Fulbright's request, had not given sufficient weight to the argument for stopping the bombing. He
feared the President was about to approve, in "some substantial
measure," the Wheeler-Westmoreland request, and he could not
bring himself to testify in support of a policy he personally felt
was wrong-headed.

Clifford was shaken when he saw the letter to the President. "I didn't realized you felt this strongly," he said to Nitze.

"From our first luncheon," Nitze replied, "you've heard me
twenty, forty times on this issue. I mean it. I haven't been saying
these things because I didn't mean them."

"I didn't quite realize," Clifford said, "the depths to which
you felt this." Then he said: "Well, for goodness' sakes, take out
that sentence."

Nitze agreed to delete his readiness to quit or, as he put
it, "not continue." But the rest of the letter went to the President. There was no acknowledgment from the White House.
From that day Nitze was never again invited to Johnson's Tuesday luncheons.

Clifford and Johnson then decided that Warnke should testify for the Defense Department. Warnke agreed, in spite of his
own feeling that the current strategy was "foolish to the point
of insanity." But Senator Fulbright, the chairman, insisted the
committee would hear only Clifford or Nitze. Clifford, finally,
went to see Fulbright privately, told him of his own rising
doubts about the Vietnam policy, and mentioned the secret reappraisal then under way. Fulbright quickly understood that

Clifford's prospect of turning the policy around might be damaged by public testimony at that moment. So he dropped the matter.

All this time Clifford's task force was meeting, and the new Secretary of Defense was asking questions of the generals:

Q. Would 206,000 more men do the job? *
A. *There is no assurance that they would.*
Q. If not, how many more might be needed—and when?
A. *No one can say.*
Q. Could the enemy respond with a buildup of his own?
A. *Yes, he could and probably would.*
Q. Could bombing end the war?
A. *Not by itself.*
Q. Would a step-up in bombing decrease American casualties?
A. *Very little, if at all. The United States has already dropped a heavier tonnage of bombs on North Vietnam than in all theaters of war during World War II. Yet, during 1967, some 90,000 North Vietnamese made their way to the South and, in the first weeks of 1968, were still coming at three to four times the rate of a year earlier.*
Q. How long must the United States go on carrying the main burden of combat?
A. *The South Vietnamese are making great progress, but they are not yet ready to replace American troops in the field.*
Q. What is the plan for victory?
A. *There is no plan.*
Q. Why not?
A. *Because American forces operate under three major restrictions: The President has forbidden them to invade the North, lest China intervene; he has forbidden the mining of Haiphong harbor, lest a Soviet supply ship be sunk; he has also forbidden pursuing the enemy into Laos and Cambodia because that would widen the war, geographically and politically.*
Q. Given these circumstances, how can we win?
A. *The United States is improving its posture all the time, the enemy can not afford the attrition being inflicted on him; at some point he will discover there is no purpose in fighting any more.*
Q. How long will this take? Six months? One year? Two years?
A. *There is no agreement on an answer.*
Q. Does anyone see any evidence that four years of enormous casualties and massive destruction through bombing have diminished the enemy's will to fight?
A. *No.*

* Clark Clifford, *Foreign Affairs*, July, 1969.

After days of this kind of questioning, always dissatisfied with the answers, Clifford became convinced that the course the United States was pursuing in Vietnam was not only endless but hopeless. "A further substantial increase in American forces," he decided, "could only increase the devastation and the Americanization of the war, and thus leave us even further from our goal of a peace that would permit the people of South Vietnam to fashion their own political and economic institutions. Henceforth, I was also convinced, our primary goal should be to level off our involvement and to work toward general disengagement."

Clifford needed allies close to the President. He found one in Harry McPherson, Johnson's speechwriter, who for weeks past had been drafting and redrafting a Vietnam speech in which the President proposed to tell the American people of the great decision then afoot. McPherson had spent a couple of weeks in South Vietnam the previous summer. He gave the President a memorandum upon his return and, in later months, came to regret it. "It was very long," McPherson later recalled, "and it was pure pessimism, dwelling on the corruptions, and the failures and inabilities of ARVN and of the government. Then it ended up: 'But it's right that we should be there.' For a thousand reasons that will have to be psychoanalyzed out of people, we couldn't believe . . . I couldn't believe . . . that it was the wrong thing to have done in the first place. I hadn't come yet to any heretical notions that maybe we ought to begin to try to turn the darn thing around and get out of there. I couldn't really believe that Lyndon Johnson, smart as he was, would have gotten us into a hopeless bog."

Sometime before Tet, McPherson had suggested that the President ought to make a speech, once again explaining the war to the people. Johnson told him to start drafting but then, as the Tet offensive materialized, he blew hot and cold. "It's too late," the President would say to McPherson. Or, "It's too early." Or, "I don't want to shake up Thieu and Ky." Not until mid-February did the President say: "Well, you really ought to do a speech now." No date had been fixed for its delivery, and the content kept shifting. From George Christian the increasingly disenchanted McPherson heard for the first time that Clifford was beginning to exercise his influence toward a different policy on Vietnam. He was elated. "It seemed too much to believe that a guy who had been the pillar of the establishment—and whom the President certainly expected to support the policy —was turning around," McPherson recalled. The two quickly formed an alliance. McPherson saw his own role as "keeping hawk stuff out of anything the President said, as far as I could, and warning Clifford of bureaucratic ambushes ahead."

The most encouraging thing he heard from Clifford, one day about the middle of March, concerned the speech he was working on, then in its fifth or sixth draft. "Leave the troop thing very flexible," Clifford said. "We're going to cut the hell out of that."

Clifford had reached one firm conclusion: The war could not be won. He was not yet sure in his own mind about the details of a new strategy. He was searching for a new approach that would cut back or cut off the bombing, end the costly search-and-destroy operations, get negotiations started, and make clear to Saigon that the United States would not remain forever in Vietnam. Nitze's quiet revolt had helped to resolve some of his doubts; so also the fact that the Joint Chiefs had not come up with convincing answers to the questions he propounded. The battle for Clifford's mind was half-won.

But the battle for the President's mind was just beginning. A politician of extraordinary skills and sensitivities, Johnson was certainly aware of the shrinking public support for Vietnam and the splintering of his own party. The President in late February had called in Dean Acheson, former Secretary of State, presidential adviser, and gnarled Cold Warrior. The President asked for Acheson's opinion of the current Vietnam situation. Acheson's unsettling reply was that on the basis of occasional briefings he had received he found it impossible to discover what was happening. "With all due respect," Acheson said, "the Joint Chiefs of Staff don't know what they're talking about." That was a shocking statement, the President responded. If it was, Acheson said, then perhaps the President ought to be shocked.

When Johnson responded that he still wanted Acheson's

judgment, the former Secretary of State stipulated that he had
to be free to conduct his own inquiry without prompting from
Rostow, the CIA, or the Joint Chiefs. The President agreed.
Acheson lost no time putting together a small team of his own,
all second-level people knowledgeable about Vietnam, and cross-
examining them. They included Philip Habib of the State Department, George Carver of the CIA, and Major General William DuPuy of the Joint Staff.

Three days after the New Hampshire primary, on March
15, Acheson sat down to lunch alone with the President and
told him what he had found. Johnson, already shaken by the
wobbly attitude of one renowned hawk, Clark Clifford, was
thunderstruck by Acheson's apparent defection. Acheson told
the President that his recent Vietnam speeches were so far out
of touch with reality that no one believed him, at home or
abroad. The Joint Chiefs, he said, were leading the President
down the garden path; moreover, what Westmoreland was trying to do in Vietnam could not be accomplished without unlimited resources and, he added, "maybe five years." In spite
of his vast respect for Acheson, the President could not bring
himself to admit that he had misled the country into a disastrous, unwinnable military adventure. Goldberg's memorandum
arrived the same day as Acheson's upsetting advice. Robert
Kennedy had entered the presidential contest, as the President
had feared he would. He felt jostled, unhappy, and he fought
back bitterly.

On March 17, barely containing his rage while concealing
his innermost thoughts, the President flew to the Middle West
for speeches before the National Alliance of Businessmen and
the National Farmers Union. In full public view, he attacked
the proponents of a less aggressive, less costly ground strategy.
"Those of you who think that you can save lives by moving the
battlefield in from the mountains to the cities where the people
live have another thing coming," the President said. It was a
passage that was bound to baffle any private citizen, business-
man or farmer, who knew little or nothing of the secret White
House discussions. Johnson called for "a total national effort to
win the war, to win the peace, and to complete the job that

must be done here at home." He added: "Make no mistake about it—I don't want a man in here to go back thinking otherwise—we are going to win." For years past, the President had strenuously denied that his goal was military victory. Not at all, he used to argue—the goal is a negotiated peace. All those nice gradations of language went out the window now. Clifford, McPherson, and all their collaborators back in the Pentagon, the State Department, and other agencies concerned feared they had lost to the warhawks. "Those hardnosed speeches," McPherson recalled, "they left me feeling it was all over."

On the edge of desperation, Clifford reached out for fresh allies. Before entering the administration, he had been a member of the Senior Advisory Group on Vietnam, the so-called Wise Men. At lunch one day in the upstairs dining room of the White House, Clifford coolly proposed to the President that perhaps the Wise Men should be heard from before the big decision was made. He was playing for time. Johnson must have suspected what was in Clifford's mind, but he agreed to call in the Wise Men on March 25 and 26. The decision would keep till then. Clifford had a more far-reaching aim, as well. Having talked privately with a number of the Wise Men, he knew they were no longer unanimous in supporting the war. Acheson's turnabout was already the talk of Washington. McGeorge Bundy, once a Harvard dean, had returned to the university on March 12 to deliver the Godkin Lectures. He had also agreed to debate the war with Professor Stanley H. Hoffman at Harvard's Sanders Theater. Bundy was determined to speak out against the proposed escalation. He so informed the President, through Walt Rostow, and the word came back that Johnson fully understood. The Harvard *Crimson* duly recorded, under a headline reading, BUNDY OPPOSES ESCALATION, the first intimation of his changed attitude.

The immediate issue, Bundy said that night, is "whether and in what measure the administration should respond to recent requests for more American troops in Southeast Asia." Bundy knew from a *New York Times* report, published March 10, that the President was weighing a request for 206,000 more troops. Having checked with Clifford, he knew the figure was accurate, and he disapproved in the blandest language he could devise. "I do not myself believe," Bundy said to the student-faculty audience, "that a persuasive case has yet been made for a significant military increase on our side." It was difficult to find the right words. As he later explained: "My principal difficulty was that I wanted to be against escalation but I didn't want to be against escalation in a way that made me lose whatever line I might have to the administration." Bundy was not yet transformed into a complete dove. When the Harvard debate moderator, Professor John K. Fairbank, put the question of negotiations, Bundy delivered the conventional administration answer: "You cannot get an early settlement which the Communists will agree to accept on their terms. You cannot negotiate short-term peace in Vietnam unless you offer surrender." For Clifford's purpose, however, it was sufficient that Bundy should oppose sending more troops to Vietnam, as he did.

The *Times* account, which prompted Bundy's second thoughts on escalation, had landed like a bomb in Saigon. General Westmoreland called in his information officer, Brigadier General Winant Sidle, and exploded: "What the hell is this all about? I never asked for any 206,000 troops." Only then did he recognize that the hasty outline of troop needs solicited by General Wheeler in February, an outline based on the assumption that the President would order a drastic change in strategy, had been fleshed out by the Joint Chiefs and put before the Clifford task force, tagged as "Westmoreland's request."

The general bitterly attributed the *Times* story to a leak by "a party in the Pentagon who wanted to prejudice the decision-making during the reappraisal of policy." In fact, the original *Times* source was not a Pentagon man, military or civilian. The information came from an unidentified, obviously well-informed, member of Congress.

The President's wrath at Ambassador Goldberg had blown itself out by March 20. There were signs, by then, that the President, despite his hard-line speeches, was opting for a peace formula. That day Goldberg came down from New York and met alone with the President, unaware of the eruption he had caused by daring to propose an end of the bombing. The President asked several questions about the Goldberg plan and, after an amicable discussion, invited the UN ambassador to meet with the Wise Men on March 25. He made a point of urging Goldberg to restate his views on the need for a bombing halt at that meeting. On March 22 Johnson announced that General Westmoreland was being relieved of his Vietnam command and would come back to Washington as Army Chief of Staff. Westmoreland was deeply disappointed. When General Wheeler flew out to meet him at Clark Air Force Base in the Philippines on March 24, he brought the news that General Creighton Abrams, Westmoreland's deputy, would take over in a few days. Westmoreland had wanted to get the job in Vietnam done himself. He felt that he was being sacrificed to propitiate the doves and to impress Hanoi with the President's sincere desire to end the war or to scale it down. It would certainly be difficult to prove the contrary.

Westmoreland also heard from Wheeler that there was not much prospect of a change in national strategy, the change both men had advocated as the basis for greatly expanding the troop commitment. The situation has clarified, Wheeler said, and major reinforcements were no longer needed. A change of national strategy appeared to him remote. There would be no large call-up of reserves. Westmoreland replied that with the arrival of the third brigade, 82nd Airborne Division, and the 27th Marine Regimental Landing Team, he could more than hold his own. The Force 5 troop ceiling had been lifted from 525,000 to 549,-500. The general said he could manage all right.

The President's shifting of Westmoreland, together with Wheeler's intimation that a wider, more aggressive strategy was all but ruled out by March 24, and the fact that the White House did nothing to dissuade Bundy from speaking out against further escalation in a public forum, strongly suggested that Johnson's own views were in transition. He appeared to sense that, in spite of his own protestations, there would have to be a change of policy. The transfer of Westmoreland at that moment made sense only if the President was going to turn down the troop request and clear the ground for that new policy. Moreover, by deciding to expose the Wise Men to Goldberg's views,

by going along with Bundy's anti-escalation attitude, he was indicating in a less dramatic way that perhaps he had taken Acheson's warning to heart. Perhaps the Joint Chiefs had indeed been
leading him down the garden path.

The mind of Lyndon Johnson had always been more subtle
than his language. Now, in the crisis of his Presidency, he was
clearly considering a return to private life coincident with the
new turn in Vietnam. The withdrawal from politics, he may have
felt, would reinforce the sincerity of whatever policy change he
decided to make.

McPherson recalls his own skepticism when the President
first hinted to him that he might pull out. They had lunched together in the Rose Garden that afternoon, toward the end of
March. The talk was of politics: of Nixon and Kennedy and
McCarthy. Abruptly, as they were going inside, Johnson reminded McPherson, who had a number of congressional messages still to draft, that he wanted them done by the end of the
following week.

"I want them good," he said. "They may be my last."

McPherson did not rise to the bait.

"You think I'm going to run, don't you?" the President said.

"Sure I do," said McPherson. The President then asked the
speechwriter, "Would you run?"

"No," McPherson replied. "But I'm not you. I'd be sick of
it by now. I know you are, but you have to run."

"Go on," Johnson said. "Why should I run?"

"Well, for one thing, because none of these other guys are
any good at getting a legislative program through Congress,"
McPherson replied. "So we just won't have any forward motion."

The President disagreed: "No, you're wrong. All of them
would do better than I next year. Bob Kennedy would do better
than I. McCarthy would do better than I. Nixon would do better than I. They always give a new boy a chance. They won't
give me a honeymoon. In the first place, with my majority, I
wouldn't want it. But even if I wanted it, they wouldn't give it
to me. It would be one more year like this one; and I don't want
another year like this."

Johnson made clear that day his awareness that the LBJ
magic belonged to the past.

"The Congress and I," he said, "are like an old couple who have seen too much of each other. We yell at each other and we scrap and we fight and we've pushed each other and shoved, and I've smelled all those dirty armpits. . . ."

Armpits were a familiar theme. In the President's vocabulary, sniffing armpits meant lobbying with members of Congress for his legislative program. He had far more to show for his lobbying than, for example, John F. Kennedy. But it rankled with Johnson that Kennedy never stooped to armpit-sniffing.

There were other occasions when McPherson or Joe Califano would come up with some new legislative notion and the President would say, "O.K. What have you done to sell it?"

The usual reply was, "Well, not very much. But we're going to write a strong message for you.'

Then the President would pour out his scorn in generous measure: "God, I was out all night and there were twenty of them [Congressmen] out there; and they were greasy and they were smelly and I had my nose in all their armpits, kissing their asses, trying to get that bill through. And what were you doing about it? Dreaming."

Califano remembers Johnson's haste about legislative messages. "Get them up faster," he would say. "I may not run." Califano did not take the President seriously, he admits. "I thought it was just a typical Johnson maneuver to get his program on the Hill fast, to get me off my ass."

His first intimation that the President might mean what he said came in late March. Johnson had asked him to fly up to New York and speak before a Democratic county leaders' meeting in Queens. Califano drafted for himself a speech that seemed just right for New York Democrats: liberal on the domestic side and "a little more pro-Israel than the State Department." Concerning Vietnam, Califano had dug out some old speeches by Senators Kennedy and McCarthy in which they were still supporting the war. To his great surprise, the President asked Califano to delete the barbs directed at McCarthy and Kennedy.

"You're a young man," the President said. "You've got a great future in the Democratic Party, a great future in the country. I may not be around here very long. And I don't want you to say anything against those guys."

Califano was touched by the President's solicitude. "He really didn't care much about McCarthy because I don't think he believed McCarthy was going anywhere," Califano explained. "But he didn't want me to say anything against Bobby. So he took it out. In his own way, he was protective of his own guys. He was just telling me: 'Don't do something you don't have to do. You don't have to do this for me.'"

During the same early-spring period, the President raised with Califano the possibility of his taking over the Poverty program. "I won't ask you to do this," Johnson said, "unless I decide to run again. If I don't run again I won't ask you to do it, but if I do run again I'd like you to do it, and I'll get you out of there by early next year."

Next day, after a strained conversation with his wife, who had had enough of her husband's 7 A. M.-11 P. M. working hours, Califano glumly agreed. "I'll do whatever you want me to do," he told the President. "As long as I am in the Government, I will do whatever you want me to do." The President, grateful for Califano's loyalty, asked what his aide thought would happen if he did not run. Califano's guess was that Robert Kennedy would be nominated and win the Presidency in November.

"Well, what's so bad about that?" Johnson responded. Califano recalls that he was astonished at the President's comment.

The President appeared satisfied that a new Kennedy Administration would make no great changes in domestic policy. As for Vietnam, Johnson apparently believed that once Kennedy was President he would realize "all the Godawful problems and it would not be a matter of just ordering guys on ships and coming home."

By March 22 the President was feeling the pressure for a public explanation of whatever he proposed to do next in Vietnam. That day he met with the inner circle of advisers to consider the speech draft McPherson had labored over for weeks. McPherson called it the "We Shall Overcome draft." He insists it was not "a belligerent, hawkish speech in any conventional use of the word." There were no threats in it. Neither did it contain any new peace initiative. The number of troops to be sent to Vietnam was left blank. It proposed, however, to call up 50,000 reservists, rejected the idea of a bombing halt without reciprocity, and proposed a surtax in line with a recommendation from Treasury Secretary Henry Fowler.

Clifford found the draft disappointing. He argued for at least a partial bombing halt by way of recouping some of the public support the President had been losing. Katzenbach and Harriman, with support from Vice-President Humphrey, contended that only a full stop would do. Harriman, like Katzenbach, did not believe the North Vietnamese would accept a partial halt. He felt the President should stop all the bombing about May 1. That would allow time for the forces in Vietnam to pull themselves together after the disruptions of Tet. At the end of an inconclusive seven-hour discussion, the President asked Rusk to sum it up.

The consensus, Rusk said, was that some form of bombing halt might be desirable as a sign of American good faith and continued interest in negotiations. The trouble was that the other side would probably not accept a partial halt and that, as responsible men, the President's advisers could not recommend a total cessation that would endanger American troops along the Demilitarized Zone. No one challenged Rusk's summation. It was accurate. It was fair. But it seemed to lead nowhere.

McPherson left the meeting unsatisfied. He had trouble sleeping that night. All night long he groped for something new, a proposal that could not be said to endanger American troops in the field and, at the same time, would permit the United States to scale down or end the bombing; something that would "put us in a better position in the eyes of the world."

Not until next morning, Saturday, March 23, as he was on his way out of the office to lunch, did McPherson's notion jell. He turned around, called in his secretary, and quickly dictated a memorandum for the President. It was not an oversophisticated notion he outlined: the President should stop all bombing north of the 20th parallel. Simultaneously he should offer to stop it entirely, all the way to the 17th parallel, if the adversary would respect the Demilitarized Zone and would not attack the major

cities, including Saigon. Talks might or might not follow. No
one could read the enemy's mind. But the offer would be there,
on the table, whenever North Vietnam decided to meet its terms.

McPherson sent his memorandum to the President about
one o'clock that Saturday afternoon. About five, when he was
getting ready to leave, the President called to ask for a second
copy. It went to Rusk, who promptly and privately relayed it to
Saigon—without McPherson's knowledge—for Ambassador Bunker's consideration. McPherson heard nothing more about the
matter for five days.

It was not, as McPherson conceded, a wholly new idea.
McNamara had pushed a similar notion the year before. "It was
the same old pebble that had been rolling around; it just happened to be dressed up in the right way at the right time," he
said.

On Monday, March 25, the Senior Advisory Group met in
the White House: Dean Acheson, George Ball, McGeorge
Bundy, Douglas Dillon, Arthur Dean, John McCloy, General
Omar Bradley, General Ridgway, General Taylor, Robert Murphy,
Henry Cabot Lodge, Cyrus Vance, who had been deputy Defense
Secretary under McNamara, was also there, as were Ambassador
Goldberg and Abe Fortas from the Supreme Court. They as-
sembled in the afternoon, read some background papers, then
went to dinner at the State Department with Rusk, Clifford,
Walt Rostow, Harriman, and William Bundy. After dinner, the
Wise Men adjourned to the Conference Room of the Operations
Center at State for a briefing by Habib, Carver, and General
DuPuy, the three second-level officials whom Acheson had cross-
questioned earlier.

Their assessment of the military-political situation in South
Vietnam and the effects of the Tet offensive struck Ball as
more candid than those he had listened to before; more candid
and, in his own view, more honest. Ball himself was hardly
surprised. His own assessment had been pessimistic long before
he heard the briefers. Habib stressed the degree to which the
Tet events had unhinged the pacification program, a development Ball took for granted. "What shocked my colleagues,"
Ball later recalled, "was that I don't think they'd had any sense

of the demoralization that it produced. I felt that the loss to the other side of areas that had been more or less under South Vietnamese control came through pretty clearly. It was exactly what I had expected. But the rest of them seemed to have been quite demoralized by this, quite shocked. They didn't realize how much until next morning."

General Taylor, on the other hand, felt that the briefers had nothing new or startling to say. "My impression," he recalled, "was that they'd said the same things over and over." What troubled Taylor was not so much the substance of the briefing as its impact upon his fellows. His own explanation was that all those solid citizens, most of them members of the Eastern Establishment, had come down to Washington persuaded in advance that Tet was a great disaster. His explanation was that they had been influenced more by reading *The New York Times* than by anything the briefers told them. Taylor later acknowledged that crediting or blaming the *Times* alone for so great a country-wide shift in thinking might be too simple, even "simplistic." But he was impressed with the transformation of men he had known for many years, men who had never flinched at tough, unpopular decisions in the past. "They had changed," he said. "We had not changed."

How far that transformation had gone did not become fully apparent until the next morning, March 26, when the Wise Men reassembled in the Operations Center around a green baize table. They were to lunch with the President at midday. First they had to agree on their recommendation. Bundy got the job of rapporteur. He was the man in the middle: committed to neither further escalation nor a total bombing halt. Thus "the indignity of taking notes" fell to him.

Ball made what he later described as "my usual pitch about the goddam futility of it all." He said the time had come to cut America's losses in Vietnam. The current policy, he said, was aimed at accomplishing the impossible, and the sooner the administration faced up to it, the better. None of his colleagues among the Elders went all the way with Ball. But he found a surprising degree of support for the general proposition that the President was trying to accomplish the impossible in Vietnam. McGeorge Bundy and Acheson were of that school. Dillon, Vance, Goldberg, and Ridgway all wanted to see a change of policy—a change in the direction of scaling down the violence, moving toward negotiations. "We were weighing," Vance later told a newsman, "not only what was happening in Vietnam but the social and political effects in the United States, the impact on the U.S. economy, the attitude of other nations. The divisiveness in the country was growing with such acuteness that it was threatening to tear the United States apart."

Taylor, Murphy, and Justice Fortas all favored the present strategy, only more so. The war of attrition was being won and must go on, they argued, with even heavier bombing. Lodge, Arthur Dean, and General Bradley were less ready to recommend a shift in strategy either way.

Clifford then asked the Wise Men how they would feel about a modest reinforcement, not the 206,000 reported in the press but something like 12,500, just enough to meet the requirements of rotation and to provide additional support for the combat forces already there. There was general agreement on that point. Dean Rusk, showing his hand for the first time, raised the possibility of a partial bombing halt. "How would you feel about one that went just down to the 19th parallel?" the Secretary of State asked. This seemed to most of the Elders an idea worth exploring. George Ball, still the great dissenter, couldn't see much hope in a partial cessation.

"I thought going down just to the 19th parallel was rather foolish," he said later, "because the significance of our bombing the North was that it was a political impediment to negotiations. The impediment would not be removed, simply by scaling it down. As long as we were attacking any of their soil, we might as well be attacking all of it."

The Wise Men broke for lunch with the President, having agreed with the ideas both Rusk and Clifford put to them: a partial cessation of bombing was worth trying, and massive escalation was out.

The President had quietly invited another luncheon guest, General Abrams, all the way from Saigon. Abrams talked for about forty-five minutes and, by all accounts, favorably impressed everyone at the table. He talked about how much more could be done to build up the South Vietnamese forces; with more training and more modern equipment, Abrams contended, they could take over greatly increased responsibilities for the defense of their own country. This was just what many of the Wise Men had been waiting years to hear. The Abrams-for-Westmoreland shift apparently portended a real change in tactics and policy, though not until the Nixon campaign that summer did it get the name "Vietnamization."

After lunch the President told Rusk and Clifford to get back to their departments. "I don't want any of my elder statesmen here to feel that they can't speak frankly to me without having any people in the Government around," Johnson said.

It was then, after luncheon, that Bundy delivered his report in behalf of the Wise Men. He reported a broad consensus that the President had set his sights too high. Without applying virtually unlimited resources, the objectives of present policy could not be achieved, Bundy said; and with public support for the war eroding, a changed policy was called for. Bradley, Murphy, and Fortas objected that Bundy's summation did not reflect their views. Acheson, seated beside the President, broke in to say that Bundy had certainly reflected *his* views. The President went round the table and was surprised at the number of defectors, including Cyrus Vance, long a special favorite of his; Bundy, Acheson, even old General Bradley. "Well, I've listened to all this," Bradley said, "and I've heard that briefing. I don't think we can do what we set out to do here with the limitations that have been set by the situation. I think, Mr. President, you're going to have to lower your sights."

There was a sharp clash between Acheson and General Wheeler, just returned from his meeting with Westmoreland in the Philippines. Wheeler took issue with Acheson's statement that U.S. policy was still bent upon a military solution. Not so, Wheeler contended; the Joint Chiefs and Westmoreland himself understood that a "classic military victory" was not possible in the special situation of Vietnam. Acheson called that disingenuous. If the use of half a million men to eradicate the Viet Cong and to drive the North Vietnamese back out of the South was

not an effort aimed at a military solution, then words had lost
their meaning.

When Ball's turn came, he spoke out for a total bombing
halt. "Well, you agree with Arthur Goldberg," the President in-
terjected. Ball replied: "As far as I understand Arthur's views,
I think they are very much the same as mine." He went on to
argue that, in his opinion, the North Vietnamese would refuse
to negotiate so long as the United States was attacking any part
of their territory. Ball was rolling on, never at a loss for words,
when Abe Fortas cut in: "What George Ball is really trying to
say, Mr. President, . . ." and went on to misstate Ball's position.
Turning to Fortas, Ball snapped: "Well, you sure as hell aren't
doing it." The President looked up, startled. Then McGeorge
Bundy volunteered to clarify the matter and stated Ball's position
accurately.

Fortas, as a sitting Supreme Court Justice, had no business
advising the President in any event, as the many lawyers round
the table had been raised to believe. Moreover, the Justice's direct
experience of military affairs and foreign policy would not have
filled an eyedropper. Finally, his reflexive hawkishness, while
it may have comforted the President, went down badly with
Ball and others, who felt the times cried out for a new policy
squarely aimed at turning the war down and, if at all possible,
ending it.

The President looked stricken when it was all over. No
more so, perhaps, than Maxwell Taylor, who said he could have
fallen off his chair when he heard Vance and Acheson speak
out. Rostow was heard to grumble that the briefers had exaggerated the effects of Tet. So the President recalled Carver and
DuPuy (Habib was out of the city) on the following day. He
wanted to hear exactly what they had told the Wise Men. They
repeated the briefing in the presence of General Abrams, but
the President was not satisfied. "You aren't telling me what you
told them," he said. "You must have given them a different
briefing." The President thereafter complained to members of
his official family that the briefers had been "reached"; he did
not say by whom. "Who poisoned the well?" the President
wanted to know.

For Clifford, who invented the stratagem of calling in the Wise Men when he felt the decision within the government slipping away from him, the turnabout was auspicious. Still he could not decipher the President's intentions. Johnson was certainly upset. The small-town Texan's acute sense of social inferiority toward eastern mandarins like Acheson and Bundy must have been a factor. The defection of Vance, always his first choice for such difficult trouble-shooting assignments as the Detroit riots, the Cyprus crisis, or trouble in Korea, must have been particularly painful. Yet the President gave no clear sign of his changing attitude.

On the morning of March 28 Clifford, McPherson, Rostow, and William Bundy met in Rusk's office at eleven o'clock. Their purpose was to polish the latest speech draft that Harry McPherson had worked up for delivery by the President the night of Sunday, March 31, two days before the McCarthy-Johnson primary vote in Wisconsin. The draft (McPherson believes it was No. 10 or 11 in a long series) was clearly out of date. It did not, for example, include the two-step bombing-halt formula proposed to the President by McPherson himself on March 23. Clifford was unhappy with the draft. "It won't do," he said. Somewhat timidly, McPherson suggested that perhaps a peace offer should be written into it, mentioning his memorandum to the President. To his great surprise, McPherson heard Rusk say, rather matter-of-factly, that the bombing-halt proposal had been sent out to Saigon and that Ambassador Bunker felt he could live with it. Clifford knew nothing of this either.

Clifford, as soon as he had read the draft, launched into a sonorous hour-long monologue. "The President," he said, "cannot give that speech. It would be a disaster." He went on to say that major elements of the American community—businessmen, the press, churches, professional groups, students, college presidents, the intellectuals—had turned against the war. What the country wanted to hear was a peace speech. "This war," he said, "is tearing the whole fabric of American life. It's destroying the confidence of the people in their government. I've heard it said that if we pulled out too quickly from Vietnam, that would encourage isolationism. I tell you frankly, the continuance of the war at this level, with no better idea than we have now of how and when it will end, will lead to the true isolationism. The American people will be repelled by the idea of further foreign adventures, no matter how vital they may be to our security. I don't want to have to go back and reargue all that's gone before. But I've never felt it as I feel it now."

He went back over his sad experience with the Joint Chiefs, asking them, "How are we going to win?"; and getting the answer that it would take an invasion of North Vietnam, Laos, and Cambodia; then asking the generals to assume they would not be allowed to invade the whole of Indochina. What then? How are we going to win it? And the generals replying, "We're not." Clifford is not an easy man to interrupt when in full spate. Rusk did not try. He remembers Clifford arguing with great eloquence that he wanted a Democratic President to make the first big step toward peace. What the speech had to accomplish, Clifford said repeatedly, was to set in motion "a winching-down of the war." The goal must be to reduce the level of violence, reduce the number of troops, reduce the number of engagements; and as the North Vietnamese responded, the United States would start another round of reductions.

For the first time, Clifford felt that Rusk agreed. He found the Secretary of State "enormously reasonable," perhaps because Rusk, on his own, had earlier come to the same conclusions. At lunchtime sandwiches were brought in. The soul-searching continued until 5 P. M. By that time the speech's opening had been turned around. Instead of: "My fellow Americans, I want to talk to you tonight about the war in Vietnam," the new opening read: "Good evening, my fellow Americans. Tonight I want to talk to you of peace in Vietnam and Southeast Asia."

McPherson remembers that session as the best he ever attended. He went back to work in a state of high exhilaration, and through the night prepared a new peace draft. It included an unconditional bombing halt at the 20th parallel and the promise of a cutback to the 17th (if Hanoi would respect the Demilitarized Zone and refrain from attacks on the cities). He sent it to the President early Friday morning, March 29. Later that day the President telephoned to check a passage on "page three." McPherson had to compare the two latest drafts before he realized that the President, guarding his options every step of the way, was working on his latest draft, the peace speech.

As for Clifford, who correctly assumed that the President knew all about the March 28 agreement between himself and Rusk, thanks to Rostow's presence at the speech-polishing session, he remembers feeling "a surge of hope." He could not see the President going against the advice of both the Secretary of Defense and the Secretary of State.

Rusk left Washington March 30 for a meeting of the Vietnam troop-contributing countries in Wellington, New Zealand. His Under Secretary, Nick Katzenbach, then took a hand in completing the fine details of the proposed peace initiative. Katzenbach preferred to draw the bombing limit at the 19th parallel. The Joint Chiefs, through Rostow, insisted on the 20th. They wanted to be free to go on bombing Thanhhoa, a railway switching point 210 miles north of the Demilitarized Zone, and Route 7 leading into Laos. Both targets were just a few miles south of the 20th parallel.

Katzenbach didn't think much of the military argument, and said as much to Rostow. When the President insisted, Katzenbach raised no further objection. He proposed, however, that instead of baldly identifying the 20th parallel as the upper limit, the President should express it in "functional terms." That was promptly translated into a speech passage that spoke of no further bombing in areas inhabited by "almost 90 percent" of the North Vietnamese population. The word was to be passed secretly to the Russians, who would relay it to Hanoi, that the 20th parallel was the upper limit. Although Katzenbach, personally, could not see the North Vietnamese accepting a partial halt, he did not want the effort needlessly jeopardized by misunderstandings.

"It's very important," he said to Walt Rostow, "that you do not deceive the North Vietnamese. If it's to be the 20th parallel, there must be no misunderstanding. Don't make the first big raid at 19 degrees, 59 minutes. Make sure that the [military] orders are consistent with the speech."

Through Friday and Saturday a small group worked with

the President, refining the speech. On Friday, Joe Califano, who had been ill at home, came in to see the White House doctor. McPherson showed him the latest speech draft, and both agreed that it was fine except for the lack of a "sock 'em" ending. McPherson offered to write one. But the President insisted the speech was "fine the way it is." The President called in a former White House aide, Horace Busby, to work with him in the final hours before air time Sunday on final revisions.

The President had invited the Cliffords, the Rostows, Jack Valenti, and Busby to watch the speech in the family quarters of the White House. The Secretary of Defense, trying without success to conceal his high good humor, knew the President would, in just a few minutes, cut back the bombing to the 20th parallel and announce that he was sending 13,500 more troops to General Westmoreland instead of 206,000. A few minutes before nine o'clock, when Johnson was to start reading his speech, he asked Clifford to have a look at two paragraphs he was adding to the speech. "I thought you'd be interested in seeing this," the President said. The surprise ending, drafted by Busby, read:

With America's sons in the fields far away, with America's future under challenge right here at home, with our hopes and the world's hopes for peace in the balance every day, I do not believe that I should devote an hour or a day of my time to any personal partisan causes or to any duties other than the awesome duties of this office —the Presidency of your country. Accordingly, I shall not seek, and I will not accept, the nomination of my party for another term as your President.

Across the land and round the world, surprise was the all but universal emotion. The young campaign workers for McCarthy and Kennedy were jubilant. Many ordinary citizens could not bring themselves to believe that Lyndon Johnson would give up power so lightly; there was talk in some circles of a slick maneuver by which Johnson would somehow contrive to be "drafted" in spite of his renunciation. But Dean Rusk and General Westmoreland knew he meant it.

Rusk got the word by radiotelephone, as he was flying to

New Zealand, that the President was adding a paragraph or two to his speech. The Secretary of State thought he knew what that meant. For about a year he had believed that Johnson would pull out in March. Rusk had heard the President say how much he admired Harry Truman for withdrawing, in March, 1952, so that other candidates would have time to prepare themselves and run for the Democratic nomination. This was the last day of March, 1968. "If it was to be done at all," Rusk believed, "it had to be done then." He flew on to New Zealand, confident that the President's decision would add credibility to his plea for a negotiated settlement, short of victory.

In Saigon it was ten o'clock in the morning, Monday, April 1. Westmoreland stepped out of a meeting in the American Embassy to take a call from General Wheeler in Washington. The President wanted General Westmoreland to know, Wheeler said, that he was about to announce what they had talked about back in November. Hubert Humphrey got the news in Mexico. He wept openly. Joe Califano, still ailing, was in his bedroom, watching television. His wife was downstairs, reading the Sunday newspapers. She knew what the President was going to say about de-escalating the war. Joe had told her. "Then the President came to the end of his speech, and he paused, and he started again," Califano recalled. "I remember shouting downstairs: 'Trudy, he's going to pull out, he's going to pull out!' So she came running upstairs and we watched him pull out together." At last, Califano knew he was free. He would not have to take over the Poverty program. Trudy Califano could look forward to seeing her husband around the house later than 7 A.M. and long before 11 P.M.

The why of Lyndon Johnson's decision to quit remains hard to pin down. There was the matter of Mrs. Johnson's anxiety about his health; his own presentiment (expressed to Westmoreland in November) that if he ran again and won he might, like Woodrow Wilson, become incapacitated. He had confessed to McPherson that he knew he would not again have his way with the Congress; that Nixon or Kennedy or McCarthy would do better because they were "new boys." General Taylor's explanation is that the President was shaken by the defections of people he had greatly respected. Taylor said, "When he found people drawing away from him as McNamara did to some extent, Clifford, Cy Vance, Acheson, it really shook him. Of all the things I could put my finger on as the proximate cause, that was it. He had decided he was a handicap in South Vietnam and deliberately withdrew for that reason."

Califano believes the underlying reason was that the President realized that he had come to symbolize a divided country, divided over the war and the crisis in black-and-white. It would have been almost as hard, Califano believes, for Johnson to campaign in the Deep South in 1968 as it was for him to visit a college campus. "I honestly believe," Califano submits, "that the President felt he had become the symbol of absolutely destructive division in the United States—and he had to get out."

Lady Bird Johnson, who certainly knew more than anyone else about the President's state of mind, provides additional details in her remarkable diary about the Johnson Presidency. By early 1967, Mrs. Johnson noted, Johnson began to lose "the bounce, the laughter, the teasing quality." In March she and Justice Fortas agreed that Lyndon "had had enough," and that he ought to announce his retirement in one year—by March, 1968. In September the President chatted at the LBJ Ranch with two old friends, Texas Governor John B. Connally, Jr. and Representative J. J. (Jake) Pickle, who represented Johnson's old district in Congress. For eight hours they discussed one theme—"Lyndon's big decision—when and how to announce that he is not going to run again for the Presidency." Pickle argued against it; Connally for it, suggesting an October announcement "to keep it from looking as if you were running out." Mrs. Johnson added her own thoughts. "I do not know whether we can endure another four-year term in the Presidency," she said. "I use the word 'endure' in Webster's own meaning, 'to last, remain, continue in the same state without perishing.' I face the prospect of another campaign like an open-end stay in a concentration camp."

The October date was set aside. The family discussed the possibility of adding it to the President's State of the Union message on January 17, 1968, but Johnson thought that such an announcement then would kill his legislative program for 1968.

Mrs. Johnson insists the final decision was not made until March 31, the afternoon of the big speech. "I think what was uppermost—what was going over and over in Lyndon's mind —was what I've heard him say increasingly these last months: 'I do not believe I can unite this country!'"

An immensely active, egotistical man, Johnson must have toyed with the notion of running for re-election, despite his earlier confidences to Westmoreland, throughout his post-Tet re-evaluation of policy. For him, it was not just a cool appraisal of policy; it was also a judgment upon himself and his Presidency. It proved to be a somber, negative judgment. The Wise Men only underscored his own appraisal. Shrewdly Johnson then snuffed out his second-term ambitions and, by adding his renunciation of power to his cutback in the bombing of North Vietnam, underlined the seriousness of his proposal. The effect, according to the Rumanian intermediaries, among others, was to persuade Hanoi that finally LBJ meant business.

Still, the President's credibility problem at home stayed with him to the end. On the night of March 31 he had announced that the bombing of the North would stop in areas inhabited by "almost 90 percent of the population." The Russians and the North Vietnamese leadership had been told privately that meant no bombing beyond the 20th parallel. The American people and the Congress, unfortunately, had not been told. Some assumed the line had been drawn at the 19th parallel, to be pulled back to the 17th if North Vietnam agreed not to abuse the DMZ and bomb the cities of the South.

Within thirty-six hours of the President's speech, Navy jets attacked Thanhhoa. This was precisely what Katzenbach feared would happen. Immediately there was an outcry in Congress. Senator Fulbright accused the administration of misleading the American people. Here were American jets bombing more than 200 miles north of the DMZ, before Hanoi could accept or reject the President's overture. State Department officials, taking their cue from Katzenbach, accused the military commanders of sabotaging the peace initiative.

Clifford, fearful that a squabble of this kind would doom the peace effort, persuaded the President to pull the bombing limit back down to the 19th parallel. Rostow and General Wheeler fought hard to reverse the decision. But Hanoi did not, in fact, misunderstand the President. It had been assured that the 20th parallel was the limit and Thanhhoa indisputably lay south of the parallel.

On April 4, to Washington's great surprise, North Vietnam accepted President Johnson's offer: a partial bombing halt in exchange for talks. Hanoi stipulated that the talks must be preliminary, their single purpose to decide when and how all the bombing would be stopped. It was a small step in the right direction, something to be grateful for in spite of the undignified squabble that followed over the place of the meetings. Washington proposed Geneva. Hanoi countered with Pnom Penh. Although the President had said time and again, to the point of world-wide boredom, that he was ready to "meet anywhere, anytime" he turned down Pnom Penh. Instead, Washington proposed Vientiane, Rangoon, Djakarta, or New Delhi. Hanoi countered with Warsaw. Again the President refused. So it went, Washington next proposing Colombo, Tokyo, Kabul, Katmandu, Rawalpindi, Kuala Lumpur, Rome, Brussels, Helsinki, and Vienna. At last Paris was agreed upon, by way of ending the foolish quibble.

Thus on May 10, 1968, in a Paris hotel building near the Arc de Triomphe, used as a military headquarters first by the Germans and then by the Americans in World War II, delegates of the United States and North Vietnam sat down together to talk of peace in Indochina.

NINE

Winching Down the War

Soon after the November election, President-elect Nixon announced that he was going to encourage differences of opinion within the new Republican Administration. When Lyndon Johnson heard of Nixon's remark, he said wearily, "If he went through many sessions with Rusk sitting at his right and Clifford at his left, he'd soon get over that feeling." The Secretaries of State and Defense had briefly overcome their temperamental and policy differences toward the end of March, 1968, and joined together in persuading the President to accept the partial bombing halt. But as the war dragged on, with no talk of peace even in Paris, they soon became polite antagonists. The President took to complaining that his two senior Cabinet officers were competing for the Nobel Peace Prize.

Their difference of outlook recalled the classic anecdote about the congenital optimist and the congenital pessimist: asked to describe a glass of water, Rusk would have said that it was half empty, Clifford that it was half full. In the push for peace in Vietnam, Clifford's inclination was to run more risks for a political settlement; Rusk's to make absolutely certain before one more step was taken that the ground underfoot was solid. They divided, for example, on whether to continue bombing south of the 19th parallel. In Paris, the North Vietnamese delegates, Xuan Thuy and Le Duc Tho, insisted (at least in their public statements) that until all the bombing was stopped, to the 17th parallel, they would refuse to discuss any other topic. Clifford supported Averell Harriman and Cyrus Vance, the American negotiators, in pressing for a total bombing halt so

the talks could get down to matters of substance. Rusk, on the
other hand, shared President Johnson's instinctive reluctance
to give up bombing the North. He rated its practical effect
higher than Clifford. Regarding the bombing halt as a blue chip,
he was reluctant to put it in play until the Communists had
given convincing proof of restraint.

The Joint Chiefs, General Taylor, and Walt Rostow all
argued that Hanoi had no real interest in peace; the only reason
North Vietnam had agreed to begin talking, they contended,
was that it was on the verge of defeat, so heavy had been its
losses during and after the Tet offensive. The argument they
made was that if the United States would keep up the military
pressure just a little longer, it could put itself in a dominant
bargaining position. True, the President's March 31 speech had
ruled out the goal of military victory. But the professional military leaders—and their principal civilian ally, Rostow—were
now behaving as if the Vietnam stalemate could, after all, be
converted into something that curiously resembled victory. In
this position, the Joint Chiefs were reinforced by Ambassador
Ellsworth Bunker in Saigon. Evidence that the adversary might
be withdrawing some of his troops or adopting less aggressive
battlefield tactics was fairly steadily discounted by Bunker and
his staff. Plain military necessity, they contended; the North
Vietnamese are hurting so badly that they have no choice.

Harriman was left to deal with the consequences of this
stubbornly negative attitude in his talks with Xuan Thuy. The
North Vietnamese would complain to Harriman or Vance:
"Whenever we attack, you say that this attack is not conducive
to an atmosphere which furthers the peace negotiations. But
when we stop, Saigon announces that we are defeated—and
forced to end the attack."

In July Clifford visited South Vietnam to see for himself
where the matter stood. He had developed a plan, soon after
the President's March 31 decision, to speed the re-equipping of
South Vietnamese forces with the M-16 rifle and other modern
weapons so that the burden of combat could progressively be
shifted to ARVN. At the same time Clifford was determined to
do everything in his power to support the peace efforts in Paris.

"I found distressingly little evidence that the other troop-contributing countries, or the South Vietnamese, were straining to relieve us of our burden," Clifford recalled after leaving office. He felt the South Vietnamese leadership was altogether "too complacent" about shortcomings in troop training and junior officer recruitment. As for the desertion rate, still at an alarming rate of 30 percent a year. Clifford was flabbergasted by Vice-President Ky's explanation that the men were deserting because their pay was too low. When Clifford asked what Saigon proposed to do about it, Ky suggested that the money the United States was going to save by cutting back its bombing campaign should be turned over to the South Vietnam. Then it could pay its soldiers more generously.

"I returned home oppressed by the pervasive Americanization of the war," Clifford wrote. "We were still giving the military instructions, still doing most of the fighting, still providing all the matériel, still paying most of the bills. Worst of all, I concluded that the South Vietnamese leaders seemed content to have it that way."

On his way home from Saigon, an exhausted, discouraged Clifford (not fully recovered from an attack of hepatitis) stopped in Honolulu to join President Johnson in one more strategy session with President Thieu. Harry McPherson, who flew out from Washington with the President, remembers carrying Clifford's bag as they walked side by side up the long driveway of the Henry J. Kaiser estate, where the President was quartered. "I want to tell you about 'them fellas,'" Clifford said. "They've got the most heavily armed police force they'll ever have around them and they're going to get killed if it's removed. And they're making millions, maybe billions, out of the war. Their interests and ours are irreconcilably in conflict."

The irreconcilable conflict Clifford saw building between Washington and Saigon threatened to doom the Paris talks and to blight Clifford's hope of "winching down the war." The Defense Secretary was deeply troubled: American casualties were still running high; "The enemy was not winning, but, I felt, neither were we"; moreover, so preoccupied was the administration with the single problem area of Southeast Asia that it could not address itself to emerging problems in other parts of the world. Clifford came to feel that the administration must bear down harder than ever before on the Thieu-Ky regime, insist that it take over a larger share of the combat burden, and that it stop obstructing even the most tentative moves toward a political settlement.

At the end of July, 1968, Harriman and Vance (lumped together in coded government communications as "Harvan") suggested a peace ploy to the President. Pointing to a noticeable midsummer lull in fighting, which the Joint Chiefs already had discounted as a period of enemy regrouping, Harriman and Vance pleaded with the President to exploit the occasion. Let him treat the lull, the two ambassadors suggested, as a deliberate act of restraint or de-escalation by the enemy. Let him respond by halting all bombing of North Vietnam. From some private indications in Paris, the two negotiators had reason to hope that such action might persuade the Communists not to launch a new offensive and perhaps to get serious about negotiations. Harriman later explained that he was trying "to pull a Tommy Thompson." During the Cuban missile crisis, Thompson, the veteran Kremlinologist, had recommended to President Kennedy that he ignore the tough rhetoric in a Khrushchev message and respond only to the hopeful hints of a possible settlement; in other words, to take the optimistic track, assume the enemy wants peace, and help him achieve it. Harriman, in effect, was urging the President to listen to his new Secretary of Defense.

Clifford, of course, backed Harriman and Vance, as did Vice-President Humphrey, who was about to be nominated for the Presidency and chafed more each day at the burden of defending the war. Katzenbach and William Bundy happened to be in Paris at the time. Moreover, *The New York Times* published an editorial on July 29 advocating a similar tactic. The President, always quick to sniff a conspiracy, evidently persuaded himself that Harriman and Vance, in cahoots with Katzenbach and Bundy, were using the *Times* to put public pressure on him. He rejected the plan without further consideration.

Vance and Harriman in the meantime had coaxed the North

Vietnamese to start meeting privately with them. The Americans kept probing for the terms of an understanding that would justify the President in stopping the bombing. Week after week they kept urging the Vietnamese to agree that, if the bombing were stopped, their side would respect the Demilitarized Zone and end the rocket-mortar attacks on cities in South Vietnam. They also kept pressing the North Vietnamese to accept the idea that no settlement could be worked out unless South Vietnam was represented at the bargaining table. If Hanoi agreed to sit down with a Saigon delegation, they kept saying, the United States would not object to sitting down with representatives of the National Liberation Front.

Such an arrangement seemed to Harriman perhaps the only way out of the negotiating impasse. The North Vietnamese were refusing to discuss any aspect of a military settlement. They clung to the threadbare fiction that only southerners were involved in the fighting; thus only the NLF could negotiate military arrangements. For their part, the men from Hanoi kept urging Vance and Harriman to discuss with them terms for a political settlement. This the American refused to do in the absence of a delegation from Saigon. And the Hanoi delegates kept announcing that they would never sit down with representatives of the "puppet regime" in the South.

Although there had been hints before, the first real sign of a more cooperative attitude came in Paris on October 11 during the eleventh secret meeting of American and North Vietnamese negotiators. The President was having his afternoon nap when a Harvan message arrived, indicating that Hanoi might be in a bargaining mood. A North Vietnamese delegate had put the question to Cyrus Vance: If we agree to sit down with a South Vietnamese delegation, would the United States stop the bombing?

Vance, in reply, had stressed the familiar conditions: there must be no abuse of the DMZ, no more rocket-mortar attacks on southern population centers. Both Harriman and Vance felt that Hanoi wanted the bombing stopped, understood the need to comply, but would probably balk at labeling these two actions as specific conditions. For years past, Hanoi had been consistently demanding an *unconditional* bombing halt. If it were quietly to accept American conditions now, there must be no embarrassing public talk about them.

Rusk and Walt Rostow briefed the President immediately after his nap on the latest development. The Secretary of State believed Hanoi's change of attitude was connected chiefly with the battlefield situation: enemy units were getting harder to find; many had slipped across the frontiers into Cambodia, Laos, or North Vietnam itself. They might just need a breather, Rusk suggested; either that or the Communists had lost the war, knew it, and were changing strategy.

Johnson showed interest together with characteristic wariness. He was not about "to trade a horse for a rabbit," the President said. But he told Rusk to draft follow-up instructions for Harriman and Vance, the instructions to be cleared beforehand with General Abrams and Ambassador Bunker in Saigon. If his men in Saigon were to object to a bombing halt on the ground that it might endanger American troops in the field, he would not go ahead. The President also instructed Rusk to send word through diplomatic channels to Premier Alexei Kosygin and First Secretary Leonid Brezhnev in Moscow that the United States would require "firm assurances" concerning the safety of the DMZ and the cities of the South before proceeding with the plan.

George Christian has observed that Johnson by this time had become "less a President than he was before." He had exactly 100 days left in the White House, and his cup was overflowing with bitterness. Congress no longer did his bidding; he had been denied the satisfaction of installing his old friend, lawyer, and personal adviser, Abe Fortas, as Chief Justice of the United States. Hubert Humphrey, his hand-picked successor, looked and sounded like a loser. The Nonproliferation Treaty had been sidetracked, awaiting the inauguration of a new President. The President's dream of a triumphal voyage of reconciliation to the Soviet Union had been blasted by the Soviet invasion of Czechoslovakia in August. Even the Gun Control Bill, which he had pressed so long and hard following the assassination of John Kennedy, had been watered down by Congress to the point where it banned only mail-order sales. Moreover, as Humphrey and Nixon campaigned across the land, Johnson was getting less attention from press and public. He had chosen to go out as a lame duck. But he had not bargained for premature oblivion.

Now at last he saw an opportunity to get the Paris talks moving; it might be his last significant contribution. The President called his senior advisers together Monday morning, October 14, though not without more irritation. The morning newspapers were reporting that McGeorge Bundy, in a speech the day before at DePauw University, had proposed an unconditional bombing halt and a gradual American troop withdrawal from Vietnam. The President had known since March of Bundy's disenchantment with the war policy. What worried him was the thought that Hanoi, in its ignorance of American politics, might assume that Bundy was speaking for his former boss, the President of the United States. The President's fear was that Hanoi might well decide the bombing was going to be stopped in any case and thus refuse a show of reciprocal restraint. The Monday-morning session, however, showed surprising unanimity. Bunker and Abrams had sent word that they agreed with Harriman and Vance: the bombing could be stopped; Saigon would send a delegation to Paris; the NLF would be welcome.

General Wheeler, just returned with Clifford from a NATO meeting in Germany, raised no objection. The weather in the Panhandle area was so bad that air strikes in any case were difficult to carry out, Wheeler said. He felt the time was right to test Hanoi's good faith. If Hanoi were later to violate the agreement, the bombing could always be resumed. President Johnson responded somewhat gloomily that it might be difficult to start bombing again, once it was stopped altogether, in view of world opinion. Dean Rusk, ever the voice of caution, agreed the peace effort should be made while warning everyone at the table that the United States had paid a heavy price in Vietnam —28,000 dead and some $75 billion till then—which should not be thrown away for what he called a dishonorable peace.

The President wondered aloud whether, by stopping the bombing in the final weeks of the presidential campaign, he would leave himself open to charges of playing cheap politics. Clifford reassured him. Turning the war around was more important than the election, he argued, and the time for action was now.

The same afternoon the President recalled his advisers together with Senator Richard Russell, the venerable Georgia Democrat. Having learned to value Russell's judgment when they served together in the Senate, Johnson wanted his approval now. So Russell listened to briefings by Rostow, Rusk, and Clifford. Rostow was able to report that President Thieu now joined Abrams and Bunker in going along with the new approach. One by one the service chiefs chimed in: General J. P. McConnell for the Air Force; Admiral Thomas Moorer for the Navy; General Leonard Chapman for the Marine Corps; Generals Bruce Palmer and Westmoreland for the Army.

There was no dissent from any quarter, Senator Russell included. His only qualm was that the President would probably be accused of playing politics. "They'll accuse you of everything in the book," Russell warned.

Johnson, skeptical to the end, finally instructed Rusk and Clifford to go ahead even though he saw no more than an outside chance the new approach would work. The bombing halt was set to be announced at midnight, October 15. The President ordered absolute secrecy in all federal departments.

In a matter of hours the presidential skepticism found vindication. From Saigon the American Embassy sent word that President Thieu wanted a twenty-four-hour delay to work out some political problems. From Paris the Harvan channel reported a hitch on the Communist side. The North Vietnamese were saying it would be impossible to hold the first expanded session one day after the bombing stopped because the National Liberation Front needed more time to get its delegation all the way to Paris. Harriman and Vance, fearing a loss of momentum, urged the President to stop the bombing anyway. The talks could start a few days later, they reasoned, after both the NLF and Saigon delegations had reached Paris. But the President's suspicions were aroused. He feared the enemy would take advantage of the bombing halt to move up more men and supplies. "I will not stop the bombing," he said, "if I do not know that serious talks will start with the Government of [South] Vietnam at the table."

Just as the arrangements for stopping the bombing began to unravel, so also the President's strict injunction to keep the move secret came to nothing. The story leaked first out of Saigon, though not in full detail. Ambassador Bunker had gone to see President Thieu three times in a single day. Washington reporters were on the telephone to their sources before breakfast time October 16. One of the authors, on television at seven o'clock that morning, reported that the total bombing halt Hanoi had been demanding since May was about to be announced. Having roused one prominent official from his bed an hour earlier, he had learned that the bombing halt, in fact, had been scheduled for announcement at midnight. In Canberra, Australia's Prime Minister Gorton confirmed that Washington had consulted him regarding a bombing cessation. In Paris that day, American and North Vietnamese negotiators held their twenty-sixth session. William Jorden, the U.S. spokesman, acknowledged "there has been movement in the talks" but refused to call it progress. Besieged by reporters seeking confirmation, the White House kept insisting (in the words of George Christian): "There has been no change in the situation, no breakthrough." In a matter of hours, other officials were saying privately, the loose ends ought to be tied up.

The President could no longer postpone telling the Presidential candidates what was about to happen. From the Oval Office, he put in a conference call to Hubert Humphrey in St. Louis, Richard Nixon in Kansas City, and George Wallace in Los Angeles. Nixon said he would make no statements that would "undercut the negotiations." Wallace promised not to "play politics and foul up the negotiations." Humphrey said thank you and little else. As the candidate of the President's party, who moreover had argued for a bombing halt, he felt the White House should have informed him ahead of his rivals.

President Thieu was still balking. Hanoi also kept asking for more time. Humphrey fretted over the delays, wondering whether the bombing would end in time to do him any good at the polls. Nixon, who had campaigned since September on the promise of a never-divulged plan to end the war, could not be sure at what moment the President would blunt that issue by stopping the bombing. It was a fretful time for all of them, not least for the President himself. Secretly, in Paris, a new target date was agreed upon. The bombing would stop on Friday, October 25. Three days later, on Monday, October 28, the delegations from Saigon and the National Liberation Front were to join the talks for the first time. That would make four parties to the negotiation. But because Saigon still refused to acknowledge the NLF, and Hanoi refused to acknowledge Saigon, Harriman and Vance had invented a transparent diplomatic fiction: There would be only two sides: "our side" and "your side." The NLF could sit on the North Vietnamese side; the South Vietnamese would sit with the Americans. Each side would have its own mythology, as Rostow put it.

Unfortunately. October 25 brought a new complication instead of talks. Hanoi sent word that before the talks could start the United States must sign a paper described as a secret "minute" attesting that President Johnson had agreed to stop the bombing "without conditions." Hanoi, in fact, had already *secretly* accepted two conditions: no abuse of the DMZ and no more rocket attacks on the cities. But the North Vietnamese leaders, after more than three years of telling the world and their own people that they would never accept conditions, were trying to save face. This time the President refused to play any more word games.

Johnson was now feeling—and showing—the strain. Campaigning for Humphrey in New York that Sunday, October 27, he said at a Democratic Party luncheon: "I wish I could give you some better news, and I wish I could tell you more than I have. . . . As eager as I am—and I work on it every day and every night and I have for many, many months—I just cannot make news until there is news. . . . What I need now is not your curiosity. I need your prayers."

After so many disappointments, the President could not place much hope in the news he had just received from Paris that Hanoi had dropped its demand for the secret minute. But he instructed Rostow, by telephone from New York, to summon General Abrams to Washington. He stressed that Abrams was to come alone. Bunker could not be spared from the round-the-clock task of holding President Thieu's hand. The President was beginning to suspect that Saigon might be stalling until the election was over in the hope that Nixon would win. He had seen evidence that Mrs. Anna Chennault, widow of the Flying Tiger commander, might be intriguing with the South Vietnamese Embassy in behalf of the Republican National Committee. Time was running out.

General Abrams reached Washington from Saigon at 2 A.M. on Tuesday, October 29. Christian recalls that the new Vietnam commander, trying hard to conceal his identity, walked into the White House "looking like a grizzled Spencer Tracy in a snap-brim hat never intended for a general." At 2:30 the President called his secret council to order in the Cabinet Room: Rusk on the President's right, Abrams on his left, Clifford, General Wheeler, Rostow, Helms, Taylor, and Harry McPherson round the table.

Abrams's report gave the President an infusion of hope. A new major attack on Saigon, the general said, could not succeed. There would be no problem about assaults across the Demilitarized Zone. Even if the North Vietnamese were to create some emergency situation after the bombing had stopped, the Army could deal with it. Johnson put the question: Could the bombing be stopped now without causing additional American and Allied casualties?

"Yes, sir," Abrams replied.

The general added that he had no reservations about the plan. It was, he said, the right thing to do.

At five o'clock, still in the darkness of early dawn, the Cabinet Room council ended. An hour later Rusk received word that President Thieu again was playing for time—three days, he complained, were not enough to get his South Vietnamese delegation to Paris. Johnson, thoroughly exasperated and bone-weary, sent word back that there could be no more delays. He reinforced the message with an implied threat to let the American people know that Thieu—not the Communists—was blocking the move toward peace.

There were other alarms during the final hours before the President was to make known his decision with a television speech on October 31. The night of October 30 a rocket attack on Saigon demolished a Roman Catholic church, killing nineteen Vietnamese. Thieu and Johnson were equally furious, until Rostow pointed out that the United States was still bombing North Vietnam. Once again the President put in a conference call to Humphrey, now in Elizabeth, New Jersey; to Nixon, in his New York apartment; and to Wallace in a Norfolk, Virginia, motel. He told them he was now prepared to end the bombing based on the understandings worked out in Paris, with the full concurrence of the Joint Chiefs, General Abrams, and Ambassador Bunker. The President reminded all three candidates that he had taken himself out of the race in the hope of restoring peace and he was not inclined to delay now because the election happened to be just a few days off. All three candidates promised to say nothing that might complicate his task.

The speech, filmed in advance by a White House crew under Commander Tommy Atkins, was delivered to the networks on the 31st, for broadcast at 8 P. M. eastern time. There was one final flurry of excitement when Channel 13 in New York City started broadcasting the speech before the agreed deadline.* Lloyd Hackler, the assistant White House news secretary, who had delivered the film to the NBC studios in Washington for electronic transmission to other networks and broadcasting stations, pulled the power plug as soon as he heard that Channel 13 was breaking the embargo. But it was too late now for presidential secrets. Every newsman in the capital knew what was about to happen; at last the suspense was over. The President who had started the bombing almost four years before was now going to end it.

With great care, the President listed all the steps that led to his decision, stressing the endorsement of General Abrams

* George Christian, *The President Steps Down*, (New York: Macmillan, 1970), page 106.

and other advisers. Then he announced: ". . . I have now ordered that all air, naval, and artillery bombardment of North Vietnam cease as of eight A. M. Washington time, Friday morning." The expanded talks, including representatives of South Vietnam and the NLF, were to open in Paris on November 6, he said, five days after the bombing ended. Reporters filed their stories, packed, and flew to Paris for the grand opening; there they waited, and waited, and waited.

The National Liberation Front promptly sent its delegation to Paris. But not President Thieu. He kept raising new objections, infuriating Johnson, who for years past had extended himself as far as any man could to protect the interests and the feelings of the Saigon regime. He suspected, but could not prove, that Thieu had been misled by Mrs. Chennault to expect better terms from Nixon. The President, though, kept his silence. Clifford, less restrained, blistered the South Vietnamese leadership at a news conference on November 12, a week after Nixon's election, for torpedoing the arrangements. President Johnson, he said, was "absolutely right" not to give Saigon veto power over the end-the-bombing plan. Asked by a reporter whether he accused Saigon of sabotage or double-dealing Clifford curtly replied: "Take your pick."

Still determined to "winch down" the war, Clifford redoubled his efforts to pressure the recalcitrant South Vietnamese. He tried to persuade the President, before he left office, to lay down a schedule for American troop withdrawals from Vietnam. He speeded the supply of M-16 rifles to ARVN and he lost no public opportunity to excoriate Thieu. Johnson, however, preferred the advice of Dean Rusk, who favored a softer, more forbearing attitude toward Saigon.

It was not until December 8 that Vice-President Ky arrived in Paris to take charge of the South Vietnamese delegation. Almost five weeks had been lost, and the momentum, as Harriman had warned the President beforehand, was never recovered.

It took more than five weeks longer to get the talks started, in spite of Ky's promise upon arrival in Paris: "I have come with all my good will to search for peace." Ky's good will had its limits, as Harriman and Vance soon discovered. He would not, for example, sit down with the North Vietnamese and the NLF at a normal, four-sided table. That would signify four separate parties to the negotiation, and he refused to stretch Saigon's good will to the point of acknowledging that the NLF had the right to sit at the table. The obvious solution—a round table—had been discussed as early as October by the American and North Vietnamese delegations. But Thieu and Ky, grasping for any excuse to delay or derail the talks, kept raising new objections almost daily.

Clifford, since his July visit to Saigon, had become convinced that the South Vietnamese leaders preferred continued war to negotiated peace. On December 15, appearing on the CBS program "Face the Nation," he vented some of his frustrations: "I am becoming inordinately impatient," Clifford said, "with the continued deaths of American boys in Vietnam. I would like to get going at the Paris conference. I would like to get started on these plans to lower the level of combat. This isn't difficult to do. I would like to start getting our troops out of there."

He made light of the squabble about the shape of the table, stressing that it was not the United States that raised objections to a four-sided table. During those last weeks in office, Clifford pressed Johnson time and again to start withdrawing troops from Vietnam, precisely the policy of so-called Vietnamization that Richard Nixon was to adopt upon assuming the Presidency. He wanted a Democratic President to get the credit for initiating two major moves toward peace: first, an end of bombing and, second, a start on troop withdrawals. It was clear to Clifford that if Johnson did not move quickly, he would forfeit the political opportunity to the Republicans. Johnson understood but, with just a few weeks left to serve, pushed one way by Rusk and pulled another by Clifford, exhausted and miserable, he simply could not muster the will to act.

The lunatic quadrille over the shape of the table finally ended on January 16, four days before Johnson yielded the Presidency to Nixon. The dispute was resolved by a predictable—and frequently predicted—agreement to use a table with no sides at all; in effect, a round table. There were to be no flags, no nameplates. No one could claim to sit at the head of the unmarked table, nor would anyone be able to complain that he was seated at the foot. Thus President Johnson yielded power after having devoted more than nine months to arranging the nice details of negotiation: the who, where, and how of the peace conference. But he was denied the satisfaction of seeing any progress toward a settlement before he left Washington for the familiar hills of Texas.

The new President, ironically, had favored American armed intervention in Vietnam back in 1954, even an air attack against Communist China—both actions that Johnson, as Majority Leader, had opposed. Nixon was an anti-Communist—proud and undaunted, all the way back to his early days as a young Congressman from California. His credentials as a hawk, as a tough talker, were impeccable, especially after his famous "kitchen debate" with Khrushchev in 1959—a sure sign supposedly that he, of all Presidents, would never be "soft" on communism. Though he richly deserved—indeed relished—his reputation as a hard-liner, the political imperatives of this complicated country decreed that Richard M. Nixon, defeated for the Presidency in 1960, humiliated in his race for the governorship of California in 1962, should doggedly climb back from political obscurity to lead his tired, confused country out of the Vietnam War. It was an exquisite irony.

In the 1968 campaign Nixon had talked of a Republican plan to end the war though he refused to define it. "I do not believe a presidential candidate now should say, 'This is what I will do in January,'" Nixon explained. The new element in his campaign speeches, new in that Johnson had not pressed such a policy despite Clifford's consistent urgings, was the stress on *Vietnamization,* or as his campaign literature sometimes expressed it, *de-Americanization* of the war.

It is a cruel irony [Nixon said] that the American effort to safeguard the *independence* of South Vietnam has produced an ever-increasing dependency in our ally. If South Vietnam's future is to be secure, this process must now be reversed.

At the same time, we need far greater and more urgent attention to training the South Vietnamese themselves, and equipping them with the best of modern weapons. As they are phased in, American troops can be phased out. This phasing-out will save American lives and cut American costs.

The 1968 edition of *Nixon: A Political Portrait* by Earl Mazo and Stephen Hess would suggest that the so-called Guam Doctrine, enunciated on a presidential trip to the Pacific in the summer of 1969, had been in his mind for many months. The biography includes an interview with the authors, recorded on May 1 and May 5, 1968. Questioned about the lessons of Vietnam, Nixon then replied that the United States was rich and strong but not so rich nor so strong that it could by itself carry all the burdens of policing the world. This was scarcely an original thought but, for Nixon, the words had the quality of divine revelation.

. . . we have only two hundred million people [Nixon said] and there are two billion people who live in the free world. We simply cannot continue—whether it's Asia, Africa, or Latin America—to carry this immense burden of helping small nations who come under attack, either externally or internally, without more assistance from other nations which have an equal stake in freedom.

We need a new type of collective security arrangement, in which the nations in an area would assume the primary responsibility of coming to the aid of a neighboring nation rather than calling upon the United States in each instance for that assistance.

Countries like Japan, for example, should assume more responsibility for dealing with future insurrections in Asia, Nixon said. He argued that whenever the United States intervened in situations of the sort, there was always the danger of a confrontation with the Soviet Union or China. If a third World War was to be avoided, the United States would have to keep such possible confrontations to a minimum.

The new administration promptly relieved Harriman of the chief negotiator's job in Paris. Henry Cabot Lodge replaced him, and Lawrence E. Walsh, a New York lawyer, was named to succeed Vance. Nixon's inaugural promise ("After a period of confrontation we are entering an era of negotiation.") left the Communist delegation unmoved. When Ambassador Lodge, at the first plenary session of the expanded talks, proposed the immediate restoration of neutrality in the Demilitarized Zone, Xuan Thuy said the first question to be discussed was ending the American war of aggression. At the second session, on January 30, 1969, the North Vietnamese added that "only on a political basis can we settle military questions." Harriman interpreted that cryptic comment as suggesting that Hanoi might be ready for a resumption of secret talks. Lodge seemed to agree, but the new administration did not allow him to build on Harriman's good will or his contacts. Nixon wanted time to develop his own negotiating position. On February 10, Le Duc Tho, the senior member of the North Vietnamese delegation, flew home to Hanoi, saying that he for one could see no difference between the Nixon policy and the Johnson policy.

One difference, related only indirectly to the Paris negotiations, surfaced oddly in Saigon. President Thieu endorsed the idea of de-Americanizing the war, but not too rapidly. On January 18, two days before the Nixon inaugural, Thieu shrewdly announced that *he* had requested the withdrawal of some United States troops in 1969, thus pre-empting the obvious "big move" of the new administration. He gave no figures. Other officials guessed that Thieu had learned enough about the new President's thinking to anticipate a 50,000-man U.S. reduction before the end of the year. Thieu insisted it was a matter of South Vietnamese forces *replacing* the Americans, not at all a matter of withdrawal. With better training and equipment for ARVN, Thieu said, there ought to be a real improvement in the fighting quality of his forces.

Unhappily, the Communist forces launched a major offensive on February 23, effectively ruling out further talk of troop withdrawals for a time. They lobbed shells into Saigon, Da Nang, Pleiku, Mytho, Ben Tre, and Vinh Binh as if to test the new President. There was heavy ground fighting northwest of Saigon, and two American outposts just south of the Demilitarized Zone came under fierce attack. President Nixon, who was on his way to Europe at the time, found himself pressed by reporters to say whether Lyndon Johnson's celebrated "understanding" with the North Vietnamese had been breached. The commitment extracted by Johnson in exchange for the bombing halt—no abuse of the DMZ and no attacks on the cities—certainly appeared to have been repudiated, or at least ignored. In that event, the United States could take the position that it was now free to resume bombing the North. But the President, with his mind on European matters, still hopeful of negotiating fresh solutions to old problems with the Russians, was not about to be rushed into a decision that might re-escalate the war. To the reporters accompanying him, he said, "They key word is 'shelling' because, if that happens, it requires some action on our part."

Even when the shelling was promptly confirmed, however, the President took no action. His goal was to begin reducing the American troop commitment, not to increase it. During the first week of the offensive, 453 Americans were killed, more dead than in the first week of the 1968 Tet offensive. In Paris Lodge warned the North Vietnamese on February 27, March 6, and again on March 13 that they could not have it both ways. The new offensive, he said, made the task of negotiating peace more difficult. But the President went through his round of appointments with the NATO Council in Brussels, his official visits to London, Paris, and Rome, discussing European affairs at each stop and nervously reading the bad news from Vietnam all the way.

He left it to former Congressman Melvin Laird, now Secretary of Defense, to warn the North and the Viet Cong that if the shelling continued there would have to be a military response. Visiting Saigon March 6–10, Laird told reporters that was not the time to talk of withdrawing American troops. Laird, the foremost champion of Vietnamization within the Nixon Cabinet, was disappointed. But he determined to press the matter again as soon as the battlefield pressures eased. On March 21, testifying before the Senate Foreign Relations Committee, Laird talked hopefully of the steps he proposed to take by way of reducing America's involvement. It all hinged, he said, upon giving the South Vietnamese forces better training and equipment. Chairman Fulbright told Laird that he sounded like "an old broken record going back to McNamara." The new administration's honeymoon period, Fulbright warned, would not last much longer. "Soon it will be Nixon's war," he said, "and then there will be little chance to bring it to an end. It is time to de-escalate and settle it." But it was not to become Nixon's war, in the sense of Nixon's political liability, for another year, not until Cambodia. Till then—Fulbright to the contrary notwithstanding —the new President enjoyed sufficient popular support to take his time about extricating the United States from the Vietnam bog.

In the sixth week of the 1969 winter-spring offensive, 312 Americans were killed. On April 3 General Abrams's headquarters announced that more Americans had lost their lives in Vietnam since 1961 (33,641) than in the whole of the Korean War (33,629). This was not the kind of statistic calculated to keep the Congress or the colleges quiet much longer. It was a Vermont Republican, Senator George D. Aiken, who started the doves fluttering with a May 1 speech. Aiken, a white-haired senior citizen whose benign smile conceals a tough-minded independence, rose in the Senate chamber that May Day to propose that the United States withdraw all its troops from Vietnam immediately. To him, the South Vietnamese looked strong enough to stand on their own feet now. He saw little danger that the South would be taken over by the Communists. "Common sense should tell us," Aiken said, "that we have now accomplished our purpose, so far as Vietnam is concerned." Senator Mike Mansfield, the Democratic leader, had long been Aiken's close friend and constant breakfast companion. He promptly commended the senior Senator from Vermont. Senator Edward Kennedy of Massachusetts joined in, along with Javits of New York and Percy of Illinois.

In and out of Washington many Americans found the Aiken idea beguiling. It seemed to them a perfectly legitimate argument that the United States had sent combat troops to Vietnam in 1965 for a limited purpose: to hold the line and prevent a quick Communist victory until the South Vietnamese could pull themselves together to fight their own battles. Now that job appeared to be done. President Thieu had about one million men under arms, rapidly being outfitted with modern American weapons. Surely the time had come to let the Vietnamese fight their own war, if they insisted upon fighting. Better still, let them settle their differences by negotiation.

The White House got the message. For several months the

more astute members of the presidential staff, drawing on their
pre-inaugural experience as lawyers, salesmen, and public-rela-
tions men, had concluded that the policy of reducing U.S. military involvement in Southeast Asia, launched so painfully by
President Johnson on March 31, 1968, was by then irreversible.
There were some bitter-enders still clamoring for "military victory" and others who refused to accept a standoff with a little
Asian nation. But most people simply wanted the war to end
and the boys to be brought home. Politicians who understood
and rode this wave of discontent could be sure of gaining or
holding power. Nixon understood.

Ever since his European swing in mid-February, designed
in part to reassure the nervous NATO allies that America's commitment to the Atlantic community remained intact despite the
continuing needs of Vietnam, the President had spent many
hours alone or with his top advisers trying to devise a successful
strategy for Vietnam and the entire Pacific area. He listened to
his advisers, though in the final analysis he never seemed to lean
on them. They included Dr. Henry Kissinger, a brilliant, incisive,
former Harvard professor, now his adviser on national security
affairs; William P. Rogers, a highly successful New York and
Washington attorney, a close friend who had been Eisenhower's
Attorney General, a born conciliator, a dove; Laird, sharp as
Wisconsin cheddar, like Nixon, an instinctive politician who
knew Clifford's instinct was sound—the war had to be "winched
down" or the country would explode; John Mitchell, a Nixon
law partner and municipal-bond specialist, who understood the
war's effect upon the economy.

By late April they reached their conclusions on two levels.
They decided to press on with Vietnamization, a program of
gradual U.S. troop withdrawal, linked with Saigon's ability to
pick up the slack. The men around Nixon believed, at the time,
that Hanoi would quickly recognize its interests were better
served by negotiating while the Americans were still in Vietnam,
and thus capable of restraining Saigon's leaders, than to wait
until the Americans were gone and the South Vietnamese were
free to frustrate any move toward a coalition government. Turning to the Pacific area, in general, the President and his men

decided that the United States, while prepared to honor its old treaty commitments, must seek where possible to persuade the Koreans and the Thais, the Taiwanese, and all of the others linked to American power and money, that they would have to do much more, on their own, to defend themselves in the future. The days of leaning upon American power had ended. This was to prove a hard lesson for many of the Asian allies.

The Nixon team thought, at the time, that it had come up with a sensible and fair plan for peace. Rogers told reporters on his first Asian visit in May that the United States was not seeking to humiliate North Vietnam, nor aiming to defeat her. The U.S. was going to get out of Vietnam one way or another, he stressed, by negotiation in Paris or by Vietnamization in Saigon, but the direction was unmistakable and unalterable. Kissinger told a group of visiting students to come back in six months, sometime in the fall; he assured them, in buoyant, upbeat terms, that they would be able to see considerable progress by then toward ending the war—or, if not that, then toward ending American participation in it.

In retrospect, those were the salad days for the Nixon Administration. The President had a peace plan, at last, and it was about to be unveiled. But the Vietnamese Communists, for whom fighting while negotiating was a rule of life, beat Nixon to it. In Paris, on May 8, a ten-point peace program was made public by Tran Buu Kiem in the name of the National Liberation Front of South Vietnam. It called for:

1. Respect for the sovereignty, independence, unity, and territorial integrity of the Vietnamese peoples, as recognized in the 1954 Geneva agreement.
2. Withdrawal of all American troops and the dismantling of all American bases.
3. Questions pertaining to "Vietnamese forces in South Vietnam," presumably Communist and anti-Communist forces alike, to be resolved "by the Vietnamese parties among themselves."
4. A coalition government to be set up in Saigon, "reflecting national concord and the broad union of all social strata" through free elections for a constituent assembly that would draw a new constitution.
5. In the period between the end of the fighting and the elections, neither side would impose its political system upon the

people; the provisional coalition government would include South Vietnamese now in exile.

6. A neutral foreign policy.

7. Reunification of North and South, by peaceful means, without foreign interference, to be accomplished step by step over a lengthy period through discussions between the two zones.

8. Neither North nor South Vietnam would join any alliance, Communist or anti-Communist.

9. Release of war prisoners to be negotiated.

10. The two parties would agree on steps for international supervision of foreign troop withdrawals.

On the following day Secretary of State Rogers produced a soft reply. The negotiation, he felt, had begun. Some parts of the NLF plan, were clearly unacceptable, he said, "but there are elements in it which may offer a possibility for exploration." On May 14 President Nixon put forward his own eight-point program for peace in Vitenam, stressing that President Thieu had been fully consulted beforehand:

1. All non-South Vietnamese forces to begin withdrawals as soon as agreement can be reached.

2. "Major portions" (otherwise unspecified) of all American, Allied, and North Vietnamese troops to be withdrawn by agreed stages over a twelve-month period. At the end of twelve months, those foreign troops still remaining in South Vietnam would move to designated base areas and engage in no combat operations.

3. All American and Allied troops left behind after the first year would be withdrawn as the last of the North Vietnamese troops left the South.

4. The withdrawals would be verified by an international supervisory body, acceptable to both sides.

5. The supervisory body would begin operating according to an agreed timetable and would participate in arranging supervised cease-fires.

6. As soon as possible, the international body also would supervise elections to be held "under agreed procedures."

7. Prisoners of war on both sides to be released at the earliest possible time.

8. All parties would agree to observe the 1954 Geneva agreements concerning Vietnam and Cambodia, as well as the 1962 Laos accords.

Ambassador Lodge formally tabled the eight-point Nixon proposal at the seventeenth plenary session of the Paris talks on May 16. On May 22, at the eighteenth session, Lodge tried without apparent success to draw the Vietnamese into a comparative discussion of the two peace plans. There were enough similarities between them, Lodge contended, to provide a basis for real negotiations. The North Vietnamese spokesman disagreed. The two programs, he insisted, were "different as night and day." But no outright rejection of the Nixon program was heard in Paris. Xuan Thuy, speaking at a Paris press luncheon on May 20, complained that the Nixon proposal did not make clear who was to organize the first elections after hostilities had ceased. If the Thieu regime in Saigon were to be in charge of the arrangements, he said, the NLF would never accept. He sounded as though he were bargaining—or so Kissinger felt.

As for the ten-point NLF plan, President Thieu said flatly during a visit to South Korea that he would "never" accept a coalition government. When a reporter asked whether he would agree to Communist participation in the elections, Thieu replied, "If the Communists are willing to lay down their weapons, *abandon the Communist ideology,* and abandon atrocities, they could participate in elections." In short, the Communists were perfectly free to take part in the elections so long as they stopped being Communists. By the standards of the Spanish Inquisition, Thieu's offer doubtless would have appeared magnanimous. In modern Vietnam, torn by a long cruel war, it tended to stiffen Communist demands that Thieu and Ky must go. It was a political war to begin with, and the Communists could hardly be expected to lay down their arms after twenty-five years of bloody struggle if Thieu and Ky were free to suppress even peaceful political activity by their opponents.

Embarrassed by Thieu's pronouncements and eager to develop some negotiating momentum, Secretary of State Rogers said at a news conference in Washington on June 5 that the United States was not wedded to any particular regime in Saigon. He added that the United States would not object to NLF participation in joint arrangements for elections so it could make sure that the "votes would be cast without coercion and counted properly."

At this point, consistent with its plan, the administration

chose to inaugurate the troop withdrawal program without waiting for agreement in Paris. President Nixon flew to Midway Island on June 8 for a five-hour meeting with Thieu and there
announced that he was going to pull out 25,000 American troops
by August 31. Defense Secretary Laird the next day held out
the promise that if the South Vietnamese continued to assume
more of the combat burden, more Americans could come home
"at regular intervals thereafter." It was a smaller troop cut than
many officials had hoped for, but a start in the direction Clifford
had pointed to during the final weeks of Lyndon Johnson's term.
The former Secretary of Defense made known that month, in a
Foreign Affairs article, his belief that the new administration had
set its sights too low. He proposed that 100,000 combat troops
be withdrawn in 1969, the rest by the end of 1970. Clifford was
willing to leave Air Force, logistics, and airlift units behind
somewhat longer to help the South Vietnamese. But his disenchantment with what Lyndon Johnson used to call "nation-
building" was total. Clifford wrote:

In the long run, the security of the Pacific region will depend upon
the abilities of the countries there to meet the legitimate, growing
demands of their own people. No military strength we can bring to bear
can give them internal stability or popular acceptance. We can
advise, we can urge, we can furnish economic aid. But American
military power cannot build nations any more than it can solve the
social and economic problems that face us here at home.

The President, questioned only about the troop-pullout aspect of Clifford's article, responded with a petty, personal attack: Why had Clifford not practiced his own preaching when
he was in charge at the Pentagon? If it was such a good idea
to withdraw 100,000 combat troops in a single year, why had
Clifford not done it while in office? Nixon must have known
that it was President Johnson, not Clifford, who had refused to
begin troop withdrawals. But he was clearly angry; the careful
show of good humor he tried to present at news conferences
had vanished. "I would hope," he said, a challenge in his voice,
"that we could beat Mr. Clifford's timetable." (He didn't.)

Toward the middle of June, 1969, a battlefield lull was perceived by the official Vietnam watchers in Washington. Infiltra-

tion of men and supplies from the North also dropped off. Secretary Rogers, back from Asia and eager to link the lull with the President's first troop withdrawal announcement, promptly drew public attention to this change on July 2, hinting that if it continued, the troop withdrawals might be speeded. In Saigon, General Abrams's headquarters reported that three North Vietnamese regiments, 7500 men strong, had withdrawn across the Demilitarized Zone. An official spokesman conceded the possibility that Hanoi *might* be reciprocating the first U.S. troop withdrawal. Casualties were dropping, too. In the week ending July 5, 153 Americans were killed, as compared with 241 the previous week. More significant, conceivably, than the apparent drop in rates of enemy infiltration was the fact that General Abrams had largely abandoned the costly search-and-destroy operations favored by General Westmoreland. Laird confirmed the tactical shift before the Senate Foreign Relations Committee on July 15. The President had given orders, he said, that field commanders were to make "the reduction of American casualties" their primary objective. When Nixon visited Saigon on July 30, during his first Far Eastern tour as President, he made the new instructions more explicit:

In July . . . [he said on November 3] I changed General Abrams' orders so that they were consistent with the objectives of our new policies. Under the new orders, the primary mission of our troops is to enable the South Vietnamese forces to assume full responsibility for the security of South Vietnam.

Before setting out on his Asian journey, the President had made an extraordinary effort to break the Paris deadlock. He asked to see Jean Sainteny, a former French official in Indochina who had known Ho Chi Minh for a quarter century. At Nixon's request, Sainteny promised to deliver a personal letter to Ho in Hanoi. It was dated July 15, 1969:

Dear Mr. President:
    I realize that it is difficult to communicate meaningfully across the gulf of four years of war. But precisely because of this gulf, I wanted to take this opportunity to reaffirm in all solemnity my desire to work for a just peace. I deeply believe that the war in Vietnam has gone on too long, and delay in bringing it to an end can benefit no one—least of all the people of Vietnam. My speech on May 14

laid out a proposal which I believe is fair to all parties. Other proposals have been made which attempt to give the people of South Vietnam an opportunity to choose their own future. These proposals take into account the reasonable conditions of all sides. But we stand ready to discuss other programs as well, specifically the 10-point program of the NLF.

As I have said repeatedly, there is nothing to be gained by waiting. Delay can only increase the dangers and multiply the suffering.

The time has come to move forward at the conference table toward an early resolution of this tragic war. You will find us forthcoming and open-minded in a common effort to bring the blessings of peace to the brave people of Vietnam. Let history record that at this critical juncture, both sides turned their face toward peace rather than toward conflict and war.

> Sincerely,
> *Richard Nixon*

Ho's reply, dated August 25 in Hanoi, was received in Paris August 30 and promptly transmitted to the White House:

Mr. President,

I have the honor to acknowledge receipt of your letter.

The war of aggression of the United States against our people, violating our fundamental national rights, still continues in South Vietnam. The United States continues to intensify military operations, the B-52 bombings and the use of toxic chemical products multiply the crimes against the Vietnamese people. The longer the war goes on, the more it accumulates the mourning and burdens of the American people. I am extremely indignant at the losses and destructions caused by the American troops to our people and our country. I am also deeply touched at the rising toll of death of young Americans who have fallen in Vietnam by reason of the policy of American governing circles.

Our Vietnamese people are deeply devoted to peace, a real peace with independence and real freedom. They are determined to fight to the end, without fearing the sacrifices and difficulties in order to defend their country and their sacred national rights. The overall solution in 10 points of the National Liberation Front of South Vietnam and of the Provisional Revolutionary Government of the Republic of South Vietnam is a logical and reasonable basis for the settlement of the Vietnamese problem. It has earned the sympathy and support of the peoples of the world. In your letter you have expressed the desire to act for a just peace. For this, the United States must cease the war of aggression and withdraw their troops from South Vietnam, respect the right of the population of the South and of the Vietnamese nation to dispose of themselves, without foreign influence. This is the correct manner of solving the Vietnamese problem in conformity with the national rights of the Vietnamese people, the interests of the United States and the hopes for peace of the peoples of the world. This is the path that will allow the United States to get out of the war with honor.

With good will on both sides we might arrive at common efforts in view of finding a correct solution of the Vietnamese problem.

Sincerely,

Ho Chi Minh

Nixon did not disclose the secret correspondence until November 3; and then he disclosed only part of it. It didn't matter. By then Ho was dead. His successors, locked in a natural struggle for power, torn between the Russians and the Chinese, were simply incapable of moving into a deeper dialogue with the United States about the shape of a possible peace settlement. Just as the President had quite deliberately interrupted the flow of the Paris negotiation, after assuming power in January, while he tried to work out his own strategy, so too Ho's successors had to rethink Hanoi's policy. The rethinking took time. But the President's advisers, facing a new challenge on Capitol Hill and the campuses, read the chill in Paris as proof that the Communists were inflexibly negative. Things then seemed to fall into place, unfortunately.

For example, the President and his advisers, as he later explained, read the Ho Chi Minh letter as a rebuff. "It simply reiterated the public positions North Vietnam had taken in the Paris talks," the President said, "and flatly rejected my initiative." That was by no means the universal interpretation, least of all among scholars trained in deciphering Communist verbiage. The President had made a specific offer to discuss the NLF ten-point program, among other proposals. Ho had written back that the NLF program was "a logical and reasonable basis" for negotiating a settlement. He had not insisted that it was the *only* basis, as he had done repeatedly in the past. Moreover, Ho had picked up the President's phrase about "common efforts" at resolving the war. This was unusual, if not unprecedented. Ho Chi Minh, the dedicated nationalist and Communist, was hardly in the habit of proclaiming "common" cause between North Vietnam and the United States.

These were clear signs of flexibility in the opinion of administration experts; not examples of malicious harping by reporters, as Vice-President Agnew later implied. There were other signs, too. The day before Ho died, on September 2, Xuan Thuy hinted that progress was possible in Paris if the President would announce a timetable for more substantial, more rapid U.S. troop withdrawals. Talking with reporters at a diplomatic reception, the Hanoi delegate said, "It is evident that if the withdrawals occur at the present rate [only the first 25,000-man cut had been announced], we cannot make a judgment. On the other hand, if Mr. Nixon withdraws forces in a considerable and rapid way, we will take account of it." Coming from the circumspect Xuan Thuy, this could have been a broad hint.

For reasons, not all of them entirely clear at this point, the White House chose to ignore these hints of flexibility. Perhaps it was a rush of anxiety on Thieu's part that his regime would collapse if the U.S. continued its troop withdrawal program. Perhaps it was Thieu's judgment that North Vietnam might collapse, without Ho, and the Allies ought to just wait. Maybe it was strong pressure from within the United States military establishment, buttressed by hawkish sentiment on the Hill, or a combination of these elements. Whatever the real reason, the administration's position seemed to harden in October, 1969. Some officials told questioning reporters a month later that Ho's letter was "obviously a rebuff." "Why obviously?" one reporter asked. "Because," a member of the White House staff explained, "Ho did not even write 'Dear Mr. President' in his letter, just 'Mr. President.' Now that's damned rude!" By that time, it was clear that the administration had lost its summertime optimism. The fall had come; winter was in the air, and the leaves were falling from the trees all around the White House.

On September 16, three weeks late by earlier estimate, the President announced that 35,000 more troops were coming out of Vietnam. By December 15, he said, the authorized manpower ceiling would be down to 484,000. The level of violence was also diminishing. On October 2 the toll for the week ending September 27 showed ninety-five dead. The following week, it was down to sixty-four, the lowest figure for any week since December, 1966. Laird and Rogers argued that the troop pullout should be accelerated. The Joint Chiefs disagreed, contending that the lower casualties merely proved that Vietnamization was working and that the enemy was hurting; "Charlie" could not muster enough power, the JCS boasted, for one more major assault. The President seemed to be listening to the military chiefs.

On the negotiating front the sparring went on without a solid blow being landed either way. The NLF had made itself over into a quasi-government. Mrs. Nguyen Thi Binh, one day the personable delegate of the NLF in the Paris talks, became overnight the foreign minister of a new provisional revolutionary government of South Vietnam. "Old wine in a new bottle," said the State Department. A "propaganda trick," said the Government of South Vietnam in Saigon. Lodge's deputy, Lawrence Walsh, told Mrs. Binh directly in Paris, "We place no significance on the manner in which you choose to style yourselves." On October 16 the North Vietnamese delegation proposed that the United States enter into "private and direct talks" with the so-called provisional revolutionary government, formerly the NLF, and still the political arm of the Viet Cong. Hanoi was clearly trying to shut out Saigon, leaving Ambassador Lodge no choice but to reject the maneuver.

The antiwar coalition—Senate doves of both parties, college students and teachers, business and professional groups across the land—was getting restless. By Kissinger's own reckoning, discernible progress toward peace was to have been expected by early fall. The administration, after all, had its "plan" for peace. But there was little progress: one modest troop cut and the promise of another, nothing more. Fulbright's increasingly skeptical Foreign Relations Committee began to consider ways of literally legislating an end to the war—by cutting the administration's purse strings, if necessary. Loyal Republicans pleaded for more time, patience, and understanding. Their pleas fell, for the most part, on deaf ears. Administration officials liked to stress that the casualties had dropped. But an ever-increasing number of legislators and ordinary citizens began to say that one death a week was one too many. The war had dragged on

too long, and the cry to end it, once and for all, went forth from
Capitol Hill through the news media into every home in the
land.

Dissent finally flowered into a mass demonstration against
the war in the streets of Washington. October 15, 1969, was
Moratorium Day. Its youthful leaders called for a peaceful protest march. Hundreds of thousands of citizens, mostly young,
converged on the capital, sang songs, listened to speeches and,
by night, walked gravely with flickering candles in their hands
around and around the White House. It was perhaps the most
powerful and impressive peace demonstration America had seen.
The Executive Mansion, its great iron gates barred and its win-
dows darkened, looked like a besieged fortress turning a blind
eye to the peace marchers.

The administration believed that such demonstrations gave
aid and comfort to the enemy. Indeed, Communist propagan-
dists had a field day exploiting antiwar sentiment in the United
States. One school of official thought, volunteered to any reporter who bothered to ask, was that the demonstrations would
lengthen the war by encouraging Hanoi to believe that if it
stuck to its course a little while longer, the United States would
give up the fight and go home, yielding South Vietnam to communism. The President himself seemed persuaded of this idea;
also the Secretaries of State and Defense.

The Moratorium leaders were so pleased with their successful, disciplined October 15 demonstration that they planned another one for November 15, in the belief that they could force
the administration to change its policy. The President, in the
heat of the moment, decided on a major gamble. He announced,
in mid-October, that he was requesting radio and television time
for a report to the people on "the entire Vietnam situation as
it exists at the time." The date he chose was November 3. His
intention was to show the doves that most Americans supported
him, not the marchers. Around the country Republican state and
county leaders urged people to watch the President and to send
him telegrams of support. The "silent majority" was to be
prodded into political action.

At 9:32 P.M. Washington time, the President spoke to a

national audience estimated at more than 50,000,000. It was a masterpiece of special pleading with something in it for every conceivable special-interest group, except draft-age students. There would be no "precipitate withdrawal" from Vietnam, Nixon said, for several reasons. First, because it would "inevitably allow the Communists to repeat the massacres which followed their takeover in the North fifteen years before." Clearly, no right-thinking American was in favor of massacres. Second, the particular victims of the massacres were likely to be "the million and a half Catholic refugees who fled to South Vietnam when the Communists took over the North." It can safely be assumed that 40,000,000 Catholic Americans would take an especially dim view of massacres directed at their coreligionists. Third, precipitate withdrawal would turn Vietnam into the "first defeat in our nation's history" and destroy confidence in American leadership round the world. Surely the great majority of Americans did not want to see their country defeated or discredited. Moreover, the President said, a defeat in Vietnam would "spark violence wherever our commitments help maintain peace—in the Middle East, in Berlin, eventually even in the Western Hemisphere." In short, Americans of Jewish, or Arab or German descent had a special stake along with the Catholics in preventing a precipitate withdrawal; *i.e*, a defeat in Vietnam.

The President did not explain why he equated withdrawal with defeat, massacre, and general disaster. What would the million-man army of South Vietnam be doing while the massacres were going on? Why, ARVN was gaining strength all the time. Nixon said:

We have adopted a plan which we have worked out in cooperation with the South Vietnamese for the complete withdrawal of all U.S. combat ground forces, and their replacement by South Vietnamese forces on an orderly, scheduled timetable. This withdrawal will be made from strength and not from weakness. As South Vietnamese forces become stronger, the rate of American withdrawal will depend on developments on three fronts.

One of these is the progress which can be made in the Paris talks. . . .

The other two factors on which we will base our withdrawal

decisions are the level of enemy activity and the progress of the training program of the South Vietnamese forces. I am glad to be able to report tonight progress on both of these fronts has been greater than we anticipated when we started the program in June for withdrawal.

Finally, the President declared he was not going to have American policy "dictated by the minority" who march in the streets carrying signs like one he had seen in San Francisco: "Lose in Vietnam, bring the boys home." He closed with a clear bid for support directed to "the great silent majority of my fellow Americans." By way of demonstrating that he had spared no effort for peace, the President in his November 3 speech also mentioned the exchange of letters with Ho Chi Minh, disclosing that Lodge had met secretly eleven times in Paris with Xuan Thuy. If the President wanted those talks to continue, disclosure at the time was a peculiar way to go about it. Xuan Thuy remarked after hearing of the disclosure: "The American representatives do not keep their promises even for little things."

As predicted by some White House aides, including USIA Director Frank Shakespeare, the "great silent majority" responded to the President's plea for unity in a massive, highly graphic way. Tens of thousands of letters and telegrams inundated the White House mailroom. On November 4, in the early morning, the President invited reporters—and cameramen—into his office. Thousands of those telegrams were on his desk—telegrams of support and encouragement. Some carried literally hundreds of Republican signatures. Unless we are to assume that Western Union does a faster job delivering telegrams of support than telegrams of criticism, it seems altogether likely that local G.O.P. clubs organized, signed, and sent their telegrams, even before the President spoke.

That evening film of the President dipping into a small mountain of enthusiastic messages led off the television newscasts. The next morning, stories of an ecstatic White House dominated the front pages. Shakespeare told a friend that the President had an "uncanny" feel for the public's mood; he was sure of widespread support. Equally important, the President was hoping the critics would now shut up and allow him to "winch down" the war in his own way.

The critics were not so cooperative as the "silent majority." On Capitol Hill dove Senators complained to reporters that the President had said "nothing new," and resumed their attacks on his policy. TV commentators and editorial writers spotted a few inconsistencies and offered some interpretations differing from the President's. The White House fumed in anger. It had counted on the massive response of the no-longer-silent majority to silence the doubters and dissenters. But the war had so sharply polarized national opinion that the stratagem was bound to fail. It became necessary for the White House to take further steps. These, most notably, included the unleashing of Vice-President Spiro Agnew.

On November 13, ten days after the President's fireside chat, two days before the follow-up Moratorium, Agnew made his name a household word by appearing on network television to denounce the television networks. The case he made was not wholly original. George Wallace had tested the same appeal in the 1968 presidential campaign. The networks, he charged, were controlled by northeastern liberals who slanted the news. It was a new twist of the conspiracy theory so fondly espoused by extremists of the left as well as the right for decades past. By what right, Agnew demanded, did these self-appointed commentators (all of whom lived in New York or Washington, who read the same eastern newspapers and who, moreover, talked with one another) dare to question the President's judgment? The effect was instantaneous and overwhelming. Thousands upon thousands of letters, telegrams, and postcards poured down upon the networks and the desks of their correspondents. The tone of many was ugly, scurrilous, defamatory. The intent was to compel silence, and for a period of weeks many network executives were cowed. Network news producers trembled about scripts that might possibly offend the administration. Certain among them searched out the blandest of "good news"—no matter how inconsequential—to replace analysis on the air.

Soon afterward Agnew broadened his attack to condemn *The New York Times* and *The Washington Post*, both critics of the Vietnam war and the President's policies in Southeast Asia. Some commentators wondered whether the administration was out to do more than simply silence its critics in the media. Eric Sevareid, for one, feared that the administration was really trying to impugn the integrity of TV news, to destroy popular respect for its product, so that if the time came when the administration had to dissemble about its Vietnam policy, it could blame the media for misrepresenting it in the first place. It could, in this way, ascribe a credibility gap to the media before the media could ascribe one to the White House.

The administration decided in the cold winter of 1969 that Hanoi was not ready to bargain and that it would not beg, implore, or beseech the Communists to be reasonable. On December 8 Ambassador Lodge resigned, announcing that he must tend to personal matters at home. Rather than appoint a successor of comparable standing, the President asked Philip C. Habib, a career diplomat who had been the chief assistant to Harriman as well as Lodge, to head the delegation. The North Vietnamese promptly accused the United States of deliberately downgrading its Paris delegation in order to sabotage the talks. The President denied that was his intention, but it was not until July 1, 1970 that he appointed the veteran diplomat David Bruce to replace Lodge. If this was not a deliberate downgrading, it surely reflected the growing conviction among many administration officials that the war would probably not end in a formal negotiation but by a slow process of simply fading away. Ambassador Habib from that point on met weekly with the Vietnamese, but, in spite of his long experience and deep understanding of the problem, Paris became for both sides a holding operation.

Thus, at the end of his first year in office, President Nixon had little or nothing to show for his diplomatic efforts at negotiating a settlement. There remained only one avenue for winding down the war by degrees: unilateral American troop withdrawals and Vietnamization. That first year he recalled 60,000 troops in all. On December 15, in another broadcast address, he announced plans to withdraw 50,000 more by April 15, 1970. Vietnamization was going so well, he said (citing the opinion

of a British guerrilla-war expert, Sir Robert Thompson), that he had decided to go ahead in spite of warnings from the military command in Saigon that enemy infiltration was increasing again.

The withdrawal rate, some 10,000 men a month, was sufficiently gradual to avoid alarm in Saigon. In Hanoi, however, it could be read as a sign that four or five years might pass before all the Americans were out of South Vietnam. On February 1, 1970, Le Duan, First Secretary of the Vietnamese workers' party, cautioned his people that they "must be prepared to fight many years more."

Defense Secretary Laird flew to Saigon again on February 10 to see for himself how Vietnamization was progressing and to get the views of the military commanders on future withdrawals. He outlined a three-phase plan for all-but-total withdrawal, giving no dates or numbers. Phase 1, Laird said, would be completed when South Vietnamese forces assumed full combat responsibility for the defense of their country. It was later disclosed that the target date for this phase was to be "the summer of '71"—if all went well. Americans would, however, continue to provide air, artillery, and logistical support. At the end of Phase 2, the Americans would turn over their airplanes, helicopters, artillery, and other support equipment to the Vietnamese. Finally, in Phase 3, the only American military presence remaining in South Vietnam would be a military assistance group, chiefly advisers, perhaps 50,000 of them. Laird did not say whether the whole three-stage process would take two years or ten.

On April 20 President Nixon announced, among other things, that 150,000 more troops would be withdrawn by the spring of 1971, further reducing the authorized troop ceiling from 434,000 to 284,000. At home, the effect of these step-by-step reductions was to buy time for the President, to make the continuing war more tolerable to the voters over the long haul. The Communists were left to guess, however, whether the United States was determined to pull out all its troops over a foreseeable period or to leave a substantial residual force in South Vietnam, say 150,000 men, chiefly concerned with air, artillery, and logistical support. There were dangers and oppor-

tunities to be measured on both sides. If, for example, the Communists came to believe that the President seriously intended a complete pullout by the summer of 1972 (just in time to boost his chances of winning a second term), they might decide to lie low, limit their attacks to South Vietnamese units, and avoid any offensive action that might have the effect of slowing or stopping the withdrawal. If, on the other hand, the adversary had reason to believe that a substantial residual force was going to be left behind, he might be powerfully tempted to attack and keep attacking in an effort to persuade American opinion that half-measures could be more costly than a clean, complete withdrawal.

More fundamental than either of these concerns was what the President perceived as his political goal in Vietnam. Like Lyndon Johnson before him, Nixon had ruled out an American defeat. He also had ruled out military victory. What he had difficulty coming to grips with was the third alternative, the only one left. This necessarily called either for partition of South Vietnam or for a sharing of power between the two contending forces, Communists and non-Communists. Reluctant to move against President Thieu, who knew that he and his closest associates could have no place in such a coalition, Nixon denied himself negotiating leverage in Paris. He appeared to believe that anything less than the survival of a non-Communist regime in Saigon, able to withstand any Communist threat, would amount to a defeat. In effect, he was holding out for the fruits of victory although the war had not been won.

Vietnamization, in short, turned out to be a poor substitute for real negotiations. It sidestepped the central issue: how to promote a realistic political accommodation between anti-Communists and Communists. Moreover, it promised no safe exit for the American military contingent because the adversary could, whenever he chose, drag out the United States involvement by launching new offensives.

Events in Cambodia soon demonstrated how precarious was the President's plan for extricating the United States from Indochina. Prince Sihanouk, always respectful of powers mightier than his own, had survived on the margins of the Vietnam War

for years past by allowing the North Vietnamese and their southern allies to use a strip of Cambodian border territory as a staging area and supply base. It was a policy more popular in other parts of the country than in the region adjoining South Vietnam, where feeling ran high against the Communist intruders.

With Sihanouk in Europe for medical treatment, and Lieutenant General Lon Nol in charge of the Cambodian Government, anti-Communist demonstrations flared up, first in Syvarieng Province up against the Vietnamese border, then in Pnom Penh, on March 7 and 11. From Paris, Sihanouk announced that the Pnom Penh demonstrations, which resulted in damages to the North Vietnamese Embassy, were part of a rightist plot aiming to destroy "the friendship of Cambodia with the Socialist camp and throw our country into the arms of an imperialist power." This was, in part, a ruse. Sihanouk himself had become increasingly concerned about Communist maneuvering within Cambodia. When he heard the news of the spreading demonstrations, he promptly broke off his Parisian rest-cure. But, instead of proceeding to Pnom Penh directly, he decided to return home by way of Moscow and Peking, determined that in both Communist capitals he would appeal for help in restraining the lurch to the right in Cambodian politics.

It was too late. On March 18 General Lon Nol became premier, and Prince Sisowath Sirik Matak, a cousin of Sihanouk, became deputy premier, in a bloodless coup that was to change the face of Southeast Asian politics and to have a profound effect upon American policy in that area. None of this, at that time, was immediately apparent. Nonetheless, within the administration, the pulse quickened almost reflexively, a Pavlovian response to this new Asian stimulus. At the Pentagon those generals who for years past had unsuccessfully urged President Johnson to invade the Cambodian sanctuaries dusted off their old recommendations. Each of them appeared personally persuaded that, with Sihanouk out and with a sympathetic, anti-Communist regime in, there should be no hesitation any longer about "cleansing" the sanctuaries. The State Department quickly perceived that a new situation had arisen but showed no enthusiasm for military action to exploit it. "Cool it," was the

instinctive response of Marshall Green, Assistant Secretary for
Far Eastern Affairs. At the White House, Kissinger's shop
quickly began to sift through various options.

On April 1, while everyone in official Washington was carefully presenting a public face of concern, but not alarm, General Abrams, at Laird's request, presented to the White House
three options for handling the Cambodian problem:

First, to permit the South Vietnamese to make more cross-
border operations into enemy sanctuaries.

Second, to help the South Vietnamese launch larger and
more effective raids by providing American artillery and air
support.

Third, to encourage the South Vietnamese to stage a full-
scale attack on the enemy base camps, and to send American
ground advisers along.

Abrams himself made no formal recommendation, limiting
himself at this stage only to the presentation of the options. A
few days later, the President saw the movie *Patton*, based on
the life of General George Patton, the flamboyant commander
of the U.S. 3rd Army in Europe during World War II. He enjoyed the movie immensely. It showed him that against all odds
determined men could accomplish miracles. Some such miracle
was needed in Southeast Asia to save the Vietnamization program, since it appeared that the Cambodian flank might be falling to the Communists. Nixon would have preferred a diplomatic
solution, of course. He sent word to Hanoi that the United States
would respect any arrangement Lon Nol could work out with
the Communists. But Hanoi, believing that the Americans had
inspired the Lon Nol coup in the first place, would not hear of
a deal with Washington.

On April 13 the situation on the ground began to deteri-
orate. Communist troops began moving westward—away from
the border areas, chopping up villages along the way, killing
and terrorizing as they slipped through the underbrush toward
the Cambodian interior. This movement caught everyone's attention, alarming some American officials in Saigon, who quickly
saw the danger to the Vietnamization program of a Communist
takeover in Pnom Penh. On April 15 General Abrams and Am-

bassador Bunker recommended U.S. military attacks into the Fishhook, a dagger-shaped Cambodian area pointed at Saigon, and into other Communist sanctuaries.

Secretary Laird, who earlier had opposed any thought of sending American troops into Cambodia, understood and supported Abrams's reasoning. The Vietnam commander argued that clearing out the sanctuaries would not be a costly operation; the Communists were evacuating them anyway, but the South Vietnamese could not do the job alone. Bunker argued that Lon Nol could not last much longer without a dramatic show of American military support.

The President listened but refused to decide for action. The French had just called for a new Indochina conference, and the Soviet UN Ambassador Jakob Malik had surprised many reporters with the comment, "Only a new Geneva conference could bring a new solution and relax tension." Secretary Rogers was intrigued. He asked the Russians privately for an elaboration, but he got none.

Meantime, Communist troops moved closer and closer to Pnom Penh. The President began to worry—not only about Cambodia but equally about his credibility in the Communist world. Soon after his inauguration, when the Communists shelled Saigon, thus violating their "understanding" with Johnson, Nixon had done nothing. When the North Koreans shot down a U.S. reconnaissance plane, he had done nothing. When the Communists ignored his negotiating "plan" in Paris, all he had done was to downgrade the talks. He began to feel crowded and haunted by the fear that he, a sensible hawk, would be seen by the Communists as an ineffectual dove. He did not want to assume a new obligation in Southeast Asia. His purpose was to wind down the war, not to scale it up again. Yet he felt that he could not let the Communists "get away with murder," as he confided to a friend one evening.

On April 17 he approved the secret shipment of 6000 captured AK-47 rifles to Lon Nol. He also approved the training in South Vietnam of ethnic Khmer troops. Two thousand Khmers who had been fighting alongside the South Vietnamese were secretly flown into Pnom Penh one night in American planes.

On April 20 he had announced that an additional 150,000 American troops would be withdrawn from South Vietnam by the spring of 1971. It was not known, only suspected at the time by shrewd administration-watchers, that this formula represented a compromise between Abrams, who wanted a delay in further withdrawals until the Cambodian situation became clarified, and Laird, who insisted on continuing the withdrawal, no matter what. Politically, the 150,000-figure, with its springtime target-date attached, was a thing of beauty. It mollified the doves by suggesting massive withdrawals would continue. It also satisfied the generals by holding up withdrawals temporarily—at least, until the current threat to Cambodia eased.

April 20 had been, for the President, a rough day. He foreshadowed his Cambodia decision, warning that if "increased enemy action jeopardizes our remaining forces in Vietnam, I shall not hesitate to take strong and effective measures to deal with that situation." Saang, a district capital eighteen miles from Pnom Penh, had just fallen to the Communists. Sihanouk patched together a new effort, backed by China and North Vietnam, to "liberate" all of Southeast Asia. Moscow formally backed off Malik's "new Geneva conference" idea. And Lon Nol asked for $500,000,000 in American military aid.

On April 22, after the President returned to Washington from San Clemente ("something was up," one aide recalls), the National Security Council for the first time formally considered military intervention in Cambodia. Although there was some discussion of an American push into the Fishhook area, most of the talk had to do with a major South Vietnamese strike into the base-camp areas.

The following day the Washington Special Action Group—known as WASAG—met to discuss Cambodia. WASAG consisted of Kissinger from the White House; Deputy Secretary David Packard, General Wheeler and Admiral Moorer from Defense; Helms from CIA; U. Alexis Johnson and Marshall Green from the State Department. They met twice that day, twice the next day, too. No decisions were reached. But almost all the talk focused on some form of Allied military action in Cambodia.

So secret were all these deliberations that no one outside

the immediate official family knew about the possibility of American military intervention. On April 24, a Friday, the President asked General Abrams to submit detailed plans for a United States drive into the Fishhook and a companion thrust by the South Vietnamese into other base-camp areas. The President had not yet decided to move, but he had narrowed his options to the certainty of a South Vietnamese strike into Cambodia and the probability of an American strike too. The President then flew to Camp David to brood upon his decision. On Saturday, Kissinger joined him by helicopter with Abrams's military plans. That night, as Secretary Rogers accused Hanoi of an "explicit and unprovoked violation" of Cambodian neutrality, and another high State Department official told reporters, "Nixon is facing his Rubicon," the President invited Laird and Attorney General Mitchell to join him on a night-time cruise up the Potomac on the *Sequoia*. They discussed the American move into Cambodia. Then they returned to the White House, where they all saw *Patton*—the President, for a second time.

Early on Sunday morning, April 26, Rogers, Laird, Wheeler, Helms, and Kissinger joined the President at the White House. The President announced that he had decided to "do something." The South Vietnamese, he said, would be unleashed against Communist sanctuary positions in the Parrot's Beak area. But what about the Fishhook? Could the South Vietnamese take on that job too? The Pentagon representatives argued forcefully that the South Vietnamese, despite the claimed progress of Vietnamization, could not handle the job without considerable American support. It would be better, more effective, they added, if American troops undertook the Fishhook operation on their own and helped the South Vietnamese in some of the other operations. The President heard that the Communists were either on the threshold of conquest in Pnom Penh, or on the verge of opening a major land route from the sea northeast toward Saigon, and they had to be stopped. With the rains coming soon, Wheeler said it was now or never.

Secretary Rogers argued against the use of American forces in Cambodia. The South Vietnamese could do it alone, he contended. Laird agreed that against some enemy base camps they could, but not against all. Rogers said the use of American troops would surely kick off a new round of campus disorders and congressional debate; it might widen the war and entangle the administration in another "commitment." He pleaded with the President not to lose sight of his major objective—American withdrawal from Southeast Asia; not to forfeit his popular support by seeming to enlarge the territorial scope of the war. Helms's position was not revealed. Laird, somewhat ambivalent at first, came down on the side of the generals. Kissinger appeared reluctant to use American power but, when he sensed the direction of the President's thinking, he is reported to have raised no challenge.

That evening the President sat alone in his office with a lined yellow pad on his lap. According to Stewart Alsop's intimate and accurate account, he scribbled down all of the pluses and minuses. He had clearly decided on some form of military action. "Time running out," he noted. He wanted to avoid an "ambiguous situation"—"if we don't move and they don't either." He knew there were "deep divisions" in the country, likely to become deeper as a result of American action into Cambodia. But, he felt, he had to act.

On Monday morning, the inner circle, minus Wheeler, met once again. Rogers suggested that perhaps the military chiefs were telling the President what they thought he wanted to hear. Unlike Acheson, Rogers did not tell the President that he was being led down the garden path by the JCS. Nevertheless, the thought haunted Nixon. He sent a personal, out-of-channels message to Abrams demanding the "unvarnished truth."

That afternoon Rogers appeared in closed session before the Senate Foreign Relations Committee. He was beset with anxious questions about a rumored large-scale American military aid program to Cambodia. No one asked about a direct military move into Cambodia. Evidently it never occurred to any Senator to ask and Rogers volunteered nothing.

That night the Secretary of State telephoned the President and told him about the committee's nervousness. Shortly thereafter Abrams cabled the "unvarnished truth" as he saw it—U.S. military action was essential. General Westmoreland chimed in.

Such an opportunity, he said, comes once in a lifetime; let us clear out the sanctuaries and thus assure the success of Vietnamization. Nixon then retired to his private office—clutching his lined yellow pad—and decided to send not only the South Vietnamese into Cambodia but the Americans as well. The next morning he told first Kissinger, then Rogers, then Laird and Mitchell. Operations were to begin on Thursday night, Washington time, and he decided to make the announcement himself in another nationally broadcast report:

This is not an invasion of Cambodia [the President said]. The areas in which these attacks will be launched are completely occupied and controlled by Vietnamese forces. Our purpose is not to occupy the areas. Once enemy forces are driven out of these sanctuaries and once their military supplies are destroyed, we will withdraw.

Withdraw he did by the end of June, although air strikes continued and American military support widened. The ostensible purpose of the operation was to protect the American flank in South Vietnam against Communist attacks from across the Cambodian border. Enemy actions there, Nixon said, "clearly endanger the lives of American troops who are in Vietnam now and would constitute an unacceptable risk to those who will be there after withdrawal of another 150,000." Some of the critics ascribed a more personal motive to the stunning Cambodian operation: the President was proving his manhood, they said; he was showing that he could be another Patton. Senator Edward Kennedy called the operation "madness"; Senator Fulbright privately told one friend that he feared for the President's sanity; Senator Frank Church said the President was slipping into another Vietnam-type commitment in Cambodia.

Although the President could not have been unaware of the deep divisions in the country, it is doubtful that he had a clear sense of the frustration and the violence his action was to loose on the American campus, or indeed of the angry reaction on Capitol Hill. His Cambodia decision touched off a fresh outburst of youthful disenchantment with the "system"—reinforced by his off-the-cuff comment at the Pentagon that some of the demonstrators were "bums." Demonstrations against the President and the war stretched from one end of the nation to the other; and, on the campus of Kent State University in Ohio, National Guardsmen killed four students, whipping up new waves of anguish, disillusionment, and despair. Hundreds of outraged citizen groups descended on Washington, demanding antiwar legislation from the Congress and compassion from the White House. The silent majority, predictably, rallied behind the President. But the polarization was fully as sharp, if not sharper, than in the time of trouble that had driven Lyndon Johnson from office two years earlier. Many thoughtful citizens feared the fabric of American society was being stretched to the outer limit, that it could easily rip apart under the pressure of one more incident.

Yet some time in May of 1970, millions of Americans seemed to pause, reflect on the moral state of their country, and decide to give the "system" one more chance. Congressmen and Senators knew that, at last, they would have to try to cut the President's purse strings; to draw a line in Southeast Asia—and say, no farther; to deprive the President of every legal basis for conducting the war save one—his constitutional responsibility as Commander-in-Chief. In a swift series of steps, Congress repealed the Gulf of Tonkin resolution, which former Under Secretary of State Katzenbach, once a professor of international law, had termed the "functional equivalent of a declaration of war." Senators George McGovern and Mark Hatfield put forward an amendment that would have cut off funds for Amercian participation in the Vietnam War by the summer of 1971. It failed to win majority support. But another amendment, sponsored by Senators John Sherman Cooper and Church, passed the Senate, 58 to 37. It denied funds to the President for keeping American forces in Cambodia, whether ground troops or advisers, and for providing the Cambodian troops with direct air support.

The House did not sustain the Senate action. More hawkish, in general, and more susceptible to White House pressure, the majority of Congressmen felt that they should not tie the President's hands in time of war. Besides, many argued, the President had kept his word, the troops were withdrawn on schedule, just as he had promised. There were members of both the Senate and the House who feared that the President would be sucked into another Vietnam-type commitment in Cambodia against his better judgment; that he would be unable to resist the easy temptation of holding off a Communist victory in a country which shares a 600-mile border with South Vietnam, much less the entreaties of a rightist general, such as Lon Nol, to help Cambodia fight a common Communist enemy.

The President, the Secretaries of State and Defense, and all of their spokesmen replied that they had learned the bitter lesson of Vietnam: big, powerful nations could get drawn too deeply into the affairs of small, weak nations; it would not happen again. They were sympathetic to Lon Nol's problems; they would help him; but Cambodia would never become another Vietnam. This concession defused some of the Congressional passion. The sudden Middle East crisis in the summer of 1970, triggered by the movement of Soviet missiles toward the Suez Canal and the combat operations of Soviet pilots over Egyptian territory, also helped to distract attention from U.S. military activities on the ground and in the sky over Cambodia. The news media, especially the television networks, which suffer from a chronic inability to focus on more than one foreign crisis at a time, helped mightily.

For all the presidential promises and protestations, however, that there would be no change in the policy of avoiding new Cambodian commitments, the policy did change step by small step. No one wanted a military association with Cambodia. Everyone worth talking to in Washington had warned against it. Yet it was with a stabbing sense of recognition that Washington gradually discovered it had been over the same ground, with equal reluctance, many years before. All the familiar landmarks were there, recalling Vietnam fifteen years earlier.

First, there was the matter of aid. By July 1, 1970, the United States had supplied Cambodia with $8,900,000 in military aid, at a rate of something like $4,000,000 a month. On August 24 the State Department announced that the U.S. would provide "up to $40,000,000" in direct military aid to Cambodia; privately, some officials acknowledged that it would probably go much higher. After a briefing by Assistant Secretary of State Marshall Green, behind closed doors, members of the Senate

Foreign Relations Committee predicted that the $40,000,000 for
military aid would "more than likely" be part of a larger package for Cambodia, including economic assistance. The total
price tag was estimated at more like $200,000,000.

Green underestimated by some $85,000,000. By mid-Novem-
ber, 1970, after the elections, the administration told Congress
that the price tag would be more like $285,000,000; and some
highly placed State Department officials privately warned that
the cost of helping the Lon Nol regime would "probably" rise
still higher. At that time they could not tell by how much.

This request came one week before the U.S. launched a
massive 250-plane strike against North Vietnam in retaliation for
the downing of an American reconnaissance plane earlier in the
month.* Chairman Fulbright of the Senate Foreign Relations
Committee planned a new round of public hearings, fearful that
the administration was again seeking a "military victory" in Indochina. The North Vietnamese boycotted one session of the Paris
peace talks, and the Viet Cong promised "retribution ten-fold
harsher."

In addition, there was the matter of the increasing American
presence in Cambodia. At the time of the Lon Nol coup, there
were exactly six U.S. officials in Pnom Penh. In weeks the number jumped to eleven, then to sixty-two. When all the promised
hardware was delivered—some officials admitted, again privately
—the U.S. presence would increase still more. Finally, there was
the matter of escalating official rhetoric, once again clearing the
ground, almost imperceptibly, for an expanding commitment
toward another small Asian country. The step-by-small-step
progression can be seen in these simple statements:

• Secretary Rogers, March 23, 1970: "Cambodia has not
made any request for military assistance. . . . We don't anticipate that any request will be made."

• Secretary Laird, April 15, 1970: "I have said often that
I will not recommend troops going to Laos or to Cambodia or
to any other place without the consent of the Congress. . . .

* The U.S. also dropped an elite force of American commandos 20 miles
from Hanoi in an unsuccessful but daring and diverting attempt to rescue
some prisoners of war.

Now I feel that very strongly." (Laird made this comment on the same day that he sent the President his endorsement of General Abrams's ideas about sending troops into Cambodia.)

• Laird, May 5, 1970: "We are not going to get involved with the Cambodian Army or with military operations in Cambodia."

• President Nixon, May 8, 1970: "I would expect that the South Vietnamese would come out approximately at the same time that we do because, when we come out, our logistical support and air support will also come out with them." (The South Vietnamese stayed.)

• Rogers, May 13, 1970: "That's correct!" The question was whether "what you're ruling out, only, is that we will not get involved directly, militarily, in supporting the Lon Nol Government."

• President Nixon, June 3, 1970: "The only remaining American activity in Cambodia after July 1 will be air missions to interdict the movement of enemy troops and material where I find that is necessary to protect the lives and security of our men in South Vietnam."

• Rogers, June 23, 1970: "It is obvious, of course, that there will be times when, in the process of interdicting supply lines or communication lines of the enemy, that that will be of direct benefit to the present government in Cambodia. . . . Obviously [air interdiction] may have a dual benefit; it may serve our purposes and at the same time serve the Cambodian government."

• President Nixon, July 1, 1970: "I am going to use, as I should, the air power of the United States to interdict all flows of men and supplies which I consider are directed towards South Vietnam."

• Vice-President Agnew, August 23, 1970: "We're going to do everything we can to help the Lon Nol government" because "the whole matter of Cambodia is related to the security of our troops in Vietnam."

• State Department spokesman Robert J. McCloskey, August 24, 1970: "The Vice-President's comments" do not "change" or "expand" American policy towards Cambodia.

One day in September, 1970, a high State Department official was lunching at the Occidental Restaurant with a dozen reporters. He mentioned, in passing, that the United States had just "loaned" Cambodia six helicopters. They had been flown into Phom Penh by South Vietnamese pilots. The reporters, many of them veterans of those days in 1965 when the Johnson Administration refused to admit that American troops were engaged in combat in South Vietnam, wanted to know how he and his colleagues in the department could maintain that the United States was not slipping into a kind of military arrangement with the Lon Nol Government.

The official pushed aside his coffee cup, stared for a moment at a wall filled with photographs of Washington celebrities, and then launched into a revealing rundown of administration thinking about this touchy subject. I know, he said, what is eating you and Church and Fulbright and all of the others. You think we are going to get ourselves stupidly involved in Cambodia as we did ten or twenty years ago in Vietnam. First we move into the sanctuaries, saying that is as far as we are going to go. Then, though we pull out our ground troops on schedule, we allow our air power to interdict enemy supply routes. We unofficially expand the definition of "interdiction" to include any Communist target in the country. We increase our embassy staff. We send military aid to Cambodia. Then economic aid. We increase our personnel still more, to take care of our expanding presence in the country. Soon we have to move military advisers in mufti into Pnom Penh to protect ourselves. The Cambodians say they are so busy fighting the Communists that they need more than our air support; they need a few advisers, then a few more, until, after a while, we are doing the fighting and they are doing the watching. Before you know it, we are fighting a no-front war stretching from Saigon to Pnom Penh.

The official paused, noting that the reporters nodded in agreement. He was stating with great precision the concern they all felt. He continued: And there are powerful reasons for my saying it will not happen. For one thing, we do not have the resources. We cannot help Cambodia the way we helped South Vietnam. For another thing, we have little congressional support. We spent much of our good will on the Hill during the Cambodian operation. And, finally, we are not fools. We have learned from Vietnam. No big country can fight a small country's wars. No big country has the right to barge into a civil war in Asia. We are aware of these problems. That is the whole point of the Nixon doctrine. We will not let it happen again. There will not be another Vietnam.

One reporter felt like asking several questions: How then do you explain the Vice-President's comment? The direct air support? The growing American aid program? But he asked none of these questions. Every man at that oval table knew that the official had opposed the move into Cambodia. It was obviously a painful presidential decision like almost every other decision relating to that long, sad war in Southeast Asia.

As the lunch broke and everyone shook hands and promised to "do this again real soon," it was clear that in the four months since the President had ordered American troops into Cambodia, much about the character of the Indochina war had changed and much, unfortunately, had remained the same. The Asian Communists, embracing Prince Sihanouk, seemed to be more united than ever before. The North Vietnamese were still stubborn. The Paris peace talks remained stalemated, despite Ambassador Bruce's arrival there. And the success of the Vietnamization program—in other words, the possibility of continued troop withdrawal at a measured pace—appeared to be linked indirectly to the survival of a non-Communist regime in Pnom Penh and more directly to keeping the Communists from rebuilding their Cambodian base camps along the Vietnamese border.

Thus the President had added burdensome new obligations in Indochina, instead of reducing them as he promised the voters in the 1968 campaign. Neither of the choices he faced was promising: whether to go against his own instincts and try to negotiate a Vietnam settlement that would allow the Communists a substantial share of power in Saigon, a share they might quickly expand into something like total control if the President's pessimism about the staying power of the non-Communist alternative was justified; or to intensify the war and see it through to something like a military victory, against heavy

odds and in the certain knowledge that the home front in the
United States could become a more immediate danger zone
than Vietnam itself for the President, his party, and his countrymen.

TEN

In the Wake of the
Clipper Ship

ON OCTOBER 9, 1970, the State Department announced softly that Cheng Heng would begin an unofficial seventeen-day visit to the United States the following day. The visit would include, a spokesman said, meetings with the President and the Vice-President, Governor Nelson Rockefeller, Mayor John Lindsay, and UN Secretary-General U Thant. There would be speeches before the Council on Foreign Relations, the Pittsburgh World Affairs Council, and the National Press Club; and a VIP tour through the North American Air Defense Command headquarters in Colorado. *Chen Heng?*

Cheng Heng turned out to be the newly appointed chief of state of Cambodia, a small, shy Asian gentleman on a most important diplomatic assignment. Cambodia had just shucked the trappings of Sihanouk's monarchy and slipped uneasily into the framework of a republic. The "free and democratic" people of Cambodia were determined, as the Cambodian Embassy put it, "to defend their national independence and drive the North Vietnamese and Viet Cong invaders from their country." Cheng Heng echoed this appropriate sentiment in his talks with administration leaders, thanking them for the "material assistance which the United States has provided during the recent difficult months." He said all the right things: that Cambodia was determined to fight the Communist invaders; that Cambodia cherished her national independence; and that Cambodia needed American matériel, not men.

The new chief of state was engaging in what the diplomats call "mutual consultation"—for Cambodia and the United States, a deepening process ever since Sihanouk lost his "mandate of heaven." On July 5, 1970, Cambodia's foreign minister chatted with Secretary Rogers in Saigon. On July 6 Assistant Secretary Green journeyed to Pnom Penh, the first high-level American official to visit Cambodia in many, many years. On August 28, behind an embarrassing phalanx of machine-gun-toting Secret Service men, Vice-President Agnew dropped in on Pnom Penh during one of his Asian tours, designed in part to launch the 1970 election campaign with some firm anti-Communist rhetoric in the company of such stalwart allies or friends as South Korea's Park, Taiwan's Chiang, South Vietnam's Thieu, and Cambodia's Lon Nol. Such "mutual consultation" is deemed invaluable in the building of an unintentional commitment.

During his Washington stay, Cheng Heng talked like a true believer in the Nixon doctrine. American officials were delighted with his performance. "Nice fellow," one high State Department official confided, "a real nice fellow, smart too." A reporter listened skeptically. "He knows that we can't do much for him," the official went on, "that we're trying to get out of Indochina." Did that mean he was going home empty-handed? "Well, not quite empty-handed," the official conceded. "We don't want this crowd to lose out to the Communists. That would be bad, real bad for Vietnam."

Cheng Heng received no formal United States commitment of any kind during his long visit. But he did receive a promise of more military aid and a modest economic assistance program. More important, he received a clearer understanding of the administration's order of Asian priorities to comfort him on his long journey back to Pnom Penh. He knew that the United States considered the survival of a non-Communist Cambodia, relatively free of enemy sanctuaries, as "important" to the evolving program of Vietnamization, meaning phased U.S. troop withdrawals from Indochina. Vietnamization in turn was "vital" to the success of the Nixon doctrine; and the Nixon doctrine was the key to lowering America's profile throughout Asia (and the rest of the world) without abandoning America's commitments.

In other words, in large, strategic terms, the United States would continue to try to "winch down" the war in Indochina—but not lose it—while, at the same time, it would try to avoid becoming embroiled in a new one. As the President told a visiting Senator during a tense moment in the Jordanian crisis of September, 1970, when it looked as though United States military intervention was close at hand: "The American people cannot stomach another war at this time."

Translated into Cambodian terms, this meant to Cheng Heng, as then related by some of his associates, that the United States would *probably* not send American troops back into Cambodia but would *almost certainly* send American planes, tanks, guns, and economic aid—and, if possible, Asian manpower—into Cambodia to help protect that newly proclaimed republic from falling under Hanoi's domination. Even in the absence of a formal commitment, there was a growing political and military association between Washington and Pnom Penh that linked their destinies and greatly complicated a possible political solution of the war.

On October 7, 1970, President Nixon seemed to acknowledge the logic of this conclusion by proposing an Indochina-wide cease-fire as part of a five-point peace plan. The Nixon proposal received wide support, thus forcing Hanoi into a defensive posture. Hanoi rejected the President's plan. But its almost universal acceptance elsewhere must have prompted some second thoughts in Hanoi about the wisdom of a policy that depends in part upon the collapse of American will power for its ultimate hope of victory. It looked like a miracle of political manipulation considering the national uproar that followed the Cambodian incursions of May and June, 1970! With one eye on the November elections and the other on Hanoi, the President focused not on Vietnam alone but on all of Indochina—in this way, widening the range of negotiating possibilities and incorporating Laos and Cambodia into any possible solution. It was perhaps only natural and obvious that after the May incursions, any proposed new solution would have to embrace all of Indochina. In his April 30 speech the President had broadened the military conflict in Indochina, at least temporarily; in

his October 7 speech he broadened the framework of a political
solution to a corresponding degree. This approach had often
been considered in the past. But it had never been formally proposed by any of the several American Presidents who agonized
over Vietnam.

The October 7 speech contained lessons for everyone: for
Hanoi, the lesson that the antiwar critics were finding less and
less political profit in attacks upon the President's policy; for
Saigon, that the President would not abandon the South Vietnamese cause, even though he could find political solace only
in a policy of continuing troop withdrawals barring any further
expansion of the conflict; for the President, that power and
popularity were the political rewards to be earned by those
leaders who projected an image of peace; finally, for everyone,
that Vietnam was no longer the bloody focus of universal attention, no longer the issue that could make or break Presidents.
The smart politician in Richard Nixon instantly recognized and
respected the wisdom of Lyndon Johnson's March 31, 1968,
decision not to seek or accept another term in office. Vietnam
simply had to be defused as an explosive issue. It had tormented
Johnson. In A White House Diary, his wife, Lady Bird, recalls
LBJ's pathetic comment of March 7, 1965: "I can't get out. I
can't finish it with what I have got. So what the hell can I do?"
It took three years of personal anguish and national tragedy before LBJ approached an answer to his question. By withdrawing from public life, he took the first major step toward cutting
an Asian obsession down to a manageable nuisance. Nixon took
several others, including a start of United States troop withdrawals, a reduction in the size of the American air and naval
armada in the South China Sea, and a gradual pulling back
from any possible confrontation with Communist China. The
effect of these steps was to change the character of the Vietnam
War and thus to make it more tolerable to the American people:
from the flashpoint of a potential world conflict involving the big
powers, down the ladder of danger to its original dimension—
that of a local war, anguishing still, brutalizing still, much too
long, but local. In fact, Nixon's historic contribution may well
prove to be not that he ended the war but that he shrank
Vietnam down to size. His rhetoric, most notably in his April

30, 1970, speech explaining the United States military moves into Cambodia, still lagged behind his actions in reducing Vietnam to realistic proportions. His occasional muscle-flexing exercises —an air raid against North Vietnam, a propaganda blast at Hanoi—troubled many of his critics, too. But it is possible to see Vietnam today for the small, not very important, divided country in Southeast Asia that it is. The American people have been allowed to take a deep breath and to draw back from their narrow concentration on Vietnam, widening their view sufficiently to perceive and appreciate other national responsibilities.

This matter of perception and perspective is critical. Vietnam so distorted our sense of priorities that other parts of the world, traditionally considered "vital" to American security, were for years all but ignored. Home-front problems such as pollution, the population explosion, the shabby state of domestic politics, the need for economic justice and racial equality were often shelved or given inadequate attention by busy officials who knew that they must first cater to the President's preoccupation with a victory-of-sorts in Vietnam. Toward the end of the Johnson years officials of both parties began to realize that much had changed in the world since America first embraced Vietnam as a special concern—almost twenty years of violent and truly revolutionary change—and the new contours of world politics required new adaptations of national policies. Even if the United States had "won" in Vietnam, as a result of a quick and powerful application of American military strength—Goldwater-style, 1964—major shifts in the nation's Asia policy would have been required anyway.

The United States first became conscious of Vietnam at a crucial moment in its history. World War II was ending. America's traditional allies, France and Great Britain, were counted among the victors, but their economies were shattered, their pride hurt, their empires disintegrating. They needed help. The Soviet Union, a wartime ally, fastened its grip on Eastern Europe, restoring Catherine the Great's old empire in the form of a Soviet satrapy. Many Washington officials had come naïvely to believe that the wartime coalition with Russia could set a pattern of postwar cooperation that would reshape the world. Their disillusionment was profound. Some saw the dropping of the Iron

Curtain in 1946 as the signal for a Western crusade against
Soviet Russia. A few politicians felt that if there ever was a time
to impose a *Pax Americana* upon the Russians and the rest of
the world, the time was then. The U.S. had suddenly assumed
new, global responsibilities for protecting Western interests
against Communist incursions in a nuclear age. Washington had
not asked for the responsibility. There was simply no one else.
Of all of the major powers, only America had emerged from the
war stronger than before. Only the U.S. had the nuclear know-
how to make atomic weapons, even though none existed in the
American arsenal early in 1947. Only the U.S. could look after
allied interests—French-colonial interests in Indochina, for instance. Only the U.S. had the economic power to help friends
recover from the ravages of war and the military might to help
them resist the encroachments of an aggressive Communist bloc.
Even Bertrand Russell, hardly an admirer of the American way
of life, was so disappointed by Stalin's rejection of the Baruch
proposals for halting the nuclear arms race that he suggested
the United States should force nuclear disarmament upon the Russians by the threat of immediate war. But President Truman and
the Congress were moving in the opposite direction. The public
mood called for bringing the boys home, cutting deeply into
military budgets, cranking up the peacetime economy. Only
after the Korean War broke out in the summer of 1950 was that
trend abruptly reversed.

One of the more baffling aspects of American policy immediately after World War II was the substantial official failure
to take full account of the sweep and power of the *new* national-
isms in Asia, Africa, and Latin America.

Many top-level officials failed to understand what Franklin
Roosevelt had sensed, perhaps intuitively; that, in much of the
world, peoples denied their own nationalist revolution by decades or centuries of colonial rule would demand independence
and the right, as Jawaharlal Nehru once expressed it, to "make
their own mistakes." There is some reason to believe—as we
have seen—that had Roosevelt lived a few years longer, both
the French and American peoples might have been spared their
long, wasting wars in Indochina.

Truman and Acheson, on the contrary, looking at the new world through their European prism, made it possible for the French to return to Indochina by subsidizing their disastrous war effort there. Oddly, some of the most sophisticated Americans had difficulty grasping the fact that nationalism was sweeping the so-called third world, that it could not long be suppressed by foreign rulers and that—leaving moral considerations aside—there could be no profit for the United States in siding with the colonialists.

Many did not see how crudely nationalistic some Americans themselves could be. Dean Rusk was a good example, pressing his forefinger down upon his desk at the height of the Vietnam War and saying that when the United States applies pressure in any situation, anywhere, it must prevail. The notion that America was somehow omnipotent, that its national interest stretched round the world, found its fullest expression in Asia.

It was a notion born of success, chiefly in Europe. The Berlin airlift had broken Stalin's blockade. The Marshall Plan had restored Western Europe from a wasteland of broken brick and stone into a prosperous and powerful community, enjoying the fruits of peace. Even in Korea, the Communists had been stopped at the 38th parallel. It was second nature to believe that Americans, once they put their hands to a problem, must solve it successfully. Just as NATO could claim to have deterred possible Soviet aggression in Europe, so SEATO would contain the Chinese in Asia. Millions of Americans were uplifted when President Kennedy, in his Inaugural Address, said: "We shall pay any price, bear any burden, meet any hardship, support any friend, oppose any foe to assure the survival and the success of liberty." For, as the Fifties yielded to the Sixties, it still seemed right and natural for Americans to believe that they would "pay any price" or "oppose any foe". They looked forward to the 1960s with optimism and a sense of omnipotence.

It took the awful frustrations and trials of Vietnam to awaken the American people to the enormous changes that had taken place all around them. The rise of the so-called developing nations—side by side with the demise of old-fashioned colonialism—was now an incontestable fact. There was the startling split in the Communist world, as China disdainfully rejected Russia's brand of Marxism. Both factors attested to the growing diversity of political institutions and to the stubborn strength of national sovereignty. There was a dispersal of nuclear know-how. Not only had the United States lost its nuclear monopoly; it had to accept a widening of the nuclear "club" to include Russia, China, France, and Britain. There was the black revolution in the United States, which cast a glaring light on the failures of American society and demanded immediate action on the home front. There was one more reason for the American people to lose heart in Vietnam. In the jungles of Southeast Asia, they learned that not everyone yielded to American pressure. That feeling of omnipotence died.

Slowly, through the late 1960s, the United States learned that it could not accomplish miracles everywhere, that old enemies could become new allies, that national priorities could be reordered—indeed, had to be reordered—that globalism no longer made sense. Alone the United States could do much but not everything; others had to be brought into the responsibility of world leadership—if necessary, even the devil. The easy moralizations of the Fifties sounded antiquated or plain silly in the Seventies. The Communists shared many American problems —pollution and drugs and poverty. Extravagant claims and unrealistic ambitions seemed foolish on either side of the increasingly transparent curtain.

Vietnam taught the United States a profound lesson in national humility. Reflecting this new mood, President Nixon declared at the twenty-fifth-anniversary session of the UN General Assembly on October 23, 1970: "This is too important a time and too important an occasion [to speak in optimistic or even extravagant terms about our hopes for the future]. The fate of more than three and a half billion people today rests on the realism and candor with which we approach the great issues of war and peace, of security and progress, in this world that together we call home. So I would like to speak with you today not ritualistically but realistically; not of impossible dreams, but of possible deeds."

Presidents Eisenhower, Kennedy, and Johnson had their "impossible dreams" about Vietnam. They believed that, with a sufficient application of American military support or outright power, a "democracy" of sorts could be built south of the 17th parallel, a non-Communist state, allied to the "free world." They believed that South Vietnam could become a textbook model of nation-building. Hubert Humphrey had once spoken of building a "great society" in Vietnam.

President Nixon, like his predecessors, is a postwar statesman raised in the spirit of the cold war; like them, he is unwilling to see parts of the "free world," especially those parts that have been soaked in American blood, fall under Communist control. In this sense Chile could "fall" but not Vietnam. Nixon, however, is also a pragmatic politician who would like to be in office when the United States celebrates its 200th birthday. He knows now that America can not work miracles in Vietnam. He knows, too, that Vietnam destroyed Lyndon Johnson. Therefore, he is fashioning his policy in the hope of achieving a "possible deed"—in his mind, the survival of a non-Communist state in South Vietnam, based upon local, loyal manpower and the support of American planes, tanks, and artillery. This is the Nixon doctrine in action—a search for ways of reducing the cost of the long and dreadful war, thus making it tolerable to the American people, without losing it quickly, or yielding it slowly, to the North Vietnamese. "We know the difference between an honorable settlement and a disguised defeat," Henry Kissinger once said. This is Nixon's aim, as publicly explained—a Korean-type settlement in Southeast Asia. Many critics contend, we believe with some validity, that such an aim is merely another "impossible dream." Maybe so. But the President intends to make it work, if he possibly can.

History may yet overtake his critics. Certain of the President's advisers say that the critics may be overestimating Hanoi's ability (not its willingness) to survive another long struggle against a South Vietnamese military machine, lavishly supported and supplied by the United States. In the history of Vietnam, they add, the North has more than once tried to impose its control over the South, and has more than once failed. Adjustments are possible. For years the North Vietnamese said they would never agree to negotiate with the Americans while any part of their country was being bombed. In 1968 they did. Later that year they said they would never sit down with representatives of the Saigon regime. They did that, too.

There can be no question that North Vietnam lost its great inspirational leader with the death of Ho Chi Minh. China may soon lose Mao Tse-tung, as Russia lost Lenin and Stalin many years ago. Thus, the Communist world, deprived of its most authoritative father figures, divided and confused in any case, may soon find itself ideologically rudderless. The old orthodoxies do not work, though they will doubtless continue to be cited in political tracts for many years to come. Moreover, in a quarter century of cruel war, the North Vietnamese have suffered grievous losses. Their economy is said to have stagnated; millions of personal lives have been disrupted and as many dreams shattered—despite the stiff upper lip on ready display for visiting foreigners. At some point, Hanoi's leadership may yet conclude that a political accommodation with the United States (and South Vietnam) would serve its interest better than interminable war. Or so the President and certain of his advisers believe. As for the critics, who know Hanoi's legendary stubbornness, they are more inclined to believe that its horrendous losses in men and matériel may only have served to steel its will and strengthen its determination to defeat the Americans—if not today, then in some more distant tomorrow. There is no crystal ball that permits the President—or his critics—to read the future in Hanoi.

After carefully tracing out the roots of American involvement, we feel that the United States will not turn its back on Asia even if it should manage in the near future to extricate itself from Vietnam. Those politicians, historians, and journalists who predict a retreat into isolation, in recoil from the agonies of Vietnam, seem to us mistaken. The United States, in our judgment, cannot be expected to abandon its interests in Asia and retreat to Waikiki. Too much American blood has been spilled, too much American treasure squandered, too many American dreams blasted. In the age of simultaneous satellite communication, moreover, distance counts for little. Americans will make their presence felt in Asia—and Asians will make their presence felt in the United States—not perhaps in all the traditional ways, but increasingly through commercial, cultural, and political interaction.

The United States can, however, be expected to lower its military profile in Southeast Asia as part of an overall Vietnam settlement. We believe that Washington also is getting ready at long last to recognize that there are no eternal enemies in this world and that peace in the Far East necessarily requires a degree of accommodation with China, assuming that the Chinese leaders are ready too. In the Fifties, such accommodation was out of the question by reason of the emotional climate in the United States. In the Seventies, it appears to be a simple necessity. Talk of a new peaceful order in Asia that ignores one quarter of the human race is a plain absurdity.

Unfortunately, Vietnam was not an aberration. The inexorable progression—from Yankee Clipper to Yangtse gunboat to helicopter gunship—suggests that Vietnam was but a terrible moment in America's swashbuckling adventures in Asia. If we are to break that progression and avoid blundering into new Vietnams, Americans will have to re-examine many of their attitudes and assumptions about Asia—and the rest of the world, never forgetting that even the most powerful of nations can exhaust and discredit themselves by overspending their resources in a dubious cause.

INDEX

INDEX